MAPPING

THE INTELLIGENCE OF ARTISTIC WORK

An Explorative Guide to Making, Thinking, and Writing

ANNE WEST

ventive grouping
the editor (or author)
og post as extended artist statement
played + preserved work
ur philosophy + teaching strategy
ing on a diet of the work
anifesto, or words to live for
immediate release
stract as convergent process
aphic inspiration
it! launch it!
ving some things unsaid
ence
iew into the studio
akes of breath
voice of now
idea of artist
tural blind spots
dden clear images
images (or objects) + their stories
ly delving
ough the lens of memory
al pursuits
ratives of place
gin piece
cestral lines
notive to begin the work
sing the matter of the world
nnotations of beauty
t quality of light
rking the dialogue with space
or
out time
ers for the road
ections + organizations of things
to my students, past, present, and future
ositioning the familiar
cess
edilection to play
mundane against the fantastic
am quotient
rking with physical materials
play of lightness + weight
ing in the questions
rshalling reference points + models
r reading list
ers of intimacy
ual hopes
ore the "beginning was the word"
gap that drives the work
oming threshold without a map
he collective sphere
ing the doubleness of the work
bidextrous word play

EXPLORING

COVER PHOTO JESSICA GREENFIELD, *MATRIX MAP*, 2011

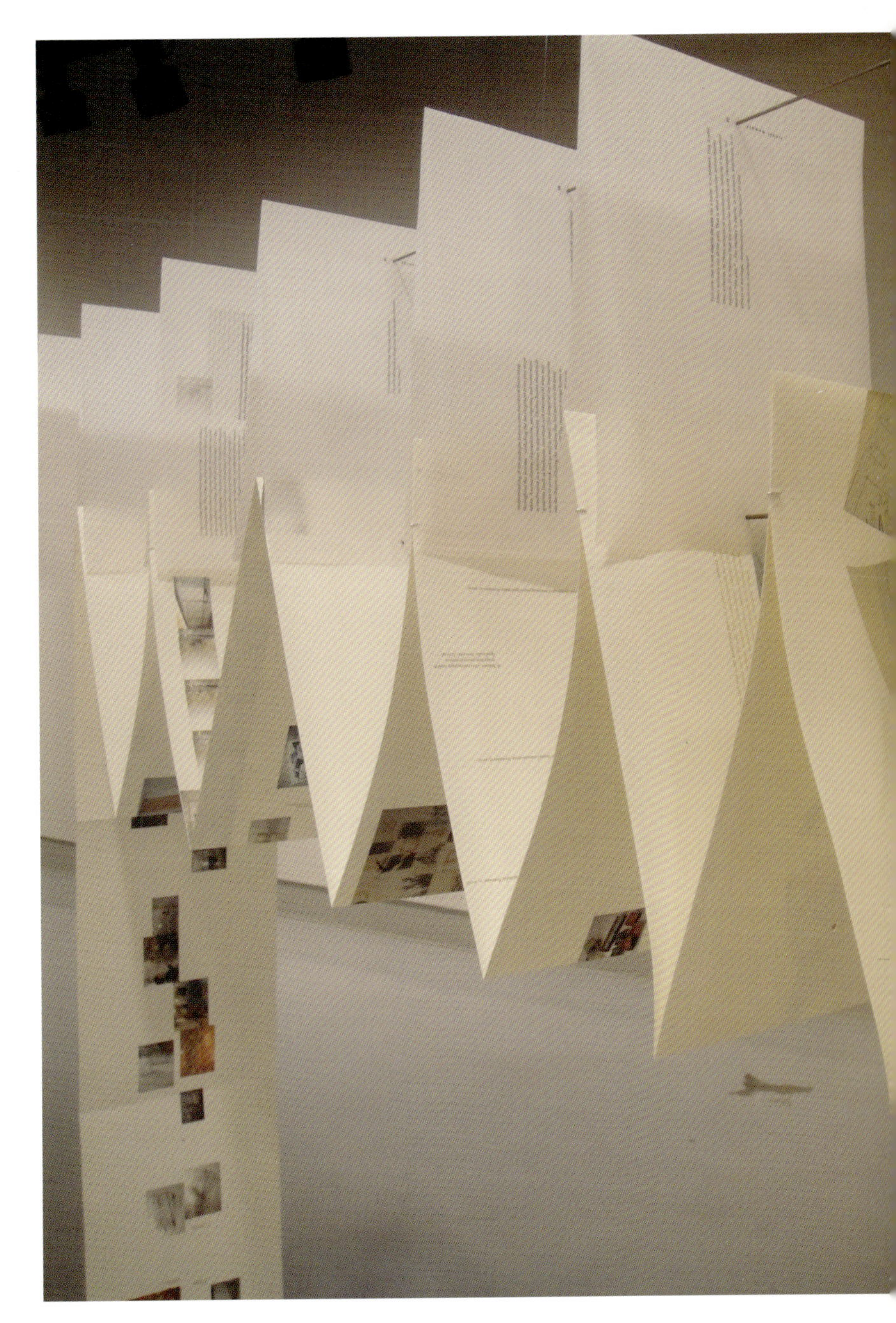

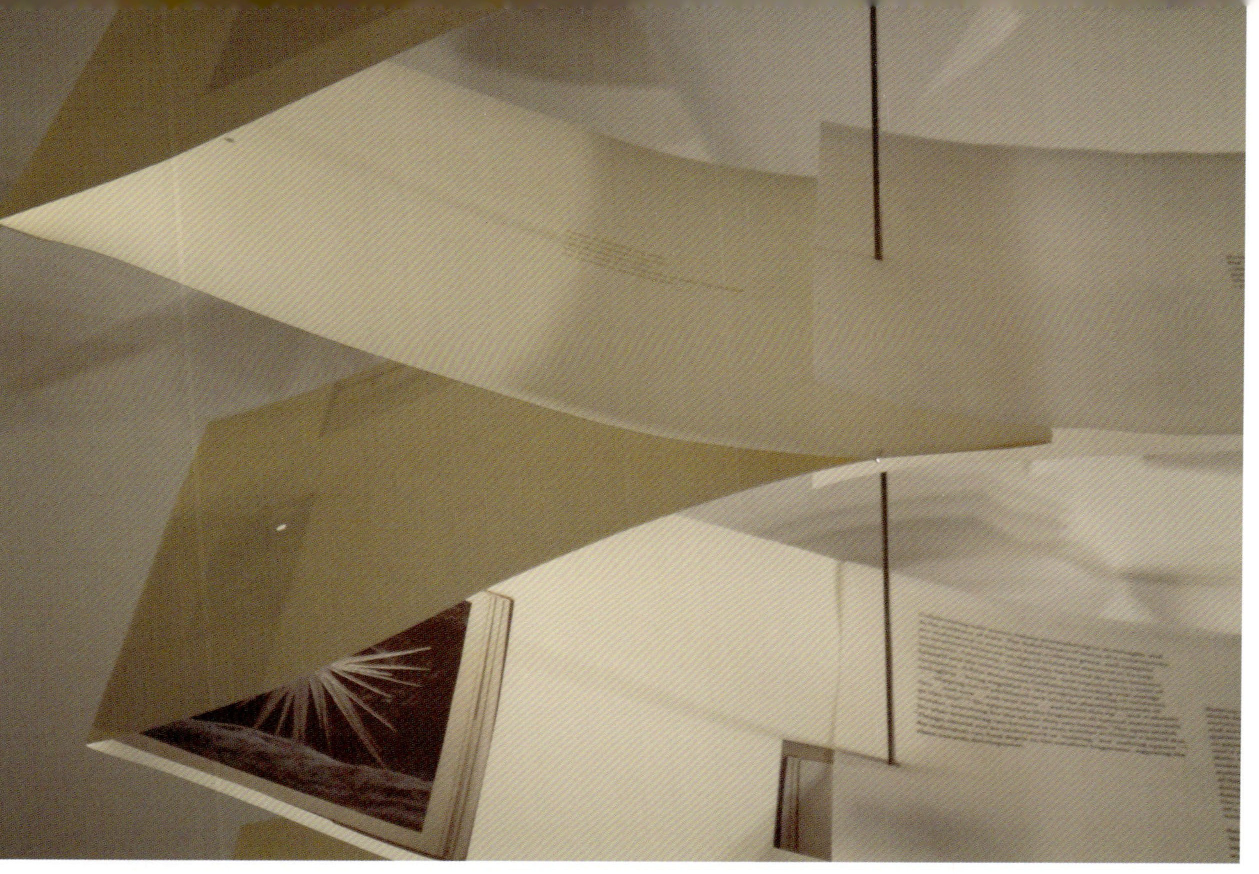

KELLY SALCHOW MACARTHUR (L AND R), *FROM EXPERIENCE TO CONSTRUCTION: FOCUSING, EXPANDING AND ROTATING THE LENS OF AWARENESS*, 2003

CONTENTS

MAPPING THE INTELLIGENCE OF ARTISTIC WORK

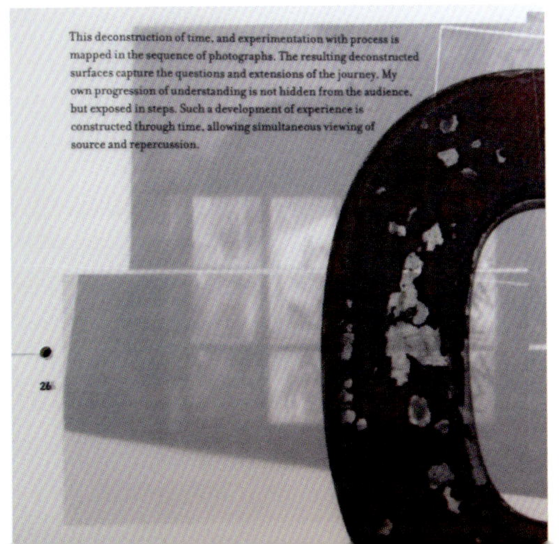

what IS MAPPING?

Mapping is a process of visualization and spatial transcription.

It draws from the picturing and structuring mind.

Mapping organizes relevant bits of information and fragments from the imagination into some kind of structure, creating a synthesis that carries understanding.

Maps are abstract conceptualizations that draw the component parts to the gestalt.

One point on a map does not mean anything unless it is seen in relation to the implied, the symbolic, and the entire sweep of the imagination.

A map can be viewed in its entirety or in its details.

Maps are enterable from any side.

We make the map, and the map makes us.

Maps are living sketches of us immersed in our work. They have the capacity to stir the imaginations of others.

Maps question and maps clarify.

Everything on a map signifies, points out a direction, intent.

The maps we generate are like eyes. They give us perspective.

Maps embody a point of view, reflecting tone, bias, curiosity, focus, choice, intelligence, and scholarship.

Maps establish connectivity.

Maps reflect multi-layered relationships.[1]

1 The writings of Charles Hampden–Turner and Denis Wood are essential to my understanding of the language of maps, mapping, and map–making. See *Maps of the Mind: Charts and Concepts of the Mind and its Labyrinths* (New York: Macmillan Publishing Company, 1982) and *The Power of Maps* (New York: The Guilford Press, 1992).

next page

2 E.M. Forster, *Aspects of the Novel*, ed. Oliver Stallybrass (Harmondsworth, England: Penguin, 1976), 99.

3 Robert Smithson, interviewed by Paul Cummings for the Archives of American Art / Smithsonian Institute, *The Writings of Robert Smithson*, ed. Nancy Holt (New York: New York University Press, 1979), 138.

how can I tell what I think until I see what I say?[2]

E.M. FORSTER

PC What about writing? When did you start?

RS That started in 1965–1966. But it was a self-taught situation. After about five years of thrashing about on my own, I started to pull my thoughts together and was able to begin writing. Since then, I guess I've written about 20 articles.

PC Do you find it augments your work, or is it separate from it?

RS Well, it comes out of my sensibility—it comes out of my observation. It sort of parallels my actual art involvement—the two coincide; one informs the other.[3]

ROBERT SMITHSON

FOREWORD

Writing, thinking, making, being: all are parts of a core studio practice, and all require supportive methodologies. The ability to write, research, and conceptualize critical discourse grounded in the realm of visual representation is a necessary skill for today's practicing artist. In a time when artwork can be anything from a prepared meal to a full-length film, the ability to communicate ideas is all the more important. Rapid developments in communications technology are leveraging the artistic, educational, and commercial value of clear and evocative writing. This fertile landscape of production has unearthed new opportunities for artists to write, publish, and distribute work, so that our insights and voices can more readily invigorate cultural conversations.

In this timely book, Anne West has cultivated a flexible, non-linear writing approach for the artist-writer. *Mapping the Intelligence of Artistic Work: An Explorative Guide to Making, Thinking, and Writing*, introduces multiple skill sets to stimulate creative thinking, by creating visual maps of interconnecting links. The heart of this book is a generous set of questions/probes that West has culled and refined from her fifteen years of graduate teaching at Rhode Island School of Design. The book is an invaluable tool for anyone interested in articulating the layers of meaning embedded in the process of making.

The Moth Press and the MFA Archive Project at Maine College of Art are committed to supporting the relationship between the acts of making and writing. West's book does just this, fostering profound growth in our making, thinking, and being, while at the same time mirroring the changing topography of the current art world and challenging our cultural habits. We thank West for the clearly articulated exercises and suggestions she shares with artists, makers, and creative thinkers, moving beyond the reach of her classroom to help us survey, excavate, and analyze our own methods, and question our own intentions.

The Moth Press is extremely grateful to the Jenny Fitch Fund and the Roderick Dew Fund for supporting our publishing projects on innovative practices. Support of this kind makes commitment to critical engagement possible.

Director/Editor
MFA Archive Project and Moth Press
Maine College of Art

KATARINA WESLIEN

JESSICA GREENFIELD, *MATRIX MAP*, 2010

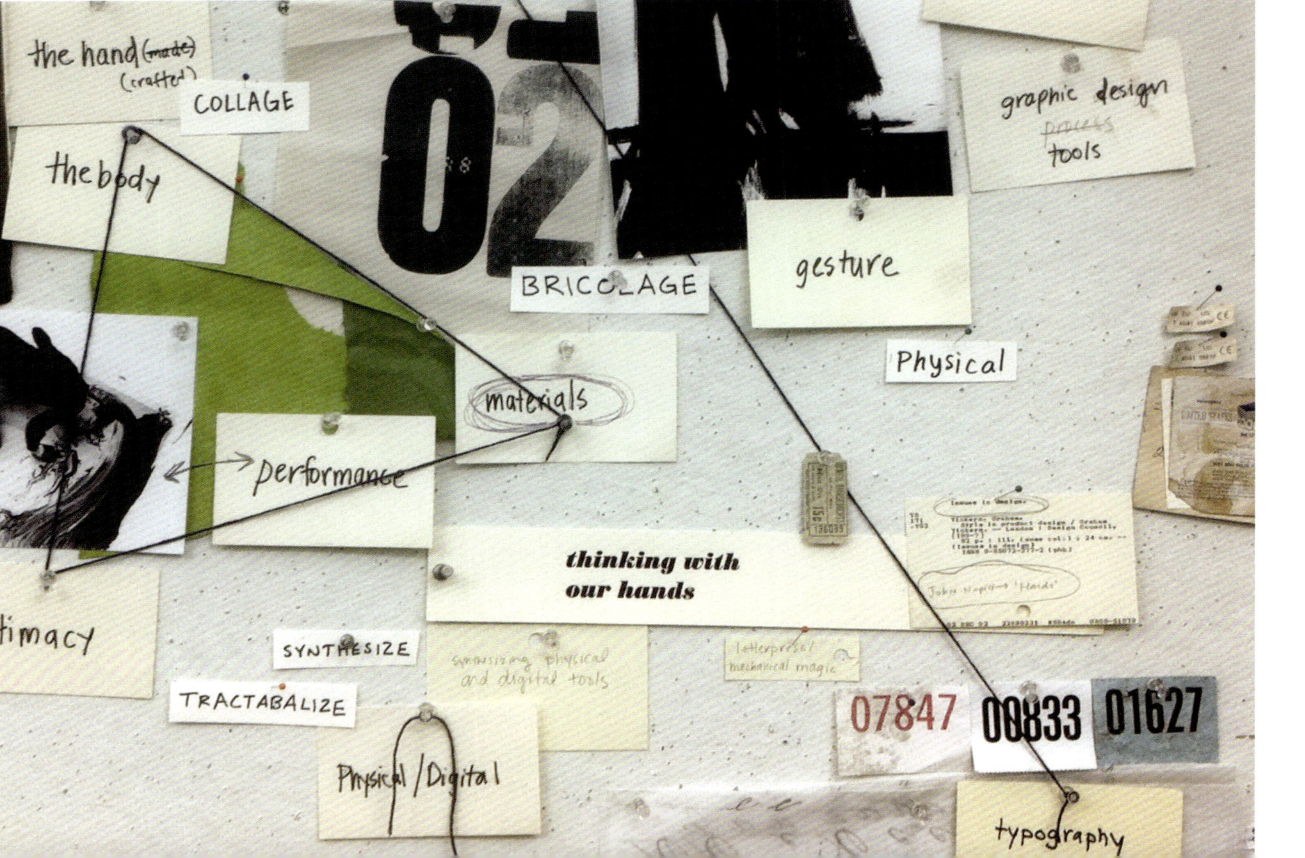

INTRODUCTION

ANNE WEST

Through mapping the experience of being an artist—our sensory world, ideas, and understanding of life—it is possible to develop a story of the imagination.

In *Six Memos for the Next Millennium*, a series of lectures written for Harvard University's Charles Eliot Norton Lectures in 1985-86, Italo Calvino speaks to six human values worthy of appreciation, nurture, and preservation by future generations. He titled his fourth memo "Visibility" and cautioned his readers about losing "the power of bringing visions into focus with our eyes shut, of bringing forth forms and colors from the lines of black letters on a white page and in fact of thinking in terms of images."[4]

Imagination, argues Calvino, is an essential instrument for knowing the self and the world. What Calvino envisions is a "possible pedagogy of the imagination," one that draws out inner vision and supports its realization. And yet, like Agnes Martin, Calvino resists conferring this pedagogy on others, claiming that we must bring "this exercise upon ourselves, according to methods invented for the occasion and with unpredictable results."[5]

I tread boldly in this book, suggesting a template for a pedagogy of the imagination—one that can be used by artists, makers, and creative thinkers to map the intelligence of our work. Through mapping the experience of being an artist—our sensory world, ideas, and understanding of life—it is possible to develop a story of the imagination. This non-linear story holds both the practical knowledge of creative process and the search for meaning. We come to listen closely to and understand the deep impressions on our imaginations, our themes, the discoveries that come through making, and the lights and shades of our particular view of the world.

Our imagination is our mental mapping system. We each see in our own way by its light—that is, through a dynamic mind that shapes a compendium of impressions formed from perceptions, facts, and signature experiences. Each outer impression is gathered and threaded together with inner feelings, memories, desires, and dreams into a net of inner-outer knowing.

Imagination is by no means a random process, but one guided at a deep level of mind by a highly structured intelligence or inner schema. At the deepest level our images form an interference pattern in the mind, weaving and connecting an inner-outer knowing into connective links and patterns. This becomes our creative matrix. By turns addressing making and writing, sensation and language, intuition and rationality, seeing and knowing, I propose that mapping through writing is a way for us to create pathways into this matrix and to illuminate inherent visual intelligence.

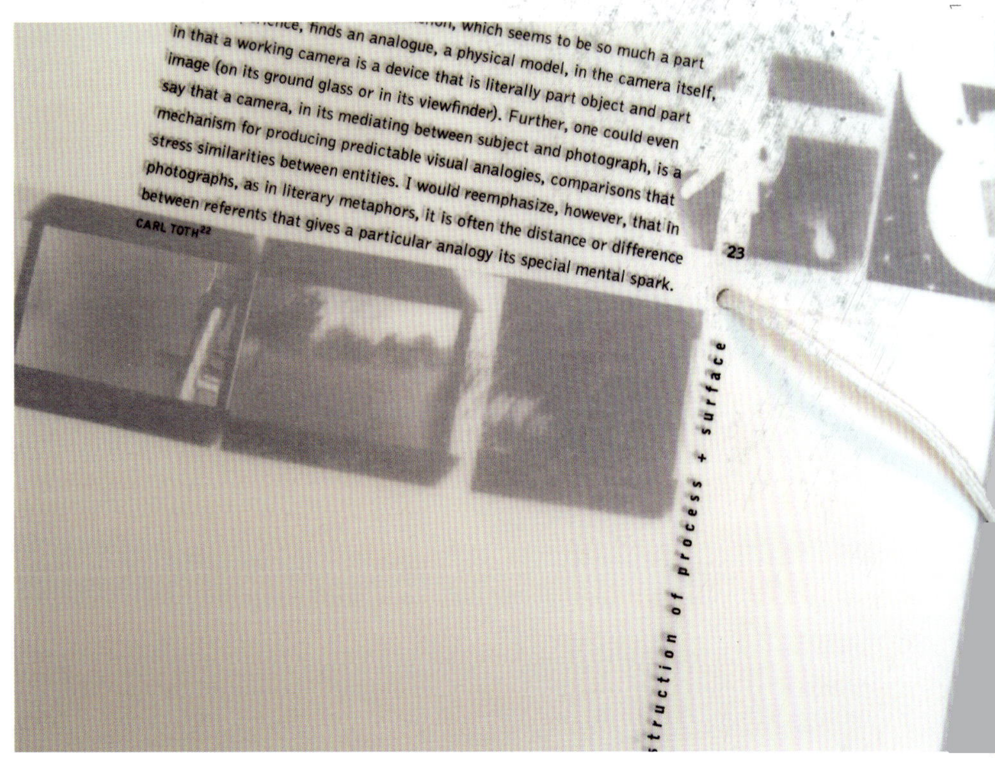

KELLY SALCHOW MACARTHUR, *FROM EXPERIENCE TO CONSTRUCTION: FOCUSING, EXPANDING AND ROTATING THE LENS OF AWARENESS*, 2003

For an artist this is the only way. There is no help anywhere. He must listen to his own mind.[6] AGNES MARTIN

We repeatedly question, listen, and write. We cull this writing by giving our thinking process objective form through systems of mapping. Connections are allowed to develop, which in turn give us the words to tell the story of our work. Mapping through writing is a complex emergent process of making sense in a "felicitous space" at the edge of knowing.[7]

4 Italo Calvino, *Six Memos for the Next Millennium* (Cambridge, MA: Harvard University Press, 1988), 81–99.

5 Ibid., 92.

6 Agnes Martin, "Beauty is the Mystery of Life," in *Agnes Martin* (New York: Whitney Museum of American Art, 1992), 10. "Mind" as used by Martin does not imply intellect. Rather it suggests receptivity to inspiration, awakened sensibility, and intuition.

7 Gaston Bachelard, *The Poetics of Space*, trans. Maria Jolas (Boston: Beacon Press, 1994), xxxv.

THE SPIRIT OF MAPPING THROUGH WRITING

For more than a decade, in various courses and contexts, I have worked with art and design students at Rhode Island School of Design as faculty guide, mentor, and companion in the process of developing and deepening their own creative voices and projects. Mapping through writing is a way to explore, understand, and explain work and process.

This book is presented as an open-ended framework for inquiry and documentation, and is meant to catalyze creative thinking, locate and build ideas, and help develop a voice for public presentation and dialogue. This book supports connecting clearly and inductively with the multiple dimensions of our vision and then developing skills to express this vision in words.

When I begin a writing session, I often hear these comments: "I am blind to my own process," "It's all a muddle," or "I experience my work as a big lump from which it is hard to extract the meaning." Know that our voice is built slowly through recognition and declaration. As the physicist Francisco Varela believes, knowledge is built in "micro worlds"—that is, in "small domains"—through a process of ongoing discovery where what we think comes about slowly and incrementally.[8] To instigate this process, I present catalyst questions that allow us to forge links with the connections that rise to the surface.

This is a book of questions. Questions stimulate an intimate and passionate conversation (both conscious and unconscious) with the work. Each question is designed to elicit a specific store of knowledge and to encourage a multi-angled approach to viewing the work. We explore life history, revisit experiences to see how they impact the work, and clarify concepts.

The process of true creative writing is rarely straightforward, efficient, or methodological. Rather it is like following the path of a strange attractor in chaos theory. The route to understanding is unpredictable, dynamic, and oftentimes messy. Revelations come through a matrix of hidden, disorderly correspondences. As we search with words, we find our vision and voice in the intimate tension between sensations and writing, the insistence of our questions and insights born from project experiments, in comments offered during conversations and critiques, and in the rigor of our research probes. We must take stock while our ideas are still new and in formation.

We must also remain open to allow meaning to arise over time. Yet, as keen witnesses with active radar, we respond in dialogue to the work and the creative process. A perspective shapes. Thought patterns become evident. A working philosophy comes into view. The

The present epoch will perhaps be above all the epoch of space. We are in the epoch of simultaneity: we are all in the epoch of juxtaposition, the epoch of the near and far, of the side-by-side, of the dispersed. We are at the moment, I believe, when our experience of the world is less that of a long life developing through time than that of a network that connects points and intersects with its own skein.[9] MICHEL FOUCAULT

practice of writing asks that we be energized by the speech of our practice. We capture it close-up, appreciate the questions, the materiality of the work, the false starts, the creative ruptures, the edges of perception we are trying to name. And we do this so that all the energy of writing can then feed energy back into the work. We are not explaining the work but writing together with it.[10]

Siphoning off the thought and the intent in the work is part of the endeavor, as is perusing the landscape of accomplishment to see both the gestalt and the connections. We write to recognize what is happening in the work, to articulate intuitions, to integrate our understanding of core themes, and to feel the weight of what we are creating. To paraphrase Wendell Berry, " Words act as fulcrums across which intelligence is endlessly weighed against experience."[11]

Telling makes demands. Writing requires honesty, a willingness to touch personal identity, and openness to exploring the depths of our imaginative waters. Writing does not allow us to hide behind the work. Writing leads to awareness and insight. Artist Eva Hesse wrote, "I thought one must know oneself to write and that always intrigued me most of all. The idea of honesty is so challenging, much more so in words than in pictures."[12]

Through a patient commitment to writing about our work, we bridge the schism between making and thinking. Rather than siphon energy from our creative practice, the process of writing allows us to make vital connections to the visions that steer our lives. We see more clearly the direction of future work and we gain confidence in explaining to others what we do and why. Mapping through writing sees the relationship between making and thinking as a holistic practice. The language of the work allows us to become part of cultural conversation.

8 Francisco J. Varela, "The Re-enchantment of the Concrete," in *Incorporations*, eds. Jonathan Crary and Sanford Kwinter (New York: Zone Books, 1992), 328.

9 Michel Foucault, "Of Other Spaces," in *The Visual Culture Reader*, ed. Nicholas Mirzoeff (New York: Routledge, 1998), 237.

10 These ideas were worked out for and first appeared in Arianne Gelardin, Patricia C. Phillips, and Mat Stevens, eds. *Speculations: A Collective Exchange on the Creative Process* (Providence: Rhode Island School of Design, Division of Graduate Studies, 2010).

11 Wendell Berry, *Standing by Words* (San Francisco: North Point Press, 1983), 10.

12 Helen A. Cooper, "Eva Hesse: Diaries and Notebooks," in Cooper et al., *Eva Hesse: A Retropective* (New Haven, CT: Yale University Press), 17.

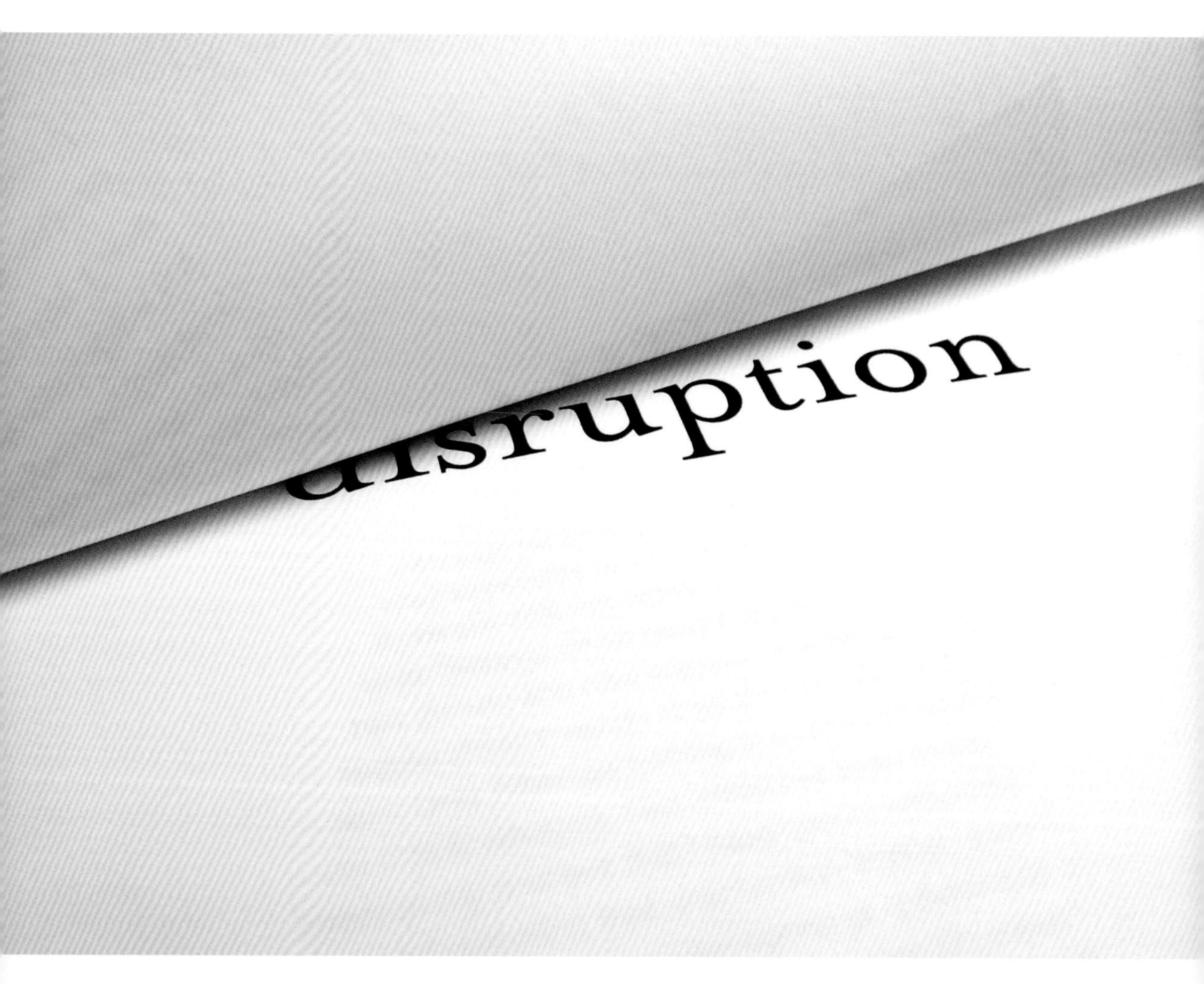

REBECCA KLEIN GANZ, *BALANCING THE BETWEEN*, 2003

seeing, making, thinking, probing, writing, naming

USING THIS BOOK

Writing is a necessary skill and a critical expectation of every artist. While most works of art are not generated from words (unless language is a feature of the work), we must nevertheless present art works using language in various public contexts. Today some form of writing—artist statement, report, grant, or residency application—is necessary for the successful working professional in the arts.

This book is for artists who wish to, or must, write about their work. It offers a guide for moving interpretively between visual and verbal language, intuition and intellect in seeking out our own voice. My intention is to support a variety of artist-writers: the autodidact involved in a personal writing process, the practicing artist preparing a grant or publication or with the gift of time a residency provides, faculty at art colleges, or the student writing a capstone document —the degree project or graduate thesis.

This book presents the practice of mapping through writing in three steps.

We explore. We chart. We communicate. While these stages are portrayed sequentially, actual practice yields a more flexible, non-linear approach whereby activities within each stage inform and re-inform the other as a view of the work unfolds. The relationships among these stages are not separate but part of a living continuum.

This book presents 75 vignettes designed to unfold the experience of mapping through writing. I liken this mapping practice to *Inuksuit*, the cairns of people-shaped standing stones that dot the Arctic tundra. Each *Inukshuk* acts as a marker, guiding travelers who are lost on the treeless Inuit terrain. Following the signposts will enable us to navigate a path through our visual thinking processes and help connect the parts together to author the story of our work.

Each vignette has a thematic focus to spark the imagination and stimulate creative thinking. They include images, commentary, catalyst questions, and samples of writing. These vignettes are tools for inquiry intended to expand and deepen an understanding of our work, and to delineate, clarify, and expose its messages. The aim is to examine the work without over-explaining it, and to keep the perspective on vision specific, intimate, thoughtful, and vibrant. Within the space of each vignette, we write and rewrite, as if rotating a prism, until our words speak the truth.

The process begins with **Exploring**. Through exploratory free-writing exercises and projects, we discover what we are doing and why we are doing it. We investigate the work from multiple viewpoints, tapping into the vocabulary of experience, opening stores of knowledge, and unlocking insights to get to the heart of what keys into the work. The section begins with a protracted examination of silence, and it culminates with the creation of a matrix map and the first round of an artist statement.

The second stage, **Charting**, initiates the verbal organization of labeling, logic, and syntax. We chart thought processes and bring connections to the surface by creating a visual map of interconnecting links. During this stage, we begin to grasp the previously indiscernible mental patterns in the work. We bear witness to the work, reflecting and questioning what it is all about. We evaluate, map relationships, and examine the webs of interconnectivity. We find a nomenclature. This section begins with an alphabetical listing of work and ends with a composite map to establish conceptual links.

In the final stage, **Communicating**, we establish our voice and bring vision and intelligence together in a coherent narrative to share with others. We respond to various forms of writing, each with its own convention—manifesto, letter to the editor, abstract. The goal of this section is to prepare a written and visual account of our work to present within the larger, cultural environment.

How much and how long?

This book was developed to support a conversation between your thinking and working process. Set your own personal course through this book. Be your own guide. Whatever your personal goals, use the book to serve your own ends, whether you are focusing on a particular work or an entire body of work. For example, you may wish to concentrate on one vignette at a time until you have completed every question. Or you may wish to dip in at will, addressing only those vignettes that are most relevant to your concerns.

Writing one page a day will give you the ability to closely examine your process and to discern a framework for your thinking. Or you may need the intense focus of several hours for a period of days or even a short residency to build momentum for insight.

As you respond to the questions, you may wish to follow the suggested writing frameworks which were developed in the context of a classroom in which they were useful.

Timed stream-of-consciousness free writes support an open exploration of ideas without concern for form. Jot down notes or sketches and exhaust what you need to express.

Considered responses encourage you to compose a developed passage that brings forth your insights. These may vary in length from one-paragraph to three pages.

Refined writings direct you to return to passages that hold promise and to focus your attention on their content and form.

Projects and field trips encourage you to create a response to a particular activity or experience intended for individual, partner, or group responses and presentations.

Diagrams, lists, and map-making enable you to synthesize and draw comparisons.

EXPLORING

map as matrix

release

let go
free-fall

reaction

other

action

participation
interaction

natural
phenomena

Rebecca Klein Ganz, *Matrix Map*, 2003

nside

unknow

ser

intention

non-intention

c

tside

enclosed

open

sile

EXPLORING
map as matrix

We begin the process of mapping with Exploring—the activity that enables us to unearth and document the underlying dynamics of our work. We plough the soil of our inspiration. The field we furrow is what I call the vision matrix. It comes into view as a multidimensional field of relations formed from autobiography, how we sense the world, what we make, how we make, and what we think. Deepening our connection to this field of knowing is an essential first step in creating a visual map of the intelligence that underlies our work.

Throughout this section we use writing to find qualities that are an authentic and accurate reflection of our creative spirit and conceptual thinking. Each writing vignette, organized according to a specific theme, is an opportunity to consider one aspect of the work. Each vignette is a launch pad for ideas, insights, and connections. At this stage, we can—and should—let go of the urge to make logical sense of our ideas. In the early stages of developing understanding, when we are immersed in the details, the process is often messy. Yet inevitably, by writing freely, by instigating movement in our thinking, each unfolding effort adds something to the process of understanding. We generate pages of writing. And as we do so, we create concentric ripples across the surface of our awareness. This activity sets in motion dynamic connections in the mind.

What we get from this process.

We get to view our work closely. We slow it down and watch it build up. We unearth important visuals, themes, avenues for research, and questions. We get a sense of the vanishing point to which our work is directed. Through the creation of a matrix map, we also get a perspective on how things fit together and what the work needs. Once we discover the threads that connect our making to our thinking, we begin to comprehend the intelligence of our work.

IN THIS SECTION

who are you?

how do you sense?

how do you make? what do you make?

how do you think? what do you think?

mapping the multiple centers alive in the work

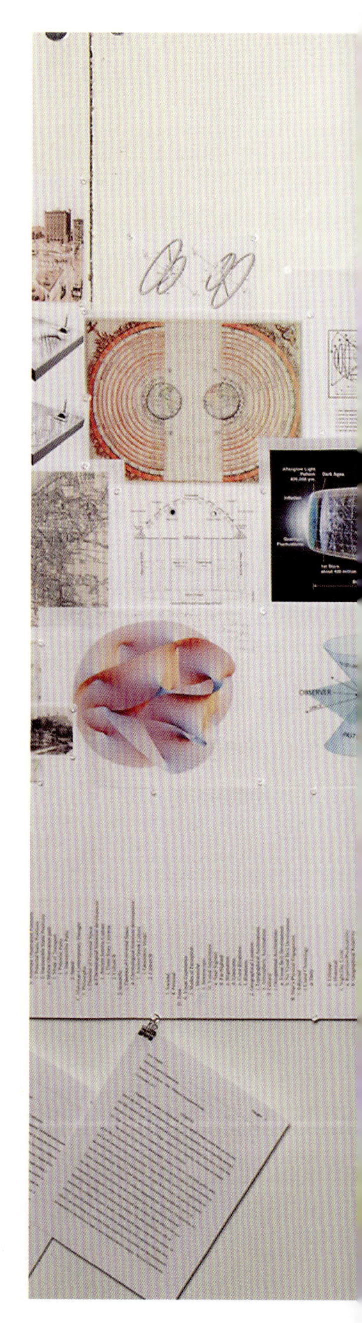

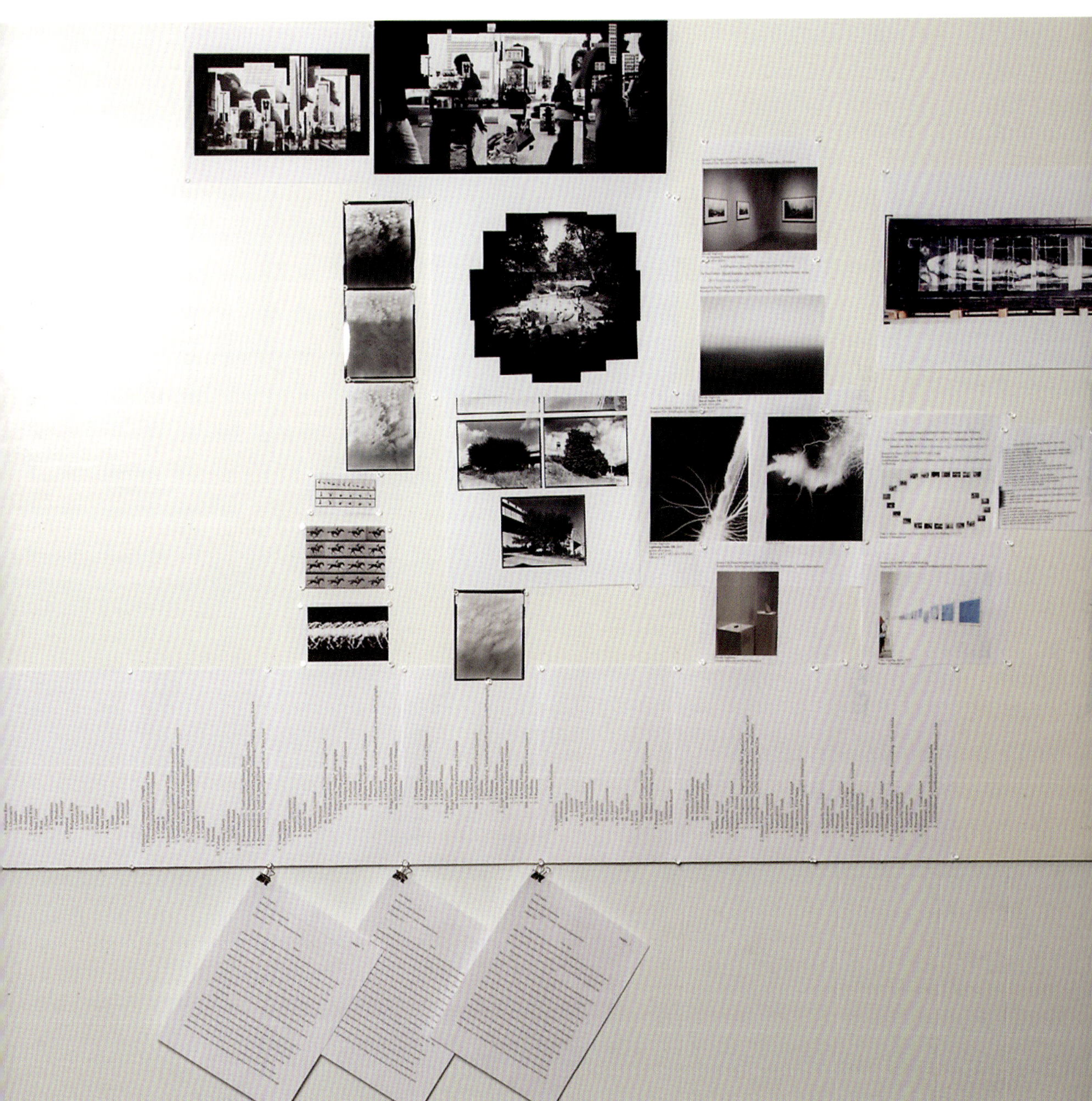

ERIC VAUGHN, *MAPPING EXERCISE*, 2011

We plough the soil of our inspiration. The field we furrow is what I call the vision matrix. ... By writing freely, by instigating movement in our thinking, each unfolding effort adds something to the process of understanding. And as we do so, we create concentric ripples across the surface of our awareness. This activity sets in motion dynamic connections in the mind.

EXPLORING
map as matrix

who are you?

silence

Through a protracted examination of silence we allow time to empty the mind and consider the threshold from which we work.

The threshold is a place of threshing + holding.[13]

Author Adrienne Rich writes: "The matrix of a poet's work consists not only of what is there to be absorbed and worked on, but also of what is missing, *desaparecido*, rendered unspeakable, thus unthinkable. ... Every real poem is the breaking of an existing silence, and the first question we might ask any poem is, what kind of voice is breaking silence, and what kind of silence is being broken?[14]

Does your work break silence?

Free write for 10 minutes.

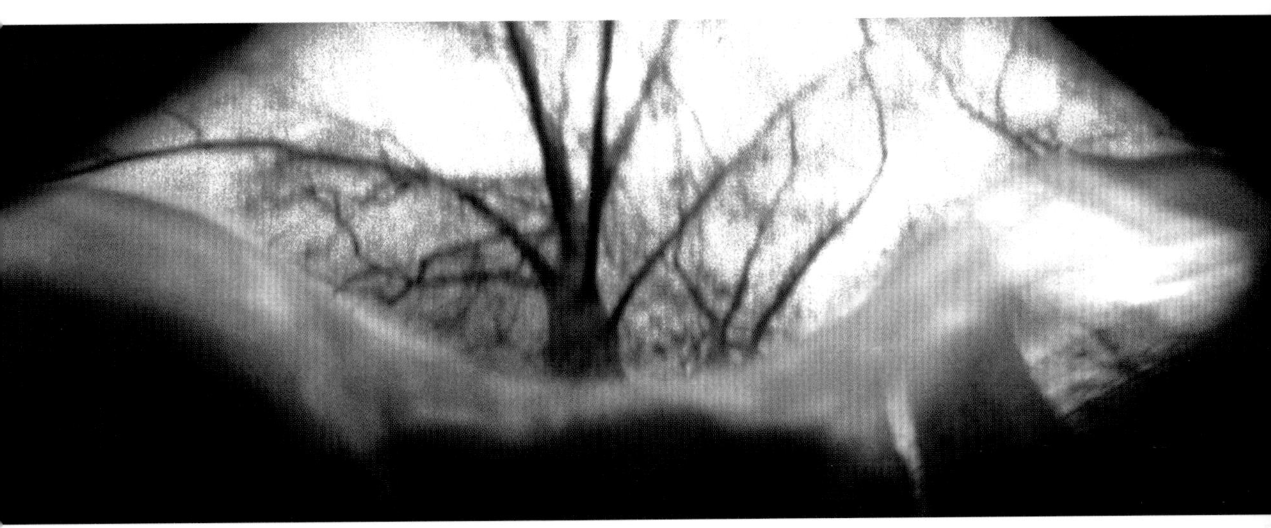

ANN HAMILTON, *FACE TO FACE 38*, 2001

>>

Many works of art are borne out of and activate a felt relationship to silence. Think of Vermeer's paintings ripe with calm reflection, the ambivalent face of silence in De Chirico's masterful architectures of stillness, the backdrops of silence in Christian Boltanski's haunting installations, or Anish Kapoor's densely pigmented voids. Silence is a signature. It is in no small part the pith, the power, and the daring of a work. If we penetrate the silence something is revealed. The negative space speaks. In silence the work's meaning is consolidated.

13 Anjali Srinivasan, "Particle Activism," MFA thesis in Glass, Rhode Island School of Design, 2007, x.

14 Adrienne Rich, *Arts of the Possible* (New York: Norton, 2002), 150.

15 Marlene Dumas, *Marlene Dumas: Give the People What They Want* (Philadelphia: Moore College of Art and Design, 1993), ii.

16 John Cage, *Silence* (Middletown, CT: Wesleyan University Press, 2002), 7–8.

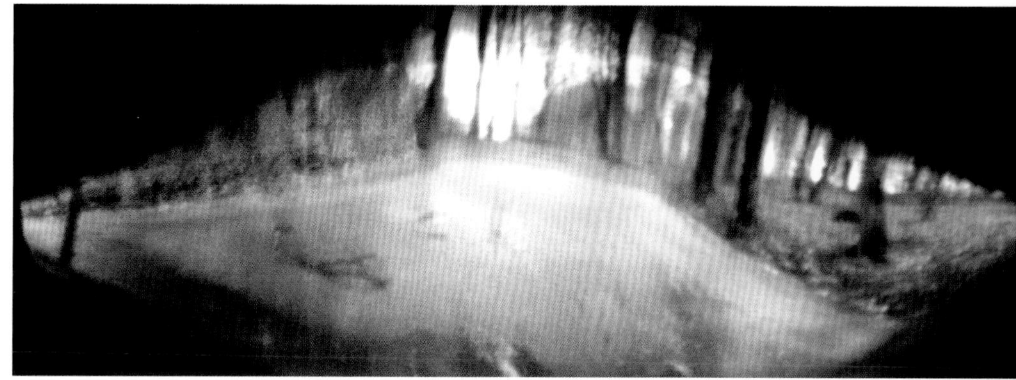

ANN HAMILTON, *FACE TO FACE 14*, 2001

Silence has many qualities. Write of one quality of silence.

What images, forms, materials, colors (or absence of color), and sense of space do you associate with silence?

Speak to the silence in your work.

Art is in love with time. It needs time, it takes time, and it steals time in order to survive in time and be quiet enough to display the silence that betrays everybody and everything.[15] MARLENE DUMAS

Try as we may to make a silence, we cannot. ... Until I die there will be sounds. And they will continue following my death. One need not fear about the future of music.[16] JOHN CAGE

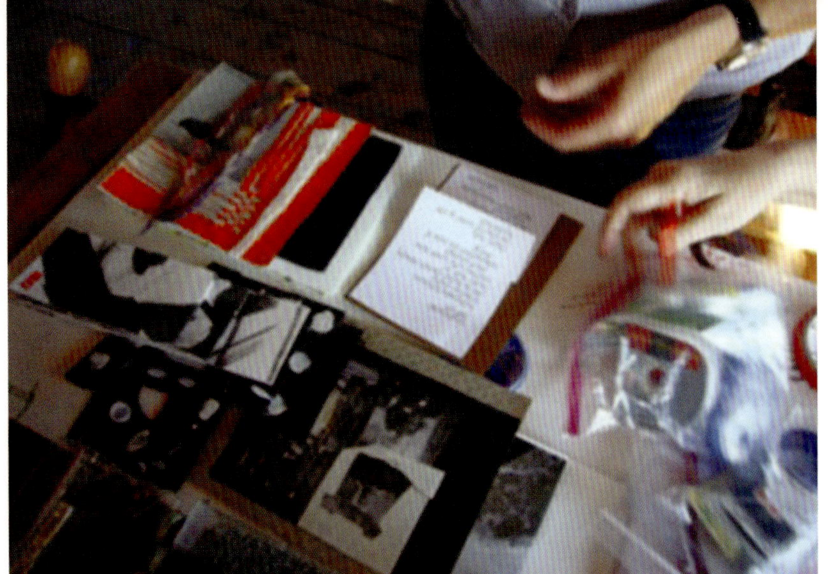

PHOTO KATARINA WESLIEN

a view into the studio

There is a central quality which is the root criterion of life and spirit in a man, a town, a building, or a wilderness. This quality is objective and precise but it cannot be named. ... The search which we make for this quality, in our own lives, is the central search of any person, and the crux of any individual person's story. It is the search for those moments and situations when we are most alive.[17]
CHRISTOPHER ALEXANDER

Work comes out of work.[18] RICHARD SERRA

The Studio as a Vital Center

The site of the studio—a place of potential and constant search—is simultaneously a physical space and a space of mind. Very little is passive in the studio. It is where a body of work propels and impassions us. Oftentimes it is an actual place where raw materials are manipulated into form. Other times, it is a site of interception or a working on location.

Step One

Bring to life the dynamics of your studio. Describe your studio space. What gives you satisfaction in the studio? What are you currently exploring there? In the spirit of Surrealist automatic writing, generate a stream-of-consciousness thought-stream of at least three pages. Keep your hand moving. Capture your mind's flow. Do not stop, read, or edit your work.

Step Two

The work we make has a particular presence and vitality when it is just completed. Convergence has occurred. Seize this moment and write a page about a work that you just completed. What were the intentions and the thoughts that guided the work? Point to some of the successes. Be honest about the limitations.

Step Three

Create a "wish list" for your work. List elements that your work may be requesting or that ignite your enthusiasm. One of my colleagues refers to this list as an opportunity for "ecstatic development."[19] What studio goals would allow for ecstasy?

Working on Location

It was very important to me when I discovered that I could actually learn from making art. Instead of being a means of dumping my feelings or ideas, it acted as a kind of vehicle for getting information. Learning how ice freezes, what the weather's like, how long it takes for rain to fall before it can leave a shadow.[20] ANDY GOLDSWORTHY

17 Christopher Alexander, *The Timeless Way of Building* (New York: Oxford University Press, 1979), ix–x.

18 *Richard Serra: Work Comes Out of Work—*Zeichnungen: Radikalisierte Klassizitat [Exhibit]. Kunstforum International no. 192 (July/August 2008), 364–66.

19 At a critique, December 2006, with Kimberly Libby, MFA in Studio Arts, Maine College of Art.

20 Andy Goldsworthy, *Hand to Earth: Andy Goldsworthy Sculpture 1976–1990*, eds. Terry Friedman and Andy Goldsworthy (New York: Harry N. Abrams, 1993), 58.

intakes of breath

As author James Hillman writes, "This quick intake of breath is also the very root of the word *aesthesis* in Greek, meaning 'sense perception.' *Aisthesis* goes back to the Homeric *aiou* and *aisthou*, which means both 'I perceive' as well as 'I gasp, struggle for breath,' and *aisthomai*, *aisthanomai*, 'I breathe in.' "[21]

Where do you go to find your intakes of breath?

Free write for 5 minutes.

Industrial designer Yann Poisson has a wonderful range of sources from which he derives inspiration:

Elvis Presley, Miles Davis, Beethoven, Chopin, Maria Callas, Pablo Picasso, big-eyed paintings, Barbie, diners, car culture, cats (not the musical), fashion (especially Jean-Paul Gautier), Chihuahuas, Mr. Potato Head, Audrey Hepburn, Tupperware, honey baked ham.[22]

> I can happily add food to my list of artistic inspirations.[23]
> SUZANNE PECK, GLASS ARTIST

List the sources from which you derive inspiration for the work.

the voice of now

Art must have a social sense, a sense of the society in which we live and thrash.[24] STANLEY KUNITZ

For it is important that awake people be awake, or a breaking line may discourage them back to sleep; the signals we give—yes or no, or maybe—should be clear: the darkness around us is deep.[25]
WILLIAM STAFFORD

Being an artist means being awake to this moment in history—the now.

What are our times asking for?

What "signals of now" does your work give off?

Free write for 10 minutes, offering a one-paragraph response to the above prompts.

21 "The Practice of Beauty," in *Uncontrollable Beauty: Toward a New Aesthetic*, ed. Bill Beckley with David Shapiro (New York: Allworth, 1998), 271.

22 From thesis writing exercise, Yann Poisson, RISD, Fall 1998.

23 From thesis writing exercise, Suzanne Peck, RISD, Fall 2009.

24 Stanley Kunitz and Genine Lentine, *The Wild Braid: A Poet Reflects on a Century in the Garden* (New York: W.W. Norton & Company, 2005), 103.

25 William Stafford, "A Ritual to Read to Each Other," in *The Way It Is* (St. Paul, MN: Graywolf Press 1998), 75.

the idea of artist

My ambition is to be a troubadour, and to just absorb the world, and try to express it in a very light way. Not in some heavy art model way with all those crushingly heavy double meanings. I'm trying to be lighter in general. I'm trying to understand things more, and produce less stuff. I think there's too much stuff in the world already. I think if I had to say what there's not enough of, I would say, probably tenderness would be one. Another would be awareness.[26]
LAURIE ANDERSON

I seem to be a verb.[27] R. BUCKMINSTER FULLER

Step One: The Idea of the Artist

What is the idea of artist that you are working out of or heading toward?

What is your artistic vantage point on the world?

Free write for 10 minutes.

Step Two: Your High-Water Marks
In the quest to communicate through our work, we must determine the durable values that sustain it. These values represent our highest goals or intentions as well as our criteria of authenticity.

Create a List
As a way of shaping your worldview and a working ethos, begin by listing the **ten most important values** that you would defend as an artist. These values may orient you, or they may set the course for your work. What matters most to you? What do you stand for? Why should anyone care?

cultural dissident
cultural leader
troubadour
social archaeologist
flâneur
orchestrator of experience
physician of culture
dreamer
revealer of mystic truths
steward
healer
facilitator
brandmaker
catalyst
informer
character
storyteller
inventor
innovator
translator
curator
visual magician

26 Laurie Anderson, interview transcript on *The End of the Moon*, last accessed November 21, 2010, http://artscenter.uhh.hawaii.edu/?Archives:2006_Season:Laurie_Anderson.

27 R. Buckminster Fuller with Jerome Agel and Quentin Fiore, *I Seem to Be a Verb* (New York: Bantam Books, 1970), 1.

cultural blind spots

Somewhere every culture has an imaginary zone for what it excludes, and it is that zone we must try to remember today.[28] HÉLÈNE CIXOUS & CATHERINE CLEMENT

Does your work bring to light a zone of exclusion or a blind spot in our culture?

Project

This project invites a simple action of improvisation. The emphasis is not so much on fabrication as on the idea of the experience.

Within 24 hours and with $15 worth of materials, create a mini exhibit of your own work in which you reveal this apparent blind spot.

Include a simple chart that offers a creative structure for seeing the content and form of this exhibit.

Did this exhibit allow you to rethink the words you use to describe your work and/or to see your work in a new context?

PHOTO BRADLEY SLADE, *SEEING THE EVERYDAY* MAGAZINE, 2011

28 Hélène Cixous and Catherine Clement, "The Newly Born Woman," trans. Betty Wind, in *Theory and History of Literature*, Vol. 24 (Minneapolis: University of Minnesota Press, 1986), ix.

sudden clear images

"I never forgot the image," claims Louise Nevelson, referring to a moment from childhood that arrested her attention. The memory image of a stack of shelves filled with glass jars containing candy registered deep in her psyche and fueled her mature works.[29]

Remember the image at the beginning of the film *American Beauty*—of the plastic bag tossed about by the wind, as if in a slow loop of time? Images claim us. Some stick in our heads and won't go away. What does it mean to follow the lead of these living images? What does it mean to probe their expressive, cognitive, and imaginative possibilities until they assume meaningful articulation both in form and in language?

"One must be receptive to the image in the moment it appears. ... The image is a sudden salience on the surface of the mind," states Gaston Bachelard.[30] Being alert to these perceptual openings and giving them presence is a way to identify our way of seeing. Virginia Woolf refers to such image experiences as "moments of being," which cut through the non-descript cotton wool of daily life and strike hard against the inner self.[31] Celebrated author E.B. White describes these encounters as seeing "sudden clear images."[32] They have dynamic value in our experience, placing a strong imprint on our visual vocabulary, bringing light into the imagination.

Images from Life

Two images remain formative in my sight and to this day have lacerating power. I call them time-lapse encounters. The first, a primordial lantern show, was the most stilling. This I encountered twenty years ago. On my way to school one morning I became fastened to the image of a bird in shadow twittering weightlessly upon the screen of my neighbor's brick wall. The bird's performance—pure energy and naked spirit—was mesmerizing. I recall being transfixed, as if in a moment of private grace. I could do nothing but pause from my real momentum, suspended in a loop of dilated time. The second image had a similar quality, with no rest or ending, and I came upon it recently. It was also played off against a casual walk. This time I was with my dog alongside a river. Nested at the base of a gentle waterfall an inflated red rubber ball spun ceaselessly, stalled from moving downstream by a rock that held it in a suspended sensitive balance.

The image is a mainstay against confusion. The image is a celebration. The image is a clarification. The image is a generative experience. The image is an event of place-making.

Step One: A Visual Encounter

Consider a visual encounter—either recent or one that has resurfaced in your awareness—when an image surprised you, seized your attention. The encounter does not have to be a mystical experience! Think of the image as a photographic afterimage that remains in your mind.

What imagery do you keep coming back to?

Free write for 5 minutes.

29 Arnold B. Glimcher, *Louise Nevelson* (New York: E.P. Dutton & Co., Inc., 1976), 27.

30 Bachelard, *The Poetics of Space*, xv.

31 Virginia Woolf, *Moments of Being* (London: Triad Grafton Books, 1976), 82–83.

32 E.B. White, *Writings From The New Yorker 1927–1979*, ed. Rebecca M. Dale (New York: HarperCollins, 1990), 21.

Step Two: Postcard Correspondence

Imagine you are on a trip and telling a friend back home about this image. You have a succinct, yet charged space in which to describe the power of this encounter.

Let the resonant impressions from this event return to your awareness. See the event reflected back. Within the space of this postcard template, write a short descriptive passage which describes in words the power of this visual encounter. Picture the encounter in words. Make the thrust of the experience vivid to the reader. Capture what invoked in you a sense of engagement with something that shaped your sensibility as an artist.

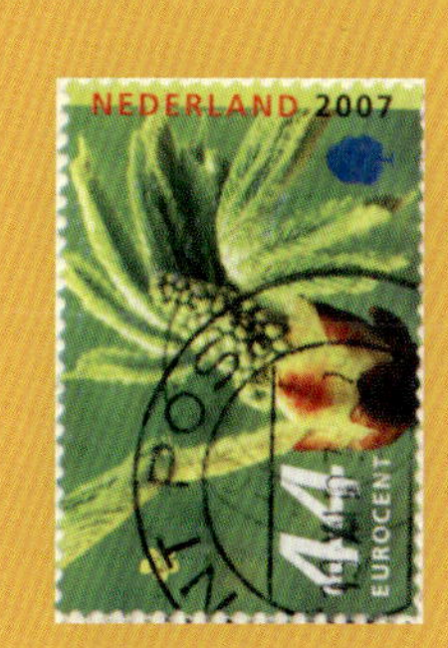

TNT POST, THE NETHERLANDS

five images (or objects) + their stories[33]

In devising a story, therefore, the first thing that comes to mind is an image that for some reason strikes me as charged with meaning, even if I cannot formulate this meaning in discursive or conceptual terms. As soon as the image has become sufficiently clear in my mind, I set about developing it into a story; or better yet, it is the images themselves that develop their own implicit potentialities, the story they carry with them. Around each image others come into being, forming a field of analogies, symmetries, confrontations.[34] ITALO CALVINO

We all have our own visual archive: online bookmarks of inspiring images, a digital image bank, a treasure box of photos and clippings, images preserved in the "deep storage" of our memory, images pinned on the office or studio wall. These images carry "implicit potentialities." They are idea spaces. They hold a seeing and knowing, and as makers and creative thinkers we must find ways to plot the intricacies of this composite world.

Sy Safransky, editor of *The Sun* magazine, refers to his office wall as his "wailing wall," which displays the "graffiti of his inner life."[35] This exercise invites you to find connections among images (or objects) you are attracted to and collect. These images (or objects) can be inspirational references that offer confident echoes of possibility, comfort images as emotional landmarks, current information you need to look at now, or a resource for ideas you are building.

Choose five images (or objects) that inform your working process.

When and how did you stumble upon these images (or objects)?
What do you relate to in them?

Describe what is relevant to an appreciation of these images (or objects).
Do they tell stories?

How have these images (or objects) served your growth as an artist?
For example, have they helped you find a stylistic visual language or figure out certain formal or conceptual issues?

Compose a 300-word response to each of the questions listed above.

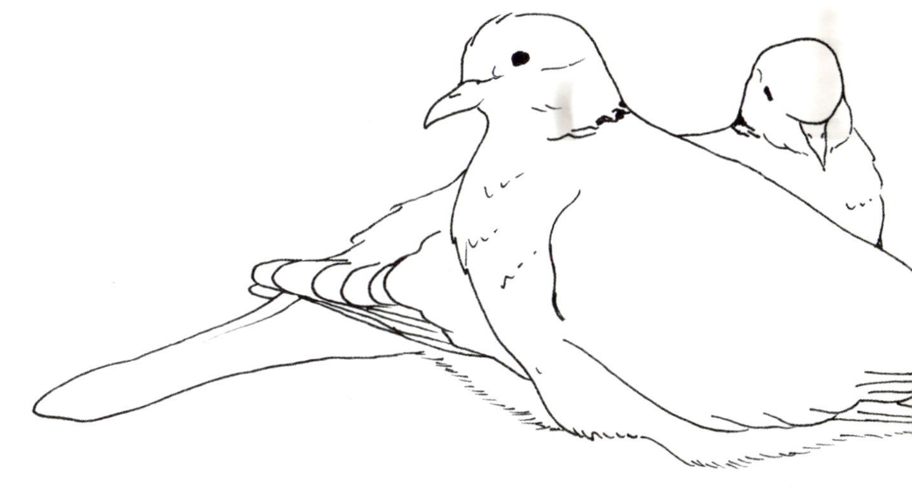

33 Inspiration for this exercise came from Betty Woodman: *5 x 7: Seven Ceramic Artists Each Acknowledge Five Sources of Inspiration* (New York: Division of Ceramic Art, School of New York State College of Ceramics at Alfred University, c1993).

34 Calvino, "Visibility" in *Six Memos*, 88–89.

35 Sy Safransky, *Four in the Morning* (Chapel Hill, NC: The Sun Publishing Company, 1993), 49–54.

>>

DRAWINGS BY OLIVIA VERDUGO, 2010

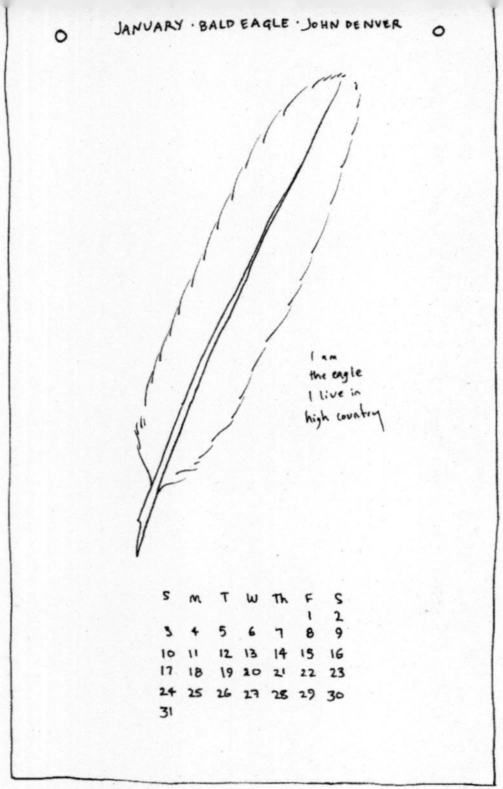

1

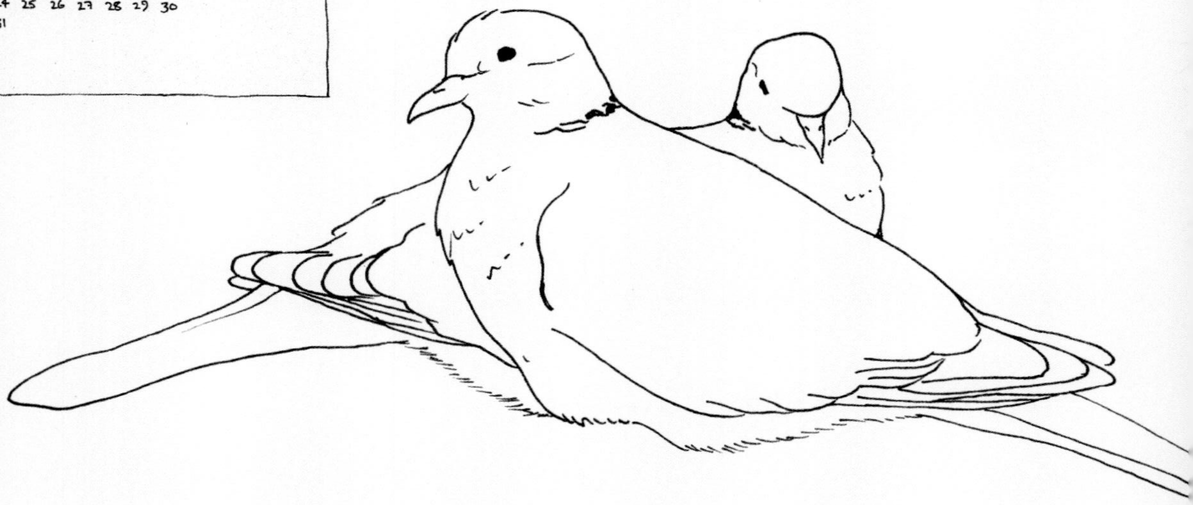

JANUARY · BALD EAGLE · JOHN DENVER

I am
the eagle
I live in
high country

S	M	T	W	Th	F	S
					1	2
3	4	5	6	7	8	9
10	11	12	13	14	15	16
17	18	19	20	21	22	23
24	25	26	27	28	29	30
31						

2

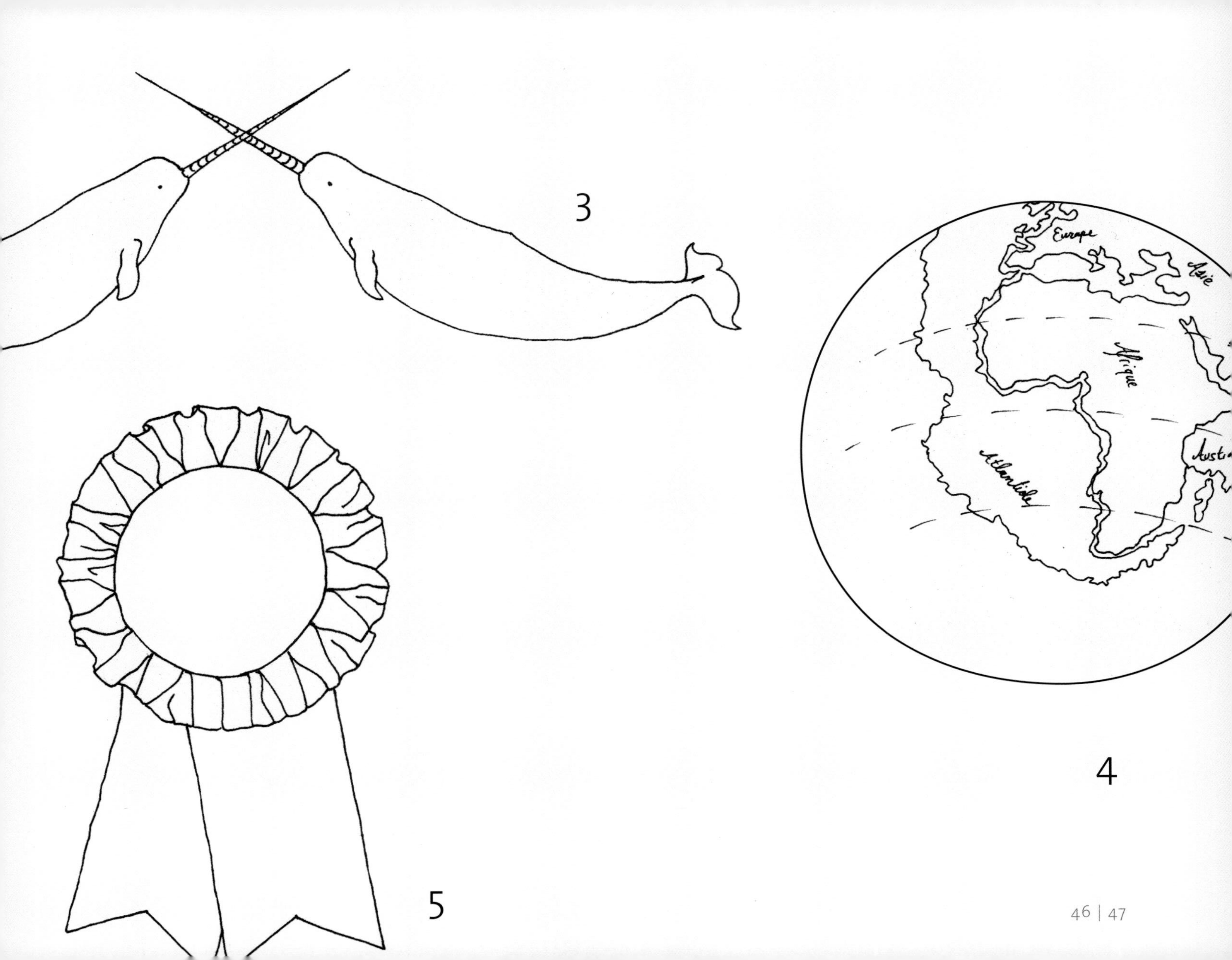
3
Europe
Asie
Afrique
Atlantide
4
5

early delving

Most artists, writers, and designers nurture a vocabulary of images, ideas, and forms throughout a lifetime. Over years a language is developed whose source of energy originated, was shaped, and given momentum in childhood. Reveries from childhood, "the indelible solitudes," as Bachelard refers to them, are a liberating force in the poetic imagination.[36]

Travel writer Barry Lopez once opened a lecture about travel with the recollection of a boyhood reverie.[37] Between the ages of six and eight he played a game that filled him with wonder and desire. Within the small space of his bedroom closet he set up a study with a table, lamp, chair, pencil, tracing paper, and his cherished *Hammond World Atlas* gifted to him by his mother. During hours of imaginative absorption in the protected solitude of this space, he traced his internal longings for adventure over the pages of his atlas, traveling widely.

Decades later, he pulled his atlas down from the shelf. What he discovered, forgotten yet still alive within its pages, were the free-spirited tracings from youth, an archive of facts of his early delving. Amazingly, the same fantasy paths illustrated from his imagination had found vivid actualization in adulthood. He got to do what he wanted to do! Exact cities had been visited, geographies had been crossed, and exploratory longings had been documented in his celebrated travel writings. These youthful inscriptions informed the development of the larger story of his life. Open to the lead of his playful curiosity, he had served a kind of apprenticeship.

Certain perceptions, recurring imagery, or themes originate in childhood, then form an objective pattern later in life. Describe an early delving that was foundational to your creative practice.

Write a one-paragraph response.

36 Gaston Bachelard, *The Poetics of Reverie: Childhood, Language, and the Cosmos*, trans. Daniel Russell (Boston: Beacon Press, 1969), 99.

37 Barry Lopez, lecture on travel at Rhode Island School of Design, February 22, 2000.

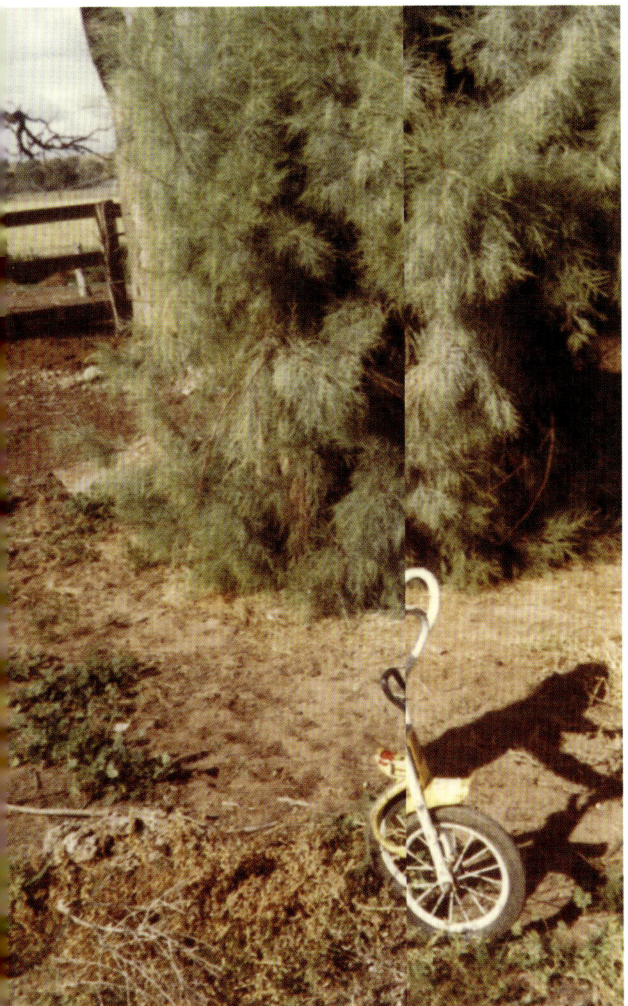

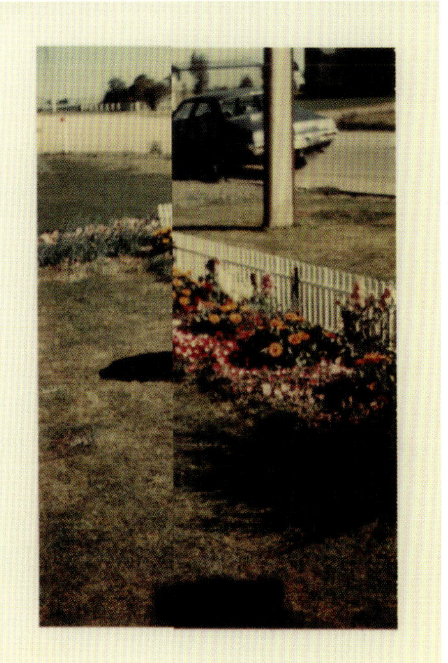

ODETTE ENGLAND, *PHOTOS OF ME WITHOUT ME*, 2011

through the lens of memory

I need my memories. They are my documents. I keep watch over them. ... You must differentiate between memories. Are you going to them or are they coming to you? If you are going to them, you are wasting time. Nostalgia is not productive. If they come to you, they are the seeds for sculpture.[38] LOUISE BOURGEOIS

Some years back I saw an exhibition at the New Museum of Contemporary Art in New York City of works by the French artist Christian Boltanski. His work explores themes of childhood and death as markers of existence.[39] In one installation, Boltanski shaped objects remembered from childhood in plasticene and carefully placed them in drawers with wire mesh. I still recall the evocative stillness that surrounded these awkward forms—the naïve, uninhibited directness of these private, yet shared memories. These works were tangible snapshots—vivid embodiments where absence and presence were condensed in solid form. While obdurate they were also mysteriously alive.

About memory and imagination, Gaston Bachelard said, they remain associated, each one works for their mutual deepening.[40] It is not so much that we are dependent on memories, but they encourage us. We are called by something tacit. Poetic understanding is in our memories. An effort of remembering can offer us coherence.

Project: Create an Object from Memory

Is there some material object or sensation that triggers a recollection? Allow this memory to come to you. Then make the object in Playdoh. Write of this memory. How has this memory informed your work?

perfect playdoh

Measure 2 cups all purpose flour,

1/2 cup salt, 1-tablespoon cream of tartar,

2 cups water (add food coloring or dry tempera before cooking).

Combine all dry ingredients in heavy saucepan. Add liquids.
On medium heat, start cooking and stirring. As it thickens into a blob, stir and mush. Stir, mush down, and cook. The longer it cooks, the less sticky it will be. After it is one big "blob," remove from heat. Knead after it cools down. Store in a plastic bag. Does not have to be refrigerated.

38 Louise Bourgeois, as quoted in Charlotta Kotik, "The Locus of Memory: An Introduction to the Work of Louise Bourgeois," in *Louise Bourgeois: The Locus of Memory, Works 1982–1993* (New York: Brooklyn Museum, 1994), 23.

39 *Christian Boltanski: Lessons of Darkness*, The New Museum of Contemporary Art, December 9–February 12, 1988.

40 Bachelard, *The Poetics of Space*, 5.

EXPLORING

PHOTO BRADLEY SLADE, *SEEING THE EVERYDAY* MAGAZINE, 2011

dual pursuits

Alongside Piet Mondrian's well-known geometric abstractions, he sustained another body of work, which critic David Shapiro refers to as his "secret." For his friends he displayed evanescent single-flower studies on a secret wall in New York City. These studies are a counterpoint in his artistic sensibility, revealing a devotion to the essential from another perspective. They are quietly sensual and suggestive of the body and "the allegorized feminine."[41]

Do you have a "secret" body of work that you are reluctant to bring to public scrutiny?

Does this work represent another pole of your artistic sensibility?

Why is it secret?

Free write for 5 minutes.

41 David Shapiro, "Mondrian's Secret," in *Uncontrollable Beauty: Toward a New Aesthetics*, eds. Bill Beckley and David Shapiro, (New York: Allworth, 1998), 307–23.

narratives of place

I was only an American Negro—
who loved the surface of Africa and
the rhythms of Africa—but I was not
Africa. I was Chicago and Kansas City
and Broadway and Harlem.[42]
LANGSTON HUGHES

Cultural geographer John Brinckerhoff Jackson notes that the expression "sense of place" originated as the Latin term *genius loci*, meaning genius of a place.[43] It was believed in ancient times that the unique quality of a place derived not so much from its character, but from the presence of a spirit that presided over it. Deep connections were made with a place through rituals of homage offered to that residing spirit. We no longer associate the "genius of a place" with a benevolent guardian. According to Jackson, now we establish a sense of a place from its vivid sensory impressions or influence. Places have moods and magic, an atmosphere of their own.[44]

If you recall places that have figured prominently in your life—landscapes from childhood, your hometown, a corner of the earth that you visited and loved, a geographical or cultural site—the commanding power of these places was established through a relationship. There are different ways of conceptualizing and speaking about the way we connect to the spirit and texture of a place. We find expression and authenticity of place through sensory cues, crystallized images, and from reasons steeped in memory and meaning. Jackson suggests that meaningful rituals—habitual rhythms of behavior in a place—inform the way we speak about a place for they give it unity and continuity. Topographical features of landscape, distinguishing structures and landmarks, people, and stories may also stimulate strong connections to place. "Patterns of sensations make up the quality of place," states site planner Kevin Lynch. These include sounds, smells, and feelings we experience in a place.[45]

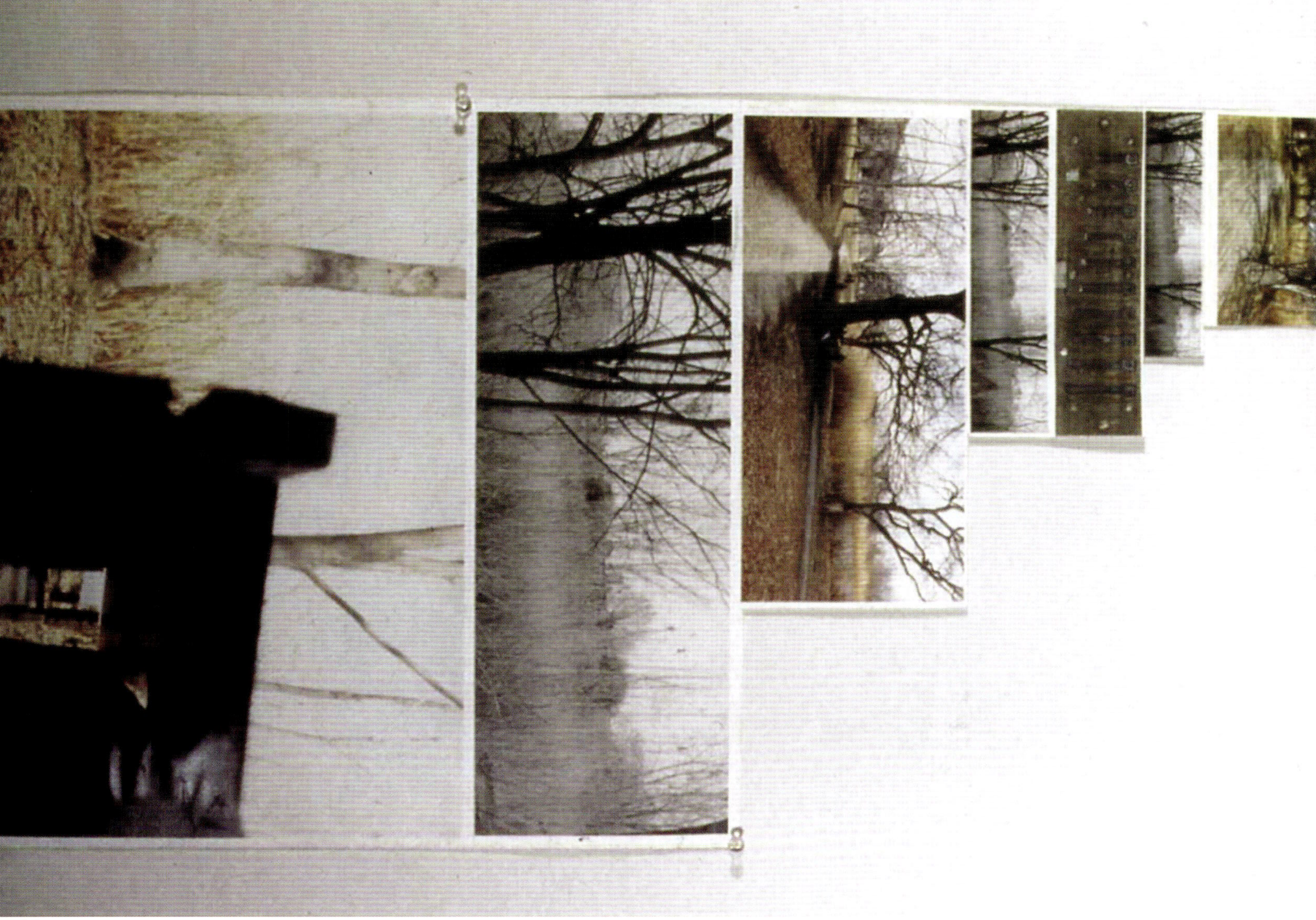

PHOTO JONATHAN L. HARRIS

Step One
Recall a place that has figured prominently in your life. Consider the way in which you have established a relationship to this place. As you build a narrative of place, engage all the senses.

How has this place affected the making of your work?

Free write for 10 minutes.

Step Two
Many artists live transient lives away from their home country. Ideas of belonging, connection, and stability established through place-making are most often replaced with themes of dislocation, displacement, or nomadism.

Are such themes prominent in your work?

Free write for 10 minutes.

42 Langston Hughes, *The Big Sea* (New York: Alfred A. Knopf, 1940), 325. As quoted in Lucy R. Lippard, *The Lure of the Local: Sense of Place in a Multicentered Society* (New York: W.W. Norton & Company, Inc, 1977), 68.

43 John Brinckerhoff Jackson, *A Sense of Place, a Sense of Time* (New Haven, CT: Yale University Press, 1999), 157–58.

44 Ibid., 158.

45 Kevin Lynch, *The Image of the City* (Cambridge, MA: MIT Press, 1980), 1–13.

46 From thesis writing exercise, Jillian Conrad, RISD, Winter 2004.

I grew up in Las Cruces, New Mexico. The Organ Mountains to the west framed the town, while the flat agricultural fields stretched out endlessly to the east. Las Cruces was, in most ways, entirely ordinary. There were suburbs, a mall, two high schools, bars, grocery stores, and a Holiday Inn. But in its humble way, Las Cruces was extraordinary.

The landscape was stark and dusty. I remember clearly the hot smell of the chili fields and searching out the cool shade of the pecan orchards. It wasn't a poor town exactly, but there was a directness and simplicity to it. Homes were out in the open, no high walls or gates. There were lots of long, straight fences and bare, plywood buildings. I didn't particularly care for the details of Las Cruces growing up; they sunk into me anyway and became my native tongue. Even now, I find myself looking for the brown stucco buildings and opening fields I grew up with. The images I have of Las Cruces are based on fact. But they are also idealized elaborations. In my memory, I've used the truth to create fiction. In my work I try to ignite this thin line between the hard facts and possibilities imagination allows.

The light of Las Cruces still influences me. A desert town where the temperature rarely dropped below 70 degrees Fahrenheit, the sun was a major presence in my life. It was everywhere and it was relentless. It blinded and scorched me. It was so bright during the day that the colors of the landscape ran together into one giant washed-out glare. But the evenings were spectacular. The sunsets against the Organ Mountains were so admired; many backyards were specifically oriented for taking them. The air cooled as the sky glowed bright pink, then faded to lilac as the sun went down. It was the perfect time of day.

As a result of these extremes, I use light and color carefully. I light my pieces to give them presence and use color to convey mood. I create an environment that is pale, almost colorless, in order to let the work be the centerpiece. There needs to be a contrast between the perimeter of the work and its center so that viewers are drawn in visually and experientially. I am creating a detailed, miniature world where the viewer's senses are heightened.[46]

origin piece

Speak to a seminal work by another artist that launched a whole set of ideas, themes, and motifs in your own work.

How is this work an axis point to your current work? How did it propel your work forward?

Free write for 10 minutes.

One student told me that her first encounter with the illusionary work of the Dutch graphic artist M.C. Escher had a significant impact on her thinking process and improved insights into her own work. His two-dimensional representations of spatial constructions helped her to understand the dynamics between micro and macro views and between the immediate and the infinite. His work represented what she wanted to realize in her architectural designs. Another student told me of a major installation by Anish Kapoor that caused her to rethink the way sculpture inhabits space and affects viewer interaction.

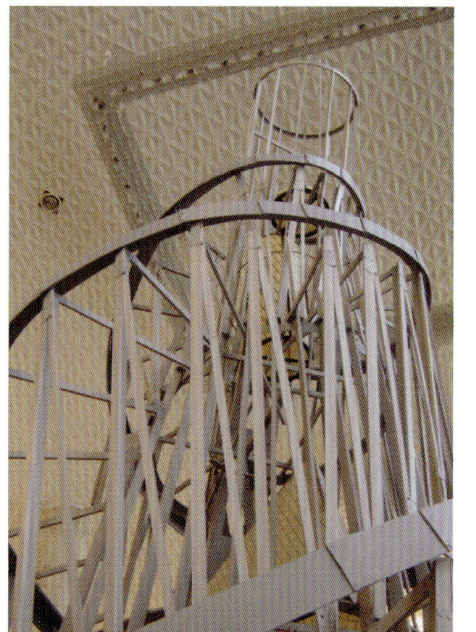

VLADIMIR TATLIN, MODEL FOR *MOMUMENT TO THE THIRD INTERNATIONAL*, 1919–20 PHOTO KATARINA WESLIEN

While I often look to artists such as Alexander Calder and Jean Tinguely for inspiration as I work, I have been watching and learning from those much closer to me throughout my life. My father and grandfather are tinkerers. They are the sorts of men who can find a solution to any problem. They are collectors and menders of many broken and over-loved items. They rescue the things that no longer work and restore them to give new life. My grandfather repairs clocks, mends toy trains and restores furniture and stained glass. His basement is like a time capsule of curiosity. My father is an innovator. He can see solutions where others see patterns and find joy in what others discard. They are often in my mind as I work, pushing me to be curious and innovative.[47]

Ancestral lines cannot be broken. Without them there is no childhood. Without them there can be no right dreams. The river flows, it is continually changing, continually moving, yet it is always a river. Now, before, after. As such, so is the line from you to your ancestors, for outside the physical there is an unbroken thread. It cannot be seen, yet can be felt. You may call it a déjà vu, an unconscious sense of familiarity about a certain place or circumstance. You may call it a certain yearning for certain foods, for certain experiences, for a certain type of person. You may call it your "nature." For what is nature but the execution of some master plan? The embodiment of some intelligence too broad or whole to be conceived of as one. And just as science discovers more about the apparent existence of a purpose or consciousness of all things, so too will they realize that what you call your likes and dislikes, attractions or repulsions, your personality expressed in your like things, is nothing more than the expression of this same thread of intelligence. And this intelligence is the wisdom of your ancestors, the wisdom of age beyond the limits of the corporeal, accumulating down through the generations. They are not so far off the track, those scientist people, when they probe into the tiny world of the unseen for this thread, yet their insistence on the use of the metaphors of the physical world will prevent them from ever really touching it.[48]

BILL VIOLA

ancestral lines

Our work is often informed by a push and pull behind the surface. Digging deep into the memory-links—the layers of history that reside in a palimpsest—can feed the imagination and strengthen emotional bonds to threads that connect you to your actual ancestors.

Write about some of these links beneath the surface. You may find a vital source of connection to ancestral lines that exist in a shared vocabulary of events, styles, foods, or products.

Free write for 5 minutes.

There is also a material sense of ancestry, as if each work is part of a family tree.

List the cumulative layers of your work from the most recent to the past.

The quality that we call beauty, however, must always grow from the realities of life, and our ancestors, forced to live in dark rooms, presently came to discover beauty in shadows, ultimately to guide shadows towards beauty's ends.[49]
JUN'ICHIRŌ TANIZAKI

47 From thesis writing exercise, Gideon Webster, RISD, Fall 2004.

48 Bill Viola, *Reasons for Knocking at an Empty House: Writings 1973–1994* (Cambridge, MA: MIT Press, 1998), 58.

49 Jun'ichirō Tanizaki, *In Praise of Shadows*, trans. Thomas J. Harper and Edward G. Seidensticker (Sedgwick, ME: Leete's Island Books, 1977), 18.

50 From thesis writing exercise, Amy Lovera, RISD, Fall 2006.

51 Tony Cragg, *In Camera* (S'Hertongenbosch, Netherlands: European Ceramics Work Centre, 1993), 14.

a motive to begin the work

Consider a body of work that has sustained you. What triggered or motivated this work? What may have changed your working direction in process?

Write a one-paragraph response.

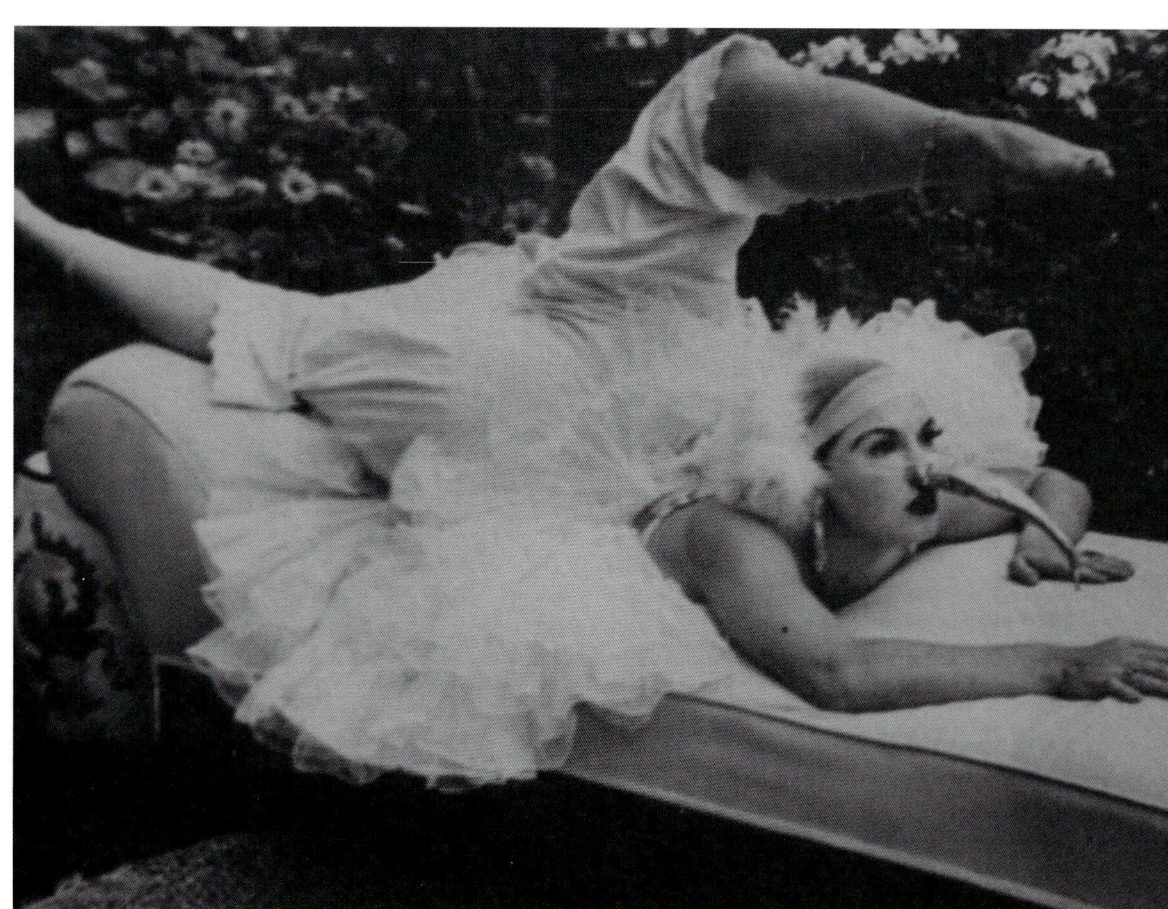

AMY LOVERA, *ANYA PETROVNA IN PETERSBURG*, 1999

I began *The Life of Anya Petrovna* on a Sunday afternoon with a friend. I had made a long pointed nose out of duct tape, wrapped my head in white ostrich feathers, and moved a Victorian chaise onto my lawn. It was playful. I posed on the chaise lounge with my legs in the air over my head; my friend took pictures. Days later, the name Anya Petrovna came to me. I knew who she was and my ideas made me giddy and anxious in a way that I never had been before. Trusting in my instinct, I began with this character and filled in the details of her life. The work unfolded from the inside out; each series of images I made would suggest another part of her story. This fictive portrait about my great aunt helped me to establish myself as a character and a storyteller. It is where I first mingled fact with fiction and where I began to use a variety of media to condense images and events into symbolic narratives. This was the seminal work out of which everything I have since made began. The real experience of knowing my family history through photographs and artifacts melded with my desire to perform.[50]

AMY LOVERA, PHOTOGRAPHER

Why is it so important to find a new language? Because the spoken language we use daily seems to be becoming worn out, exhausted, reduced to banal utilitarianism, dictated by commerce and other power systems. One only has to consider two aspects of this problem to realize that one cannot leave the creation of language to utilitarian interests. Finally there is the fact that the word "poetry," which can or should be regarded as the creative cutting edge of language, was originally a Greek word, which simply meant "to create," and was not exclusive to the written or spoken word. And secondly, that philosophy, "the love of knowledge," has been for too long defined by language. The idea being of course that what one thinks, one speaks and vice versa. This gives the spoken word an extremely dominant role in describing thought and knowledge. The problem I have with that is, that when I dream, I don't dream in words. I dream in images and colors, in events and for that there is a fantastic language available. A language which forms itself at the same highly sensitive level at which we can perceive. A picture, an image, or a form cannot be expressed with a thousand words—not even with a million. In addition, associated with our perception we have a huge vocabulary of responses even to the smallest and subtlest things, which are in a sense erotic responses to the world we live in. And that is really what making sculpture and looking at sculpture is all about. Trying to understand the physical world and to use it, as a language is really a sign of the loving respect for the material we exist in and are made of.[51]

TONY CRAGG

EXPLORING

map as matrix

how do you sense?

sensing the matter of the world

A human being is a bundle of very delicate receptor organs and at the same time an image-generating organ equipped with a vigorous memory-playback system. An image generated in the human brain is a spectacle orchestrated through multiple sensory stimuli and revived memories.[52] KENYA HARA

The sensing body is not a programmed machine but an active and open form, continually improvising its relation to things and to the world.[53] DAVID ABRAM

In his luminous book *The Spell of the Sensuous: Perception and Language in a More-Than-Human World* David Abram emphatically calls us to awaken our sensing body to the animate qualities of the "life-world." Abram centers us in matter by invoking the capacity for eros, the creative yearning found in the sympathetic perception of the sensuous physicality of the world. His scholarly work is rooted in the study of phenomenology, the branch of philosophy that sketches a view of existence where humans are not objectively separate from the life-world but rather are fully engaged as perceiving subjects. To be fully human our physical sensory-perceptual potentialities must be engaged and lived through dynamic embodiment.

Memories of my aunt's sealskin coat still trigger feelings and strong sensations. The heightened awareness of the ample, resilient softness of the generous skin of the coat on my face opened up a world. It was literally a thick coat of perception, a "landscape of touch" that I was rubbing up against.[54] I was enveloped in a quality of closeness. Yi-Fu Tuan refers to the sense of touch as a "proximate" sense, for it brings the world closest to us. This heightened awareness of the tactile is my first sensory memory, and I was equivalent to the sensation. The interaction between touch and texture was reciprocal. I was it and it was I. Eros was born there.

Sensual Perception

Particular sensations of the physical world garner strong impressions. Because of their emphatic richness, they stand out, becoming distinct within a field of perception. In the catalogue for the exhibition “Searchlight: Consciousness at the Millennium” at the California College of the Arts, the authors speak at length about what it means to attend to an “irreducible quality of perception,” or *qualia*. Some artists distill and heighten our awareness of *qualia* in their works by amplifying certain colors, sounds, and textures. This opens us to a “ flood of *qualia* and a flood of accompanying emotions.”[55]

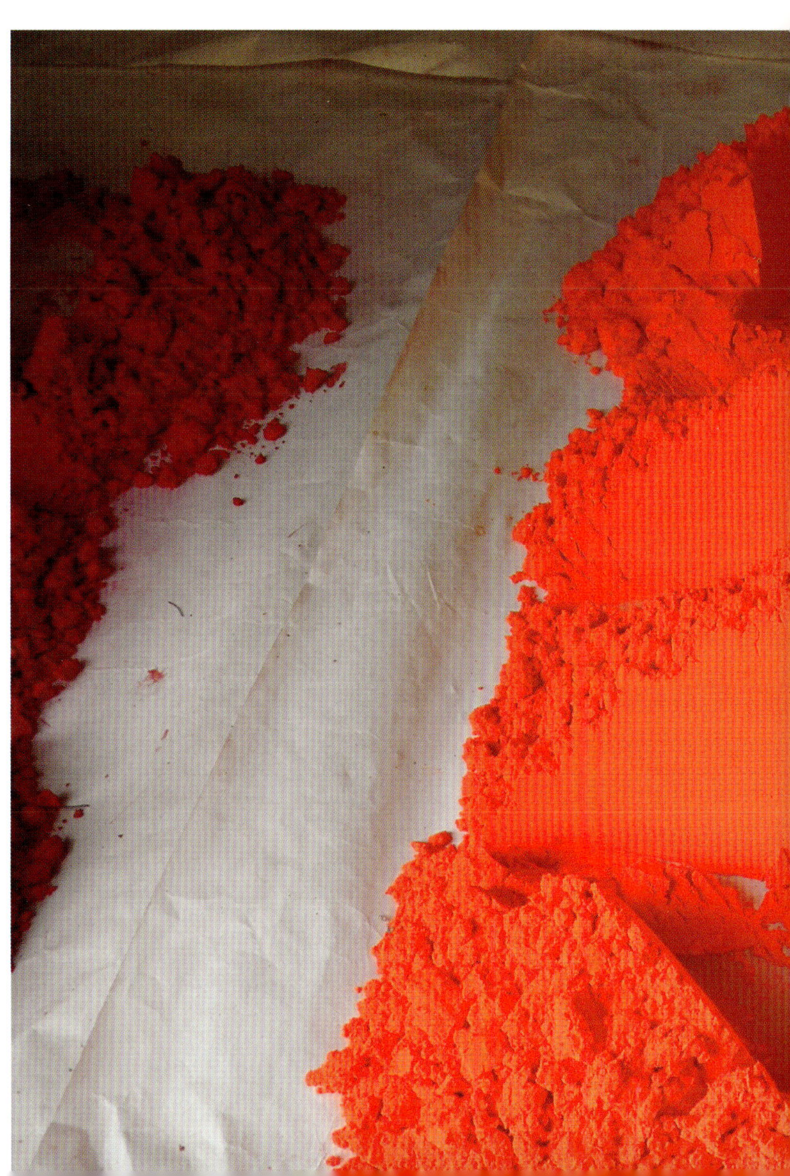

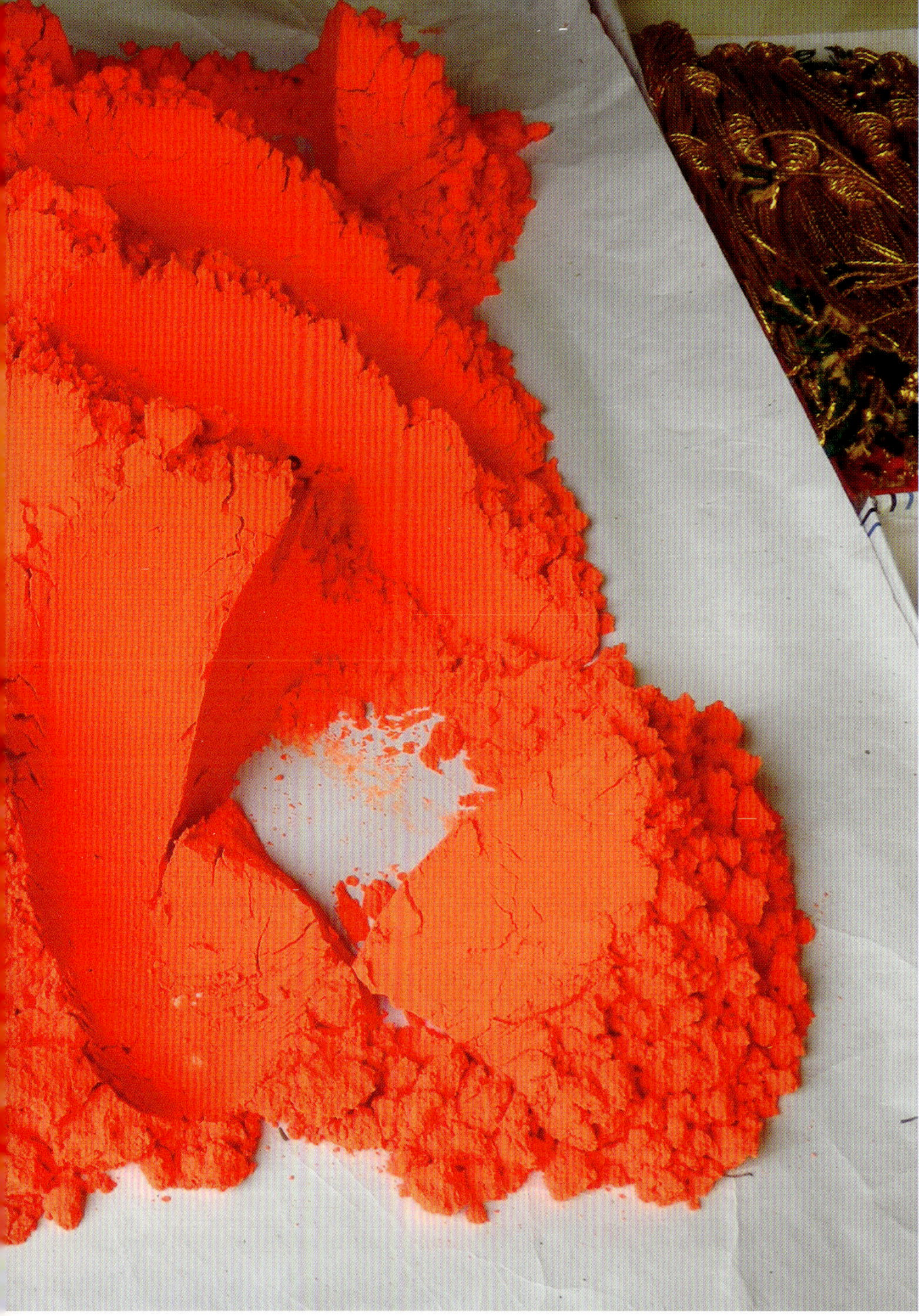

PHOTO KATARINA WESLIEN

Where is the corporeal body in your work? Does your work restore intimacy with the senses?

Recall a response to the world where a particular physical sensation became the locus of your perception.

How do you now understand this perception and how has it served to amplify sensory communication in your work?

Free write for 15 minutes.

Describe one of your works in which a particular quality of perception was stimulated. As you write, think sensually. Trust your sensual intelligence. Dilate the sensory details. Link the reader to the who, the what, the where, the why, the when, and the how of the experience and insight.

What were you trying to say by heightening this quality?

How did others respond to the work?

What was its impact on their experience?

Free write for 10 minutes.

I thought the first feeling must have been touch. Our whole sense of procreation has to do with touch. From the desire to be beautifully in touch came eyesight. To see was only to touch more accurately. These forces within us are beautiful things that you can still feel even though they come from the most primordial, non-formed kind of existence.[56] LOUIS KAHN

52 Kenya Hara, *Designing Design* (Baden, Switzerland: Lars Müller Publishers, 2007), 156.

53 David Abram, *The Spell of the Sensuous: Perception and Language in a More-Than-Human World* (New York: Vintage Books, 1996), 49.

54 Yi-Fu Tuan, *Passing Strange and Wonderful: Aesthetics, Nature and Culture* (Washington, DC: Island Press, 1993), 35–69.

55 Lawrence Rinder and George Lakoff, "Consciousness Art: Attending to the Quality of Experience," in *Search Light: Consciousness at the Millennium*, ed. Lawrence Rinder (New York: Thames and Hudson, 1999), 25–62.

56 Louis Kahn, *Louis Kahn: Essential Texts*, ed. Robert Twombly (New York: W.W. Norton, 2003), 268.

connotations of beauty

All artwork is about beauty; all positive work represents it and celebrates it. All negative protests the lack of beauty in our lives.[57]
AGNES MARTIN

How do you respond to Martin's statement?

How do you feel when you see, feel, or hear something beautiful?

Write a passage that encapsulates your sense of visual beauty. Is beauty more than a veil, a gloss to decorate, or a means of enchantment? Do you associate it with class values, indulgence, decadence, or something else?

Does beauty have two faces; a push and pull between appreciation and disgust?

Does it have any connection to authentic emotion?

What is your commitment to beauty?

Who taught you what beauty is?

Free write for 15 minutes.

Beauty hides behind the scenes. ... If we want to find it, we must demolish the scenery.[58] MILAN KUNDERA

We should rescue beauty and pleasure...repossess beauty for our own ends and reinterpret it for our own purposes.[59] FELIX GONZALEZ-TORRES

57 Agnes Martin, "Beauty Is the Mystery of Life" in *Agnes Martin*, (New York: Whitney Museum of American Art, 1993), 10.

58 Milan Kundera, *The Unbearable Lightness of Being* (New York: HarperCollins, 1984), 110.

59 Amada Cruz, "The Means of Pleasure," in *Felix Gonzalez-Torres*, ed. Julie Ault (Gottingen: Steidl Publishers, 2006), 56.

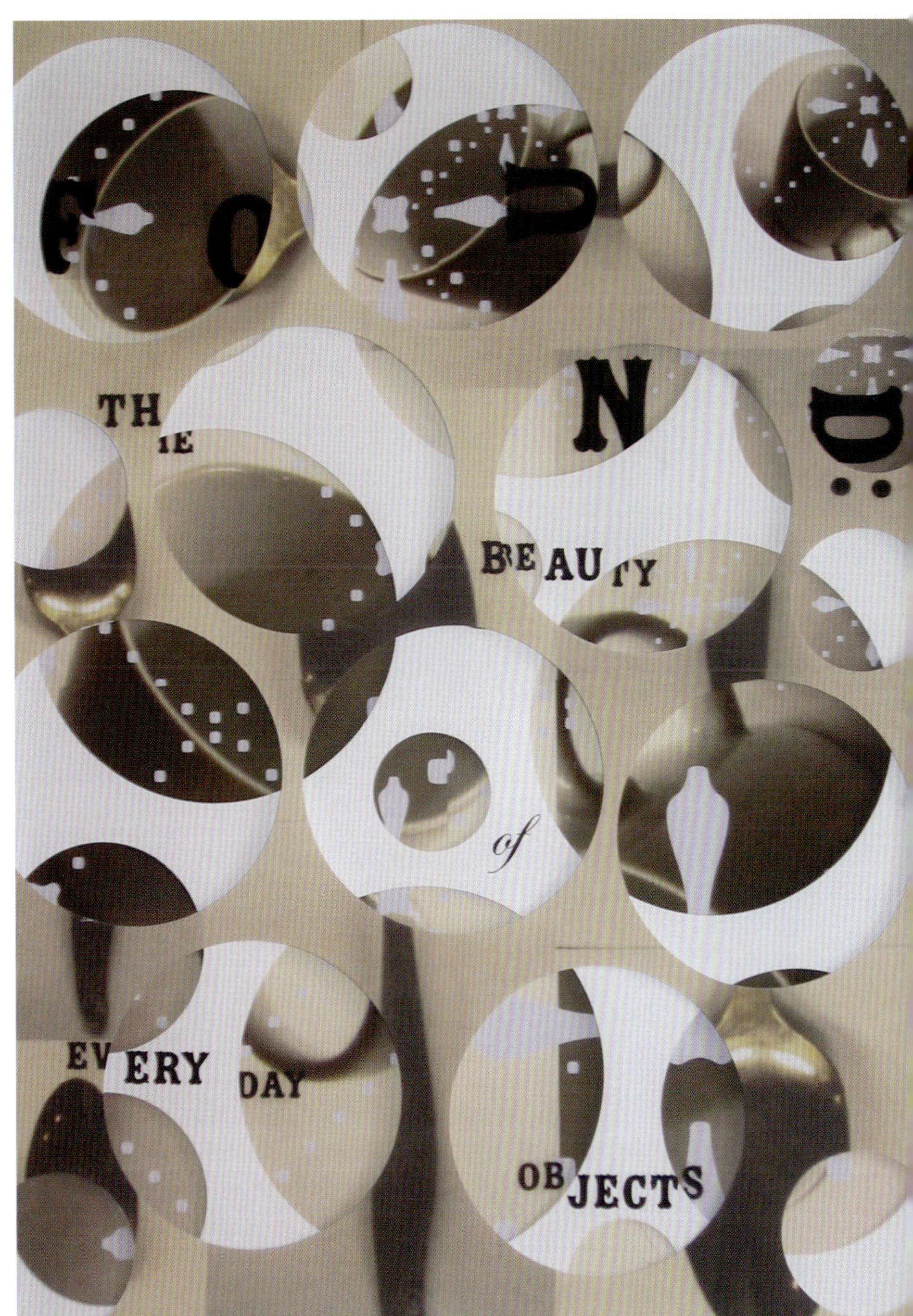

PHOTO CLAUDIA MIDDENDORF

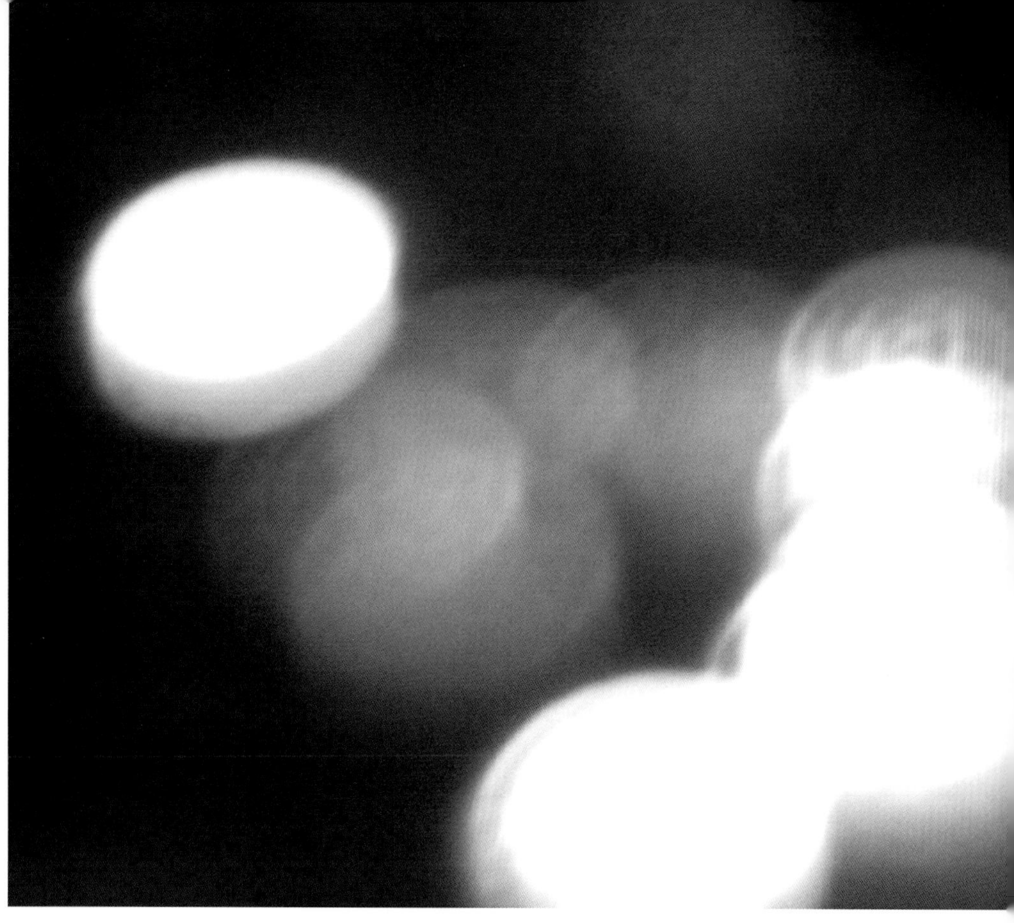

that quality of light

Perhaps only Greek has a verb expressing that fusion of perception and imagination (which is essential). On the surface, this verb means only "to notice"; but it carries with it overtones of "white," "bright," "radiance," "glitter," "shimmer." Within me there was an outright longing for this radiance, which is more than any sort of viewing. I shall always long for that kind of seeing, which in Greek is called *leukein*.[60] PETER HANDKE

All material in nature, the mountains and the streams and the air and we, are made of Light which has been spent, and this crumpled mass called material casts a shadow, and the shadow belongs to Light.[61] LOUIS KAHN

PHOTO CLAUDIA MIDDENDORF

We cannot discuss vision without an awareness of light. Light is what allows us to see.

Visual perception depends on illumination. Things are brought to life and into visibility because of this core natural phenomenon. Shifts and chromatic nuances created by light can be a source of wonder and inspiration. They can be powerful conveyers of energy, space, movement, mood, memory, color, or spiritual phenomena.

An event of sunlight is a living element in space. Each physical space changes depending on how much light is let in. Light has different qualities or densities. Clear, intense, blasted light has one effect while dimmed light has another. For example, there is a special radiance to high autumn noon light concentrated on an object and an eerie ambience to the blueness of television emissions in a darkened room.

Light is also connected to material attributes. Translucent or transparent materials will hold light in a work. Think of the way light rushes into a transparent object.

When closely observing light, it cannot be experienced without tracing the movement of its complementary dance partner, shadow. There is always the fact of shade or almost shade, penumbra caught in the underside, the folds. The Italians have a word for the arrangement of light and dark elements. Both aspects are collapsed into one concept—*Chiaroscuro* [Italian: *chirao*, bright, light from the Latin *clarus*, clear + *oscuros*, from the Latin, *obscurus*, dark].[62]

Here we a see a rich array of words that capture different qualities and densities of light. Use this list to map the sense and quality of light in your work.

Write a 200-word passage that defines the role and quality of light in your work.

I worked with the leaves and light that changed dramatically each day—from dark overcast to an intense autumn brightness that only came on a clear day after heavy rain.[63]
ANDY GOLDSWORTHY

And so it has come to be that the beauty of a Japanese room depends on a variation of shadows, heavy shadows against light shadows—it has nothing else.[64] JUN'ICHIRŌ TANIZAKI

60 Peter Handke, *Across*, trans. Ralph Manheim (New York: Macmillan, 1987), 96.

61 Kahn, *Louis Kahn: Essential Texts*, 275.

62 *The American Heritage Dictionary of the English Language*, 4th ed., s.v. "chiaroscuro."

63 Goldsworthy, *Hand to Earth: Andy Goldsworthy Sculpture 1976–1990*, 64–65.

64 Tanizaki, *In Praise of Shadows*, 19.

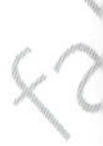

vivi

misty

radiant

brilliant

shadowy

flaring

sharp

silvery

murky

twinkling

steely

glinting

working the dialogue with space

The traditional art object, be it a painting, a sculpture, a piece of architecture, is no longer seen as an isolated entity but must be considered within the context of this expanding environment. The environment becomes equally as important as the object, if not more so, because the object breathes into the surrounding and also inhales the realities of the environment no matter in what space, close or wide apart, open air or indoor.[65] FREDERICK KIESLER

Step One: In Collaboration with Space

How we construct our experience of space depends on the lens through which we read it. It may be a boundless fourth-dimensional space-time continuum as conceived by modern physicists, an abstract geometrical construct, or a psychological situation.

What specific spaces intrigue you?

How do you experience these spaces?

Does your background inform how you see space?

How do you situate your work in space?

If your work is an event in space, what is the conceptual and physical relationship of the work to the space?

Free write for 10 minutes.

Voice. Volume. Space.

Step Two: What calls out to us from your works?

Adrienne Rich, in her essay "The Muralist," cites the writing of artist Elizabeth Catlett regarding the burden of intentionality that must accompany one's work.
Catlett writes:

1. what are you calling attention to?

2. what energy/action does your creation feed?

3. what reach will your creations (voice/images) have; & where are you directing their force?

4. what counts for connection?[66]

Free write for 10 minutes, responding to each of Catlett's questions.

In a site-specific installation at the Art Gallery of Ontario some years ago, German artist Lothar Baumgarten used words as power elements in space. He set the names of four Native American bands in prominent red lettering along the cornice of the gallery's atrium, a space often used for elite receptions. His overt gesture heightened awareness of a deep-seated historical/cultural tension. The atrium became more than a benign backdrop. It became a living canvas for the construction of a new image, activating a striking shift of conscious reclamation. Words became markers for human presences often forced into invisibility by the history-making practices of the art establishment. Here they were made visible against the background of the classical, pristine space.

Your works are acts of saying and are understood and evaluated in relation to the space they occupy. As a means to understand the assertion of your works, consider how they actively exist in space.

Consider the primary purpose of the work. Is it meant to stimulate, ignite sensory awareness, entertain, inform, educate, negotiate, advocate, agitate, interrupt, or denounce?

Assign specific words to accompany the power of your work in space.

65 Frederick Kiesler, "Second Manifesto of Correalism," as quoted in "Installations, Environments, and Sites" *Theories and Documents of Contemporary Art: A Sourcebook of Artist's Writings*, eds. Kristine Stiles and Peter Selz (Berkeley: University of California Press, 1966), 510–11.

66 Adrienne Rich, *What Is Found There: Notebooks on Poetry and Politics* (New York: W.W. Norton, 1993), 52.

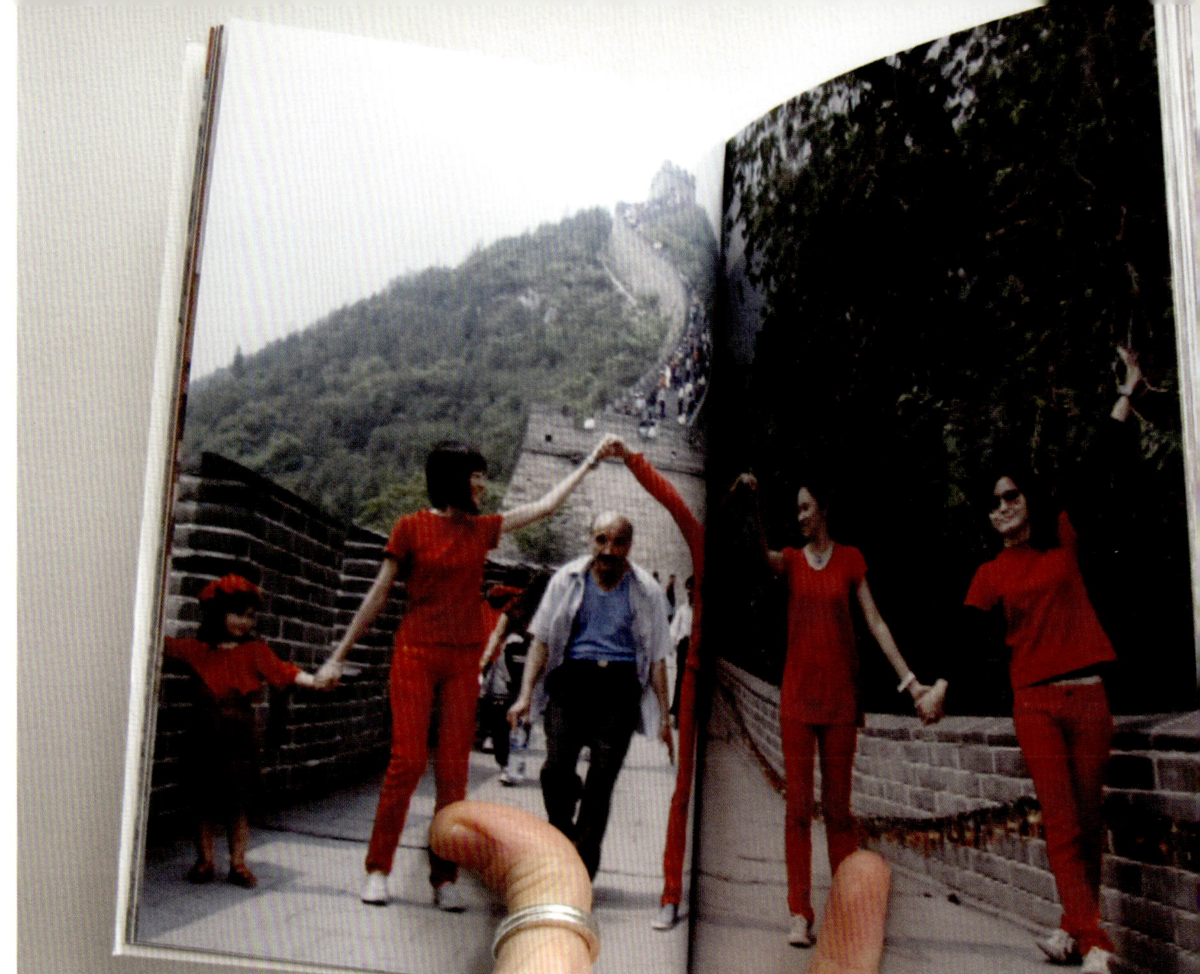

color

Color has lure, potency, and tangible effect.

The distinct presence and nuance of a color can generate energy, attitude, or mood, involving the eye in a dance of the harmonious or dissonant. Whether used alone, layered, or placed in unusual juxtapositions, colors generate a unique map. Think of the bold lushness of the saffron cloths used by Christo and Jean-Claude to wrap the thresholds for *The Gates Project* in Central Park (2005), the subtle, shimmering shifts of color of Mark Rothko's canvases, or the rich, saturated yellow hues of pollen in Wolfgang Laib's ethereal installations.

Emerald green. Vermillion. Spring green. Phthalo blue. Dioxazine purple. Ultamarine blue. Sapphire. Currant. Cobalt blue. Indigo. Amber. Dusty yellow. Blood red. Red ochre. Cadmium red. Burnt siena. Zinc white. Lamp black. China white. Malicious magenta!

Is color a major element in planning and executing your work?

Does color drive your aesthetic?

How have you developed your color palette?

How do you test your colors?

Do you use color expressively, conceptually, compositionally, perceptually, or symbolically?

What are the materials and context in which color is given a voice in your work?

Does culture influence your involvement with color?

ASTRID AL MKHLAAFY, *TAISHAN RED*, 2009

Free write for 10 minutes.

My artist grandmother lived for a love of color. We nicknamed her the purple grandmother. She cultivated violets. Her favorite suit was Parma violet, and in her closet was a slinky purple dress with a tag reading "Bury me in this." When you entered her home you became part of her living canvas and thus subject to her color protocol. Hues and tints were acceptable, shades not. If you arrived for a visit subdued in dark blue or brown, she'd lop a geranium plant on your lap or wrap one of her pink mohair shawls around you. Color expressed her artistic emotions. It was her rule of spirit, her life speech.

Do you have a color story to tell?

>>

Artists and writers throughout time have extolled the importance of color.

Color is not so much a visual as a tactile medium.[67]
MARSHALL MCLUHAN

a color chorus

One day, a young boy met a fairy and asked her if she could satisfy his every wish. "Yes," the fairy answered, "but on one condition. You must never think of the color sea green." "Is that all?" asked the boy, already sure he was on his way to happiness. "That's enough!" said the fairy, and with that she disappeared. But then something strange started happening. No matter how hard he tried, the boy was unable to get the color sea green out of his mind. Time passed, and not only did his various wishes not come to pass, but his life became more and more impossible, until finally, now grown, he seemed simply to wander the world, seized by desperation, convinced that he had been the victim of an evil spell.[68] MANILIO BRUSATIN

Know that there are several kinds of black colors. There is a black which is soft, black stone; it is a fat color. … Then there is a black which is made from vine twigs; these twigs are to be burned; and when they are burnt, throw water on them, and quench them; and then work them up like the other black. And this is a color both black and lean; and it is one of the perfect colors which we employ; and it is the whole. … There is another black which is made from burnt almond shells or peach stones, and this is a perfect black, and fine. There is another black which is made in this manner: take a lamp full of linseed oil, and fill the lamp with this oil, and light the lamp. Then put it, so lighted, underneath a good clean baking dish, and have the little flame of the lamp come about to the bottom of the dish, two or three fingers away, and the smoke which comes out of the flame will strike on the bottom of the dish, and condense in a mass. Wait a while; take the baking dish, and with some implement sweep this color, that is, this soot, off on to a paper, or into some dish; and it does not have to be worked up or ground, for it is a very fine color. Refill the lamp with the oil in this way several times, and put it back under the dish; and make of it in this way as you need.[69]
CENNINO D'ANDREA CENNINI

No color has a neat unambiguous symbolism but yellow gives some of the most mixed messages of all. It is the color of pulsating life – of corn and gold and angelic haloes – and it is also at the same time a color of bile, and in its sulphurous incarnations it is the color of the Devil.[70] VICTORIA FINLAY

Blue is sad, blue is memory and nostalgia, but blue is also affrontery and impudence. And this is what I love about the colour. The most expensive of colours. Blue is prize. No public one. Intimate prize. Blue says: outrageously and absurdly: I am yours or you are mine! And no other colour can judge us. No simple colour can judge jewel. There's an impromptu by Schubert, which talks of this. And Charlie Parker became Bird because he knew about blue.[71] JOHN BERGER

On top of all this I present a fine case of colored hearing. ... The long *a* of the English alphabet. ... Has for me the tint of weathered wood, but a French *a* evokes polished ebony. This black group also includes hard g (vulcanized rubber) and *r* (a sooty rag being ripped). Oatmeal *n*, noodle-limp *l*, and the ivory-backed hand mirror of *o* take care of the whites. I am puzzled by my French *on* which I see as the brimming tension-surface of alcohol in a small glass. Passing on to the blue group, there is steely *x*, thundercloud *z*, and huckleberry *k*.[72] VLADIMIR NABOKOV

The eye is strongly attracted by light, clear colours, and still more strongly attracted by those colours which are warm as well as clear; vermillion has the charm of flame, which has always attracted human beings. Keen lemon-yellow hurts the eye in time as a prolonged shrill trumpet-note the ear, and the gazer turns away to seek relief in blue or green.[73] WASSILY KANDINSKY

67 Herbert Marshall McLuhan, *Essential McLuhan*, eds. Eric McLuhan and Frank Zingrone (London: Routledge, 1995), 48.

68 Manilio Brusatin, *A History of Colors* (Boston: Shambhala, 1991), v.

69 Cennino d'Andrea Cennini, *The Craftsman's Handbook*, trans. Daniel V. Thompson, Jr. (New York: Dover, 1954), 22–23.

70 Victoria Finlay, *Color: A Natural History of the Palette* (New York: Random House, 2002), 203.

71 John Berger and John Christie, *I Send You This Cadmium Red...A Correspondence Between John Berger and John Christie* (Barcelona: Actar, 1999), n.p. Correspondence dated April 4, 1997.

72 Vladimir Nabokov, *Speak, Memory* (New York: Vintage International, 1989), 34.

73 Wassily Kandinsky, *Concerning the Spiritual in Art*, trans. M.T.H. Sadler (New York: Dover, 1977), 24.

>>

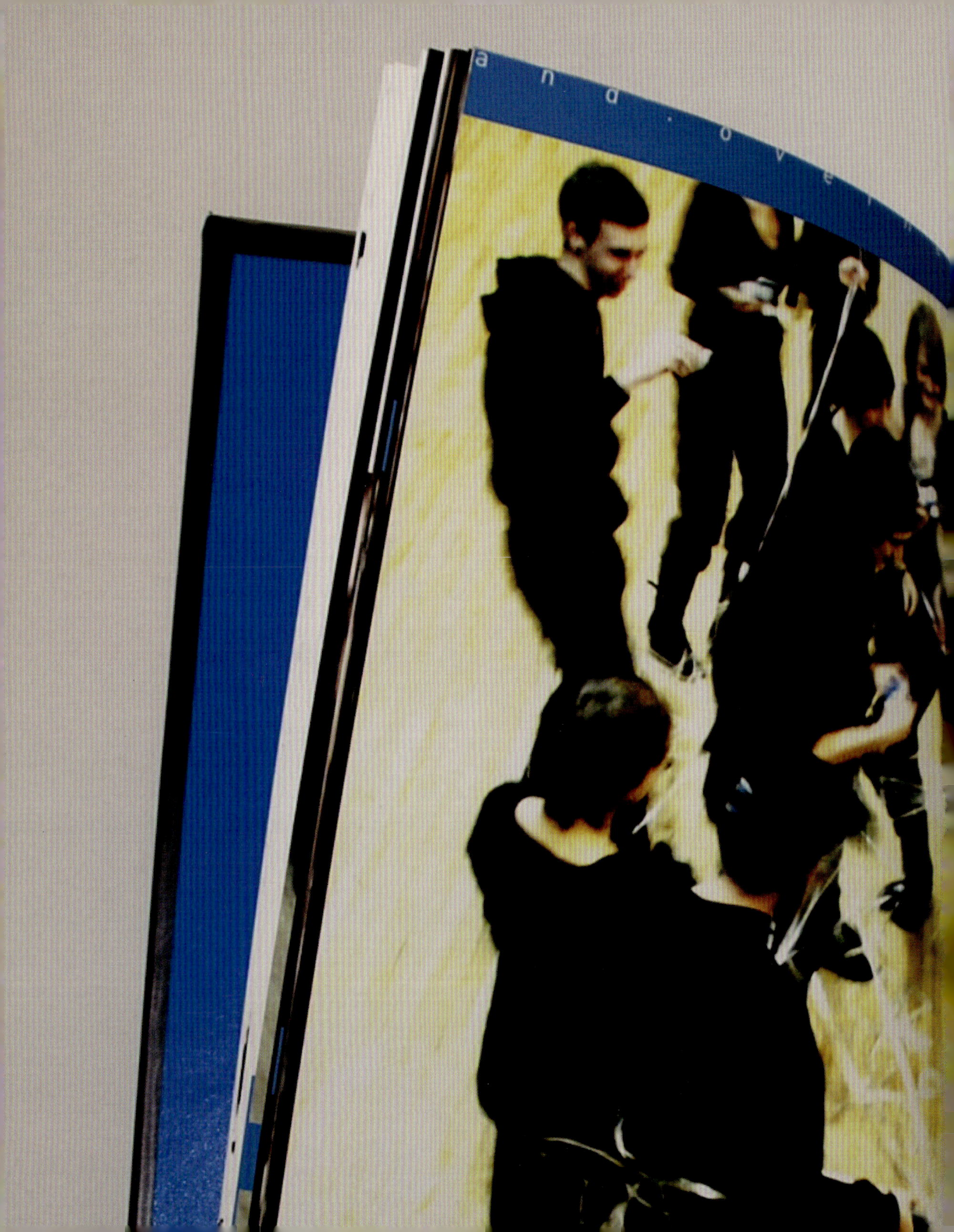
and

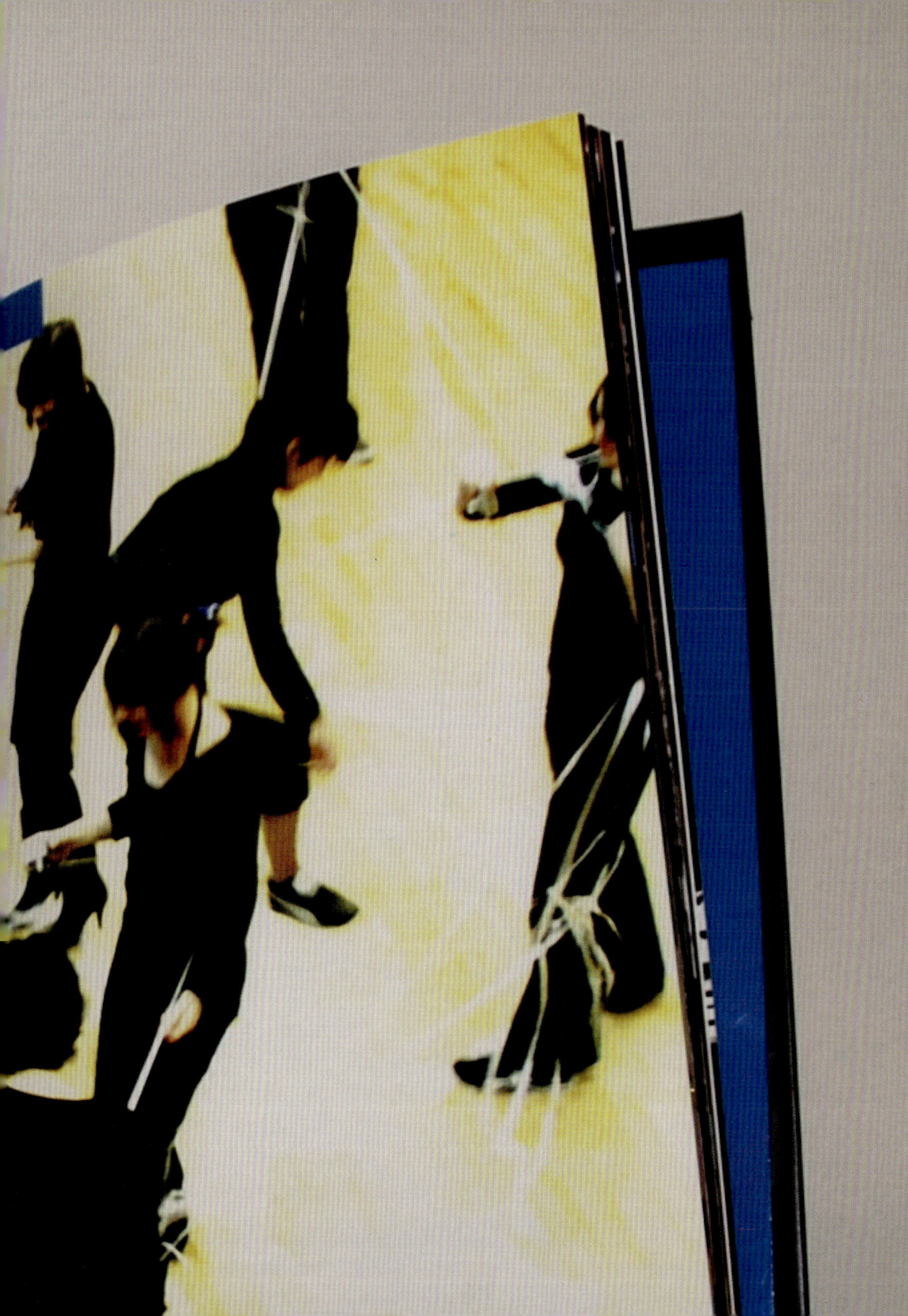

ASTRID AL MKHLAAFY, *STRETCH*, 2006

about time

Each of these buildings has a history created by its own fiction and need to demonstrate its philosophy of existence. That fiction is part of the debris of history. My images connect with that debris. They attempt to connect with the beginning or the end, with a deep and lost memory between here and there.[74] ANSELM KIEFER

Is time long or is it wide?[75] LAURIE ANDERSON

In his canonic essay, *The Monastery and the Clock,* Lewis Mumford calls the clock the most important machine of our culture.[76] He speaks of the pervasive and strict effect of the clock upon the rhythms of life. With the clock, categories of time and space underwent an extraordinary change. Born out of the context of the Benedictine monastery in the 7th century when the bells were rung seven times a day, obedience to the canonical hours dictated the routine and the strict regiment of the monks. The habits of the monks were correlated to a desire for order and the clock determined the monastic day. What was gained was mechanical efficiency and certainly not organic, bodily free choice. Against the erratic fluctuations and pulsations of worldly life, temporal order took hold of the mind. Surprise, caprice, and irregularity were put at bay.

According to Mumford, with the clock we begin to think within an abstract framework of mechanical, divided time. The division of hours into sixty minutes and of minutes into sixty seconds becomes the norm. It is the clock that makes modern progress and efficiency possible. All organization of work and the study of motion are based on the clock. Capitalism embraces this ordered rhythm to the day and as Benjamin Franklin keenly reminds us, "Time equals money."

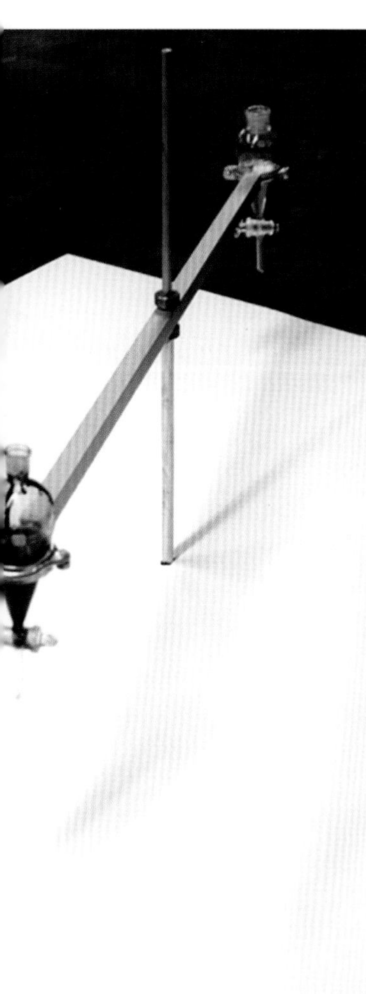

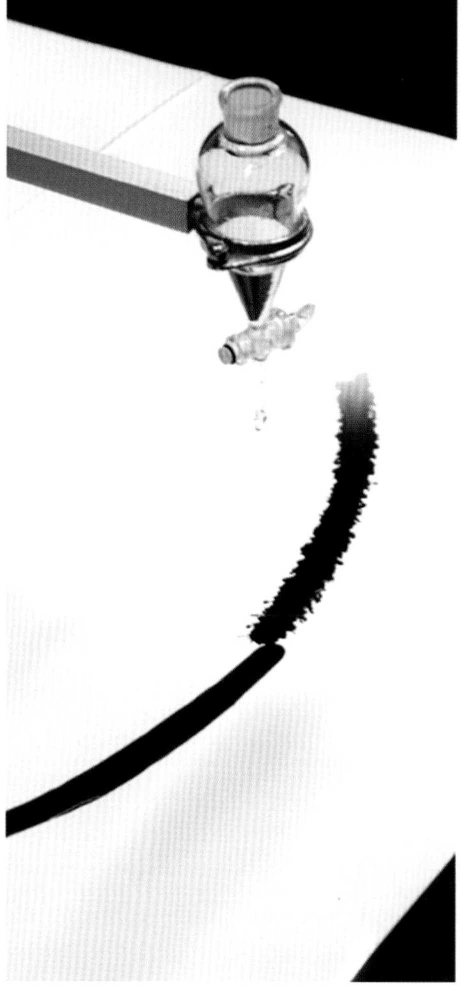

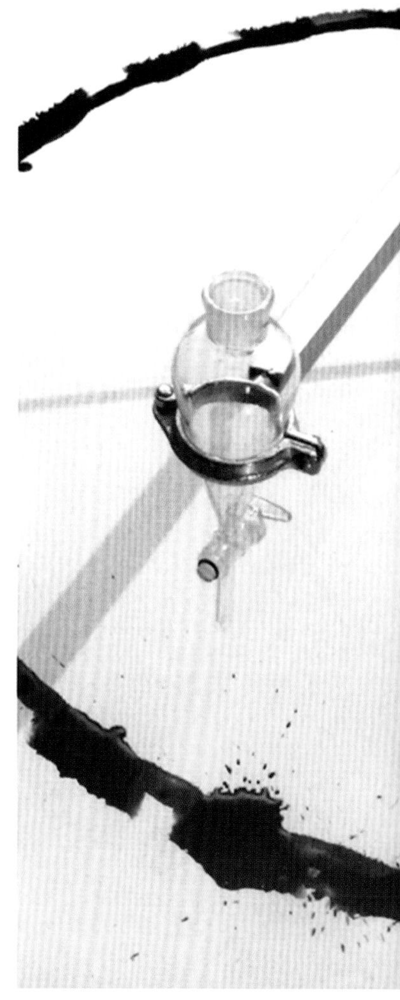

BOKYUNG JUN, *DRAWING MACHINE*, 2006

74 Anselm Kiefer, *Heaven and Earth* (Modern Art Museum of Fort Worth, Texas, September 25, 2005–January 8, 2006), 41.

75 Laurie Anderson, "Same Time Tomorrow," *The Ugly One With The Jewels*, Warner Bros. Records, 1995. Compact Disk.

76 Lewis Mumford, "The Monastery and the Clock" in *Technics and Civilization* (New York: Harcourt, Brace & Co., 1934), 12–17.

>>

Time sequencing. Time keeping. Time serving. Time accounting. Time rationing

BOKYUNG JUN, *DRAWING MACHINE*, 2006

Time signatures.

Consider the idea of time or tempo. How do you move through time?

How do you perceive time?

What are the different temporal constructs that you work with?

Offer a perspective on the way time works or comes into play in your work. List as many elements or images as possible. Does it appear as layers of overlapping timelines, time-lapse sequences, repetition, intervals, frameworks of divided time, fragments, progression, duration, time loops, organic cycles, impermanence, entropy, evidence of time's debris, the vastness of timelessness, or time standing still?

How do your materials determine the way you measure or approach it?

Free write for 15 minutes.

orders for the road

All our activities are linked to the idea of journeys. And I like to think that our brains have an information system giving us our orders for the road, and that here lie the mainsprings of our restlessness.[77] BRUCE CHATWIN

Not to find one's way in a city may well be uninteresting and banal. It requires ignorance—nothing more. But to lose oneself in a city—as one loses oneself in a forest—that calls for quite a different schooling. Then, signboards and street names, passers-by, roofs, kiosks, or bars must speak to the wanderer like a cracking twig under his feet in the forest, like the startling call of a bittern in the distance, like the sudden stillness of a clearing with a lily standing erect at its centre.[78]
WALTER BENJAMIN

There may be days when you feel mired in nothingness. Every effort to work is a strain. Your mind has deserted you. Each attempt to bring forth an idea is an extraction by force. I have learned in these times that it is important to pause and be aimless. It is at these times that I walk.

Somewhere I read, "Where the feet walk centers poetry." This is another way of saying that by placing the mind and body in movement it is possible to approach the heart of things from another direction. Walking helps to ignite the senses and to open self to external stimuli. To walk is to cultivate a wandering intelligence where we are placed in fresh relationship with the world and happenstance. When walking, thoughts are allowed to be free. We entrust ourselves to chance. Anywhere, anytime the unpredictable may appear. All we need to do is to stay open to it.

Wandering has often taken form as art. The 19th century flâneur's purposeless idling and strolling about town allowed for spontaneous thinking. Henry David Thoreau walked without expectation believing a magnetism pulled him along to take the "right walk." European *Situationists* ignited this spirit of discovery to enact what they called the "dérive" (or "drift" from the Dadaist term "dérive"), as a critique of modern, consumer culture.[79] Their practice was to float through the city, seeking out the

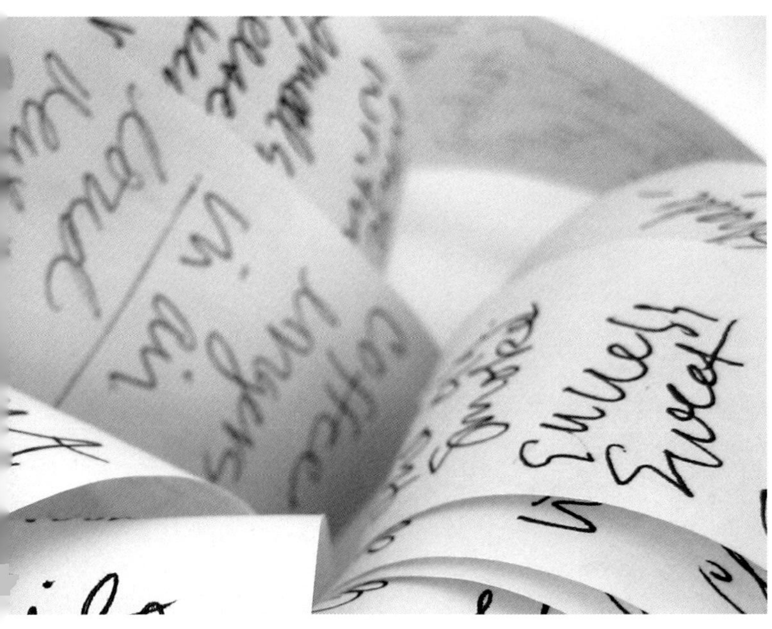

PHOTO MICHELLE HAYS

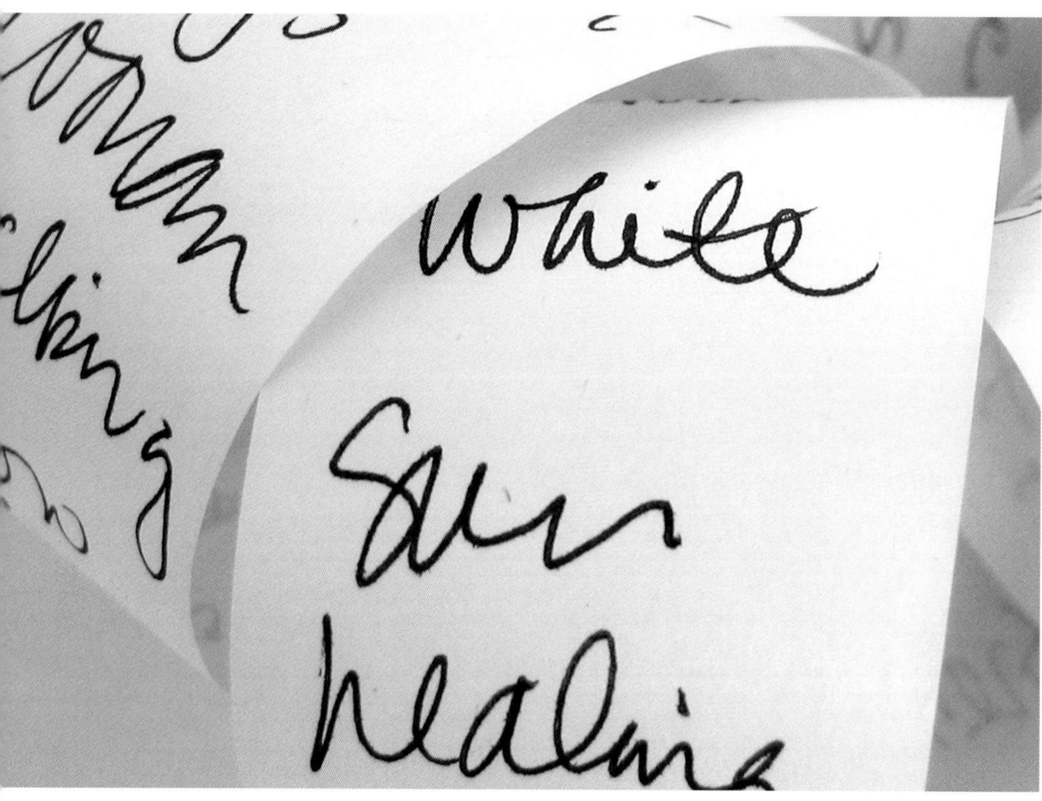

PHOTO MICHELLE HAYS

unknown in situations, opening to whatever "ambiance" they came in contact with. In this way they exposed themselves to a whole spectrum of emotions encountered by chance in the unconscious zones of the city. Sailors "gunk hole." They meander, following wind and weather, surrendering to a path that is not superimposed.

Walking also helps to generate a felt connection to internal, body intelligence. Some of the greatest intellectual and artistic discoveries have been informed by walking. Beethoven used this technique to allow inspiration to come to the surface. He always walked with a notebook in which to work out the development of his themes.

Project: The Walking Map

Make walking part of your work. For a few solid hours every week permit yourself the freedom to be opened by the outside world. Begin by taking a walk around the block with your mapping notebook, camera, or a smartphone with a GPS locator. What do you encounter?

Project: Create a Real-Time Recording of What You See and Hear

This is a form of automatic writing in real time and space. Commit to paper or video recorder the sounds, pedestrian comments, images, and sense impressions. Map these jottings or impressions. Trace the flow of the walk, recreating the journey within a spatial field. Vary the speed, cadence, scale, and volume of the words and images according to the experience of the walk. Remember: experience within time and space is a matrix and not a linear sequence.

Project: A Long-Thought Walk

In *Drinking the Rain* Alix Kate Shulman writes, "Think long thoughts, I read in a strange book with a fuchsia cover. ... Each of our thoughts is too short. Until you have experience from your own observation of the difference between long and short thoughts, this idea will mean nothing."[80]

Take an idea that is currently alive in your mind on a long-thought-walk. Use your mapping notebook or just a stream of paper from an adding machine to track a thought for twenty minutes or so. When you arrive home again, transpose the rich intricate and interwoven aspects of this extended thought into a written passage.

77 Bruce Chatwin, *Anatomy of Restlessness*, ed. Jan Borm and Matthew Graves (New York: Penguin Books, 1996), 106.

78 Walter Benjamin, "A Berlin Chronicle," in *One-Way Street and Other Writings* (London: NLB, 1979), 298.

79 Francesco Careri, *Walkscapes: Walking as an aesthetic practice*, ed. Gustavo Gili (Barcelona: n.b. 2002), 94.

80 Alix Kates Shulman, *Drinking the Rain* (New York: Penguin Books, 1995), 5–57.

ways
woman
walking

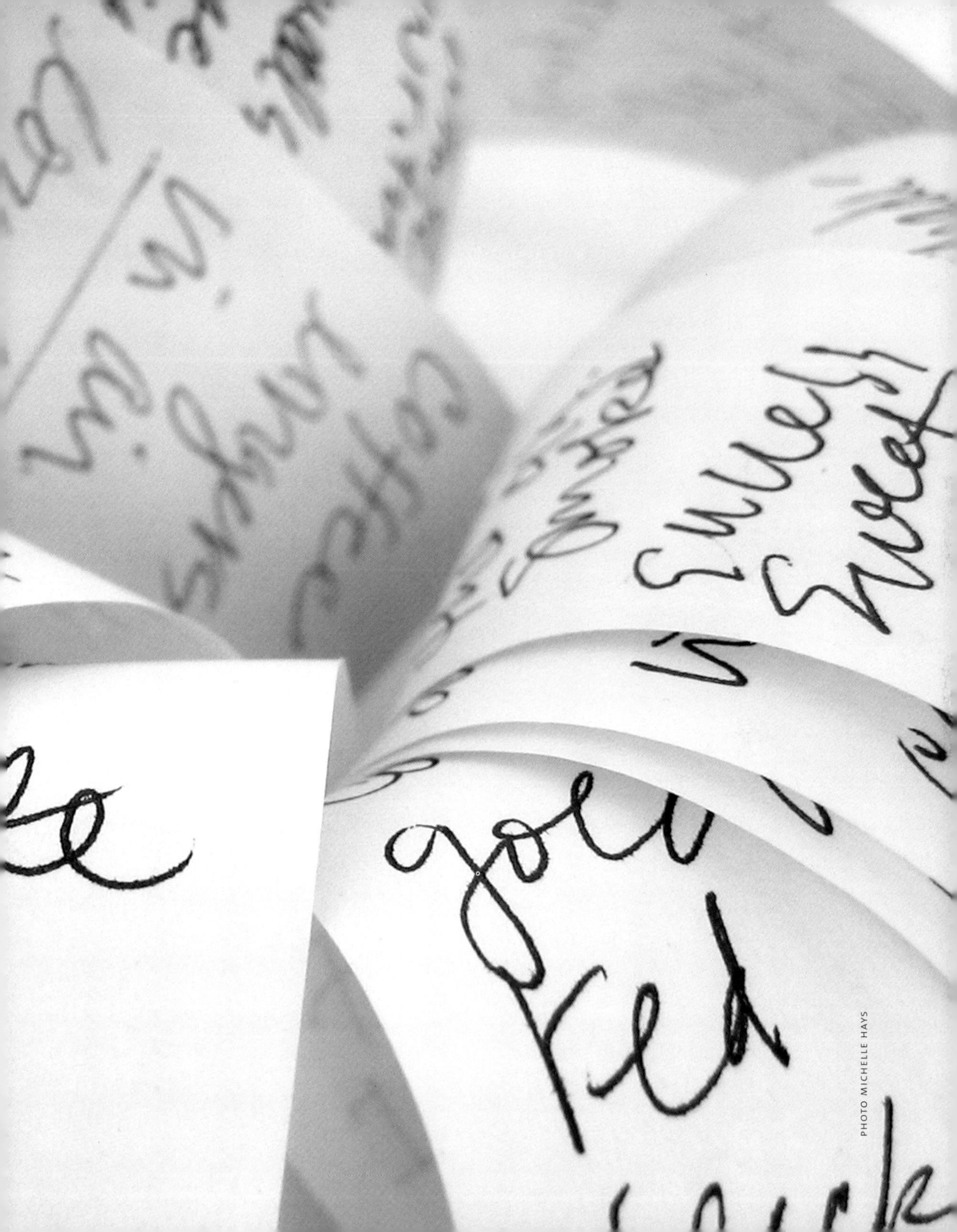
PHOTO MICHELLE HAYS

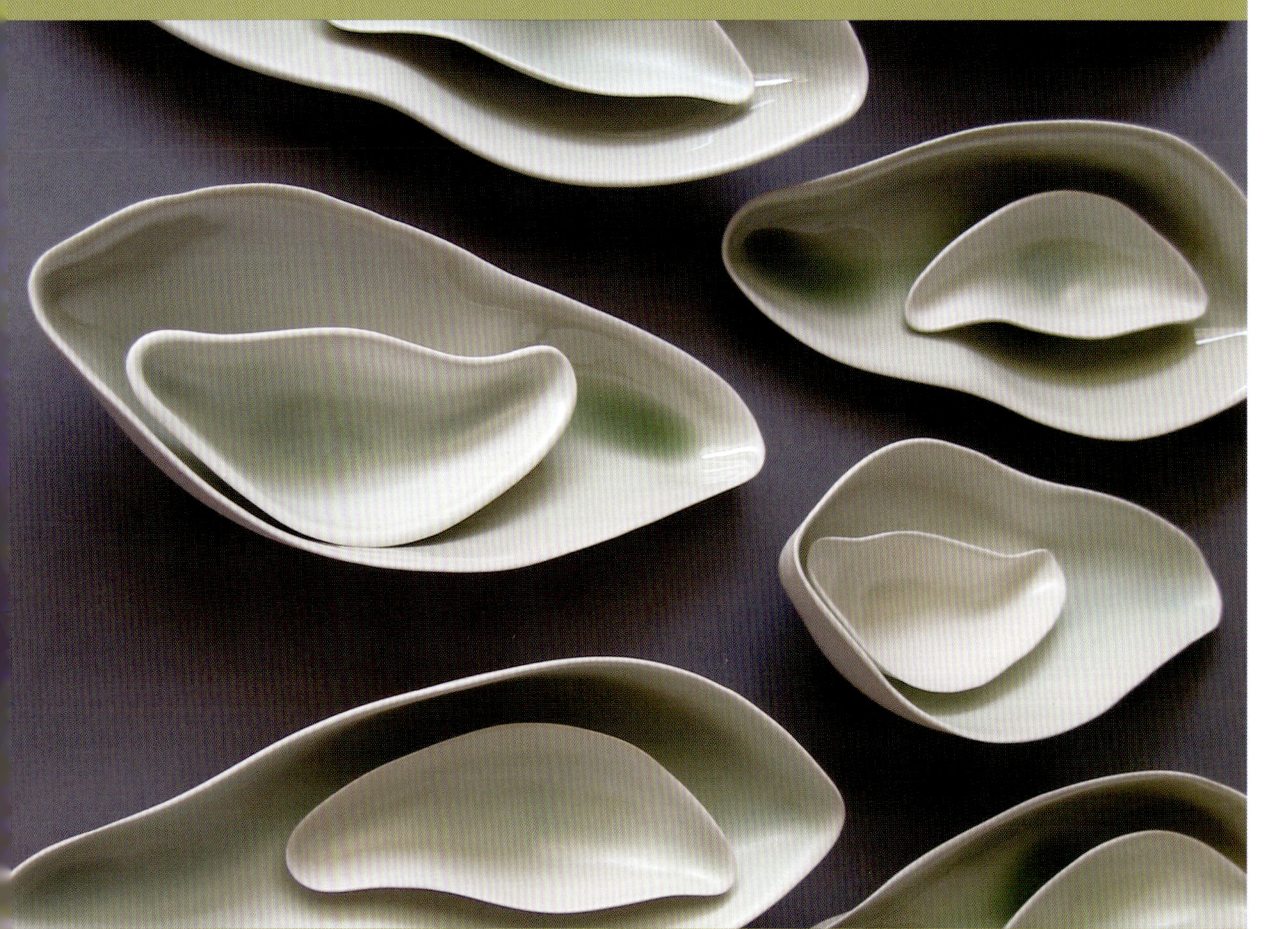

ASYA PALATOVA, *CHANT*, 2004

EXPLORING
map as matrix

how do you make?
what do you make?

collections + the organization of things

What is decisive in collecting is that the object is detached from all its original functions in order to enter into the closest conceivable relation to things of the same kind.[81] WALTER BENJAMIN

The items we collect map our horizon of significance.

Collecting is the focus of many artists' practice. Joseph Cornell's shadow boxes are one example. Mnemonic containers—miniature *wunderkammer*—their nonlinear array of elements offers a view of his personal cosmology. Artist Mark Dion, well known for his work with collections, explores issues of classification and technologies of display. With hundreds of objects he finds in the back storage of institutions, he creates new cosmologies—simple allegories—for their reinterpretation. He loves to bring obsolete objects to life again, to mix things up, and to stimulate compound relationships, so that the barriers between disciplines blur. A wonderful new language emerges through the structure of his collections.

One of the most powerful exhibitions to raise consciousness around museological practices was Fred Wilson's *Mining the Museum* (1994) for the Maryland Historical Society in Baltimore. An artist of African-American and Carib Indian ancestry, Wilson assumed the role of artist/curator, excavating the museum's storerooms and transforming our relationship to the displayed objects. Through acts of juxtaposition and irony, his astute pairings revealed institutional collecting policy and racial bias.

Make a list of your collections. They may be tactile collections or digitally based.

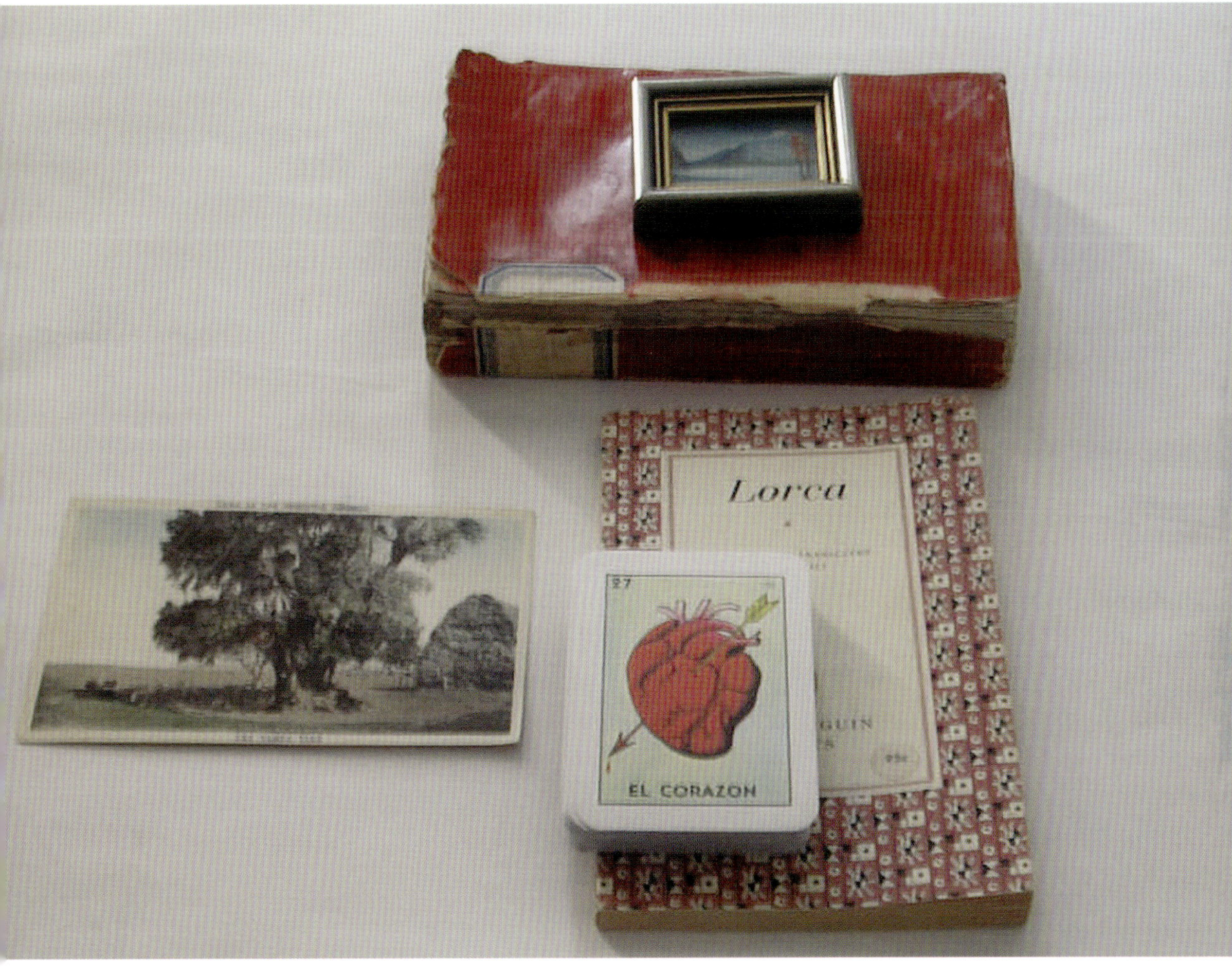

PHOTO CLAUDIA MIDDENDORF

81 Walter Benjamin, *The Arcades Project*, ed. Rolf Tiedemann, trans. Howard Eiland and Kevin McLaughlin (Cambridge, MA: The Belknap Press of Harvard University, 1999), 204.

82 Roger Cardinal, "The Case of Kurt Schwitters" in *The Cultures of Collecting*, eds. John Elsner and Roger Cardinal (Cambridge, MA: Harvard University Press, 1994), 75.

83 From thesis writing exercise, Jonathan Lashley, RISD, Spring 2007.

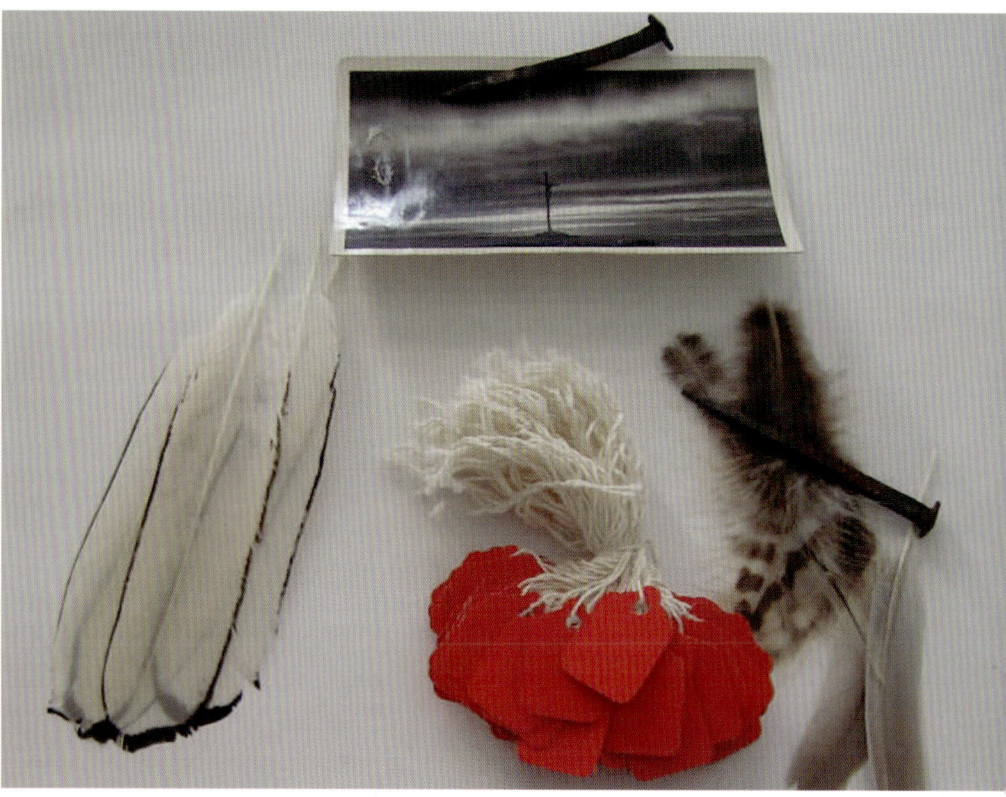

PHOTO CLAUDIA MIDDENDORF

Is the principle of collecting a focus in your work?

If the spirit of collecting is central to your artistic practice, why do you collect?

How do you create an archive or memory inventory?

Do you draw upon examples from other collectors to inform your practice?

Do you reframe your collections to create a new narrative? If so, what is your editing process?

What taxonomy—classification or ordering structure—do you employ when assembling and/or structuring your objects for display?

Free write for 15 minutes.

Kurt Schwitters, the great Modern collage artist, had an obsession for collecting. If the museum curator represents our greatest desire to preserve and order objects of exquisiteness and rarity, then Schwitters is his opposite. He was hardly a tasteful or nuanced discriminator; in fact, the artist was truly a collector of what everyone else dismisses. Known primarily for his collages, the artist absorbed the most fleeting of objects—a torn flier here, a bus ticket there—and saved them, rearranged them, and presented them all over again to remind us that these material remnants so easily discarded are important symbols and narratives of our times. My fascination with Schwitters extends beyond his extensive collecting of the everyday (or everything) into his *Merzbau* projects, where he obsessively built environments that housed and incorporated his found objects. Using his own home as a departure point and indeed leaving it as little more than a shell within to hold the transformations, the artist built up and deconstructed the interior with 3D shapes and cuts to house what he referred to as his "spoils and relics." The *Merzbau* was a palimpsest, constantly being carved and re-walled with nooks and hidden spaces, and curated, in a sense, with an unlimited variety of objects. As time progressed, objects were often completely obstructed by additions to the projects, so that some contents remained only in the memory of the *Merzbau* in one of its earlier states. The *Merzbau* was completely personal to Schwitters, yet completely allusive in its meaning and far from singular in its narrative. Roger Cardinal, an art historian writes, "Eventually coinciding with the entire house, the *Merzbau* constituted a multi-functional environment, at once dwelling, studio, storehouse, exhibition space, walk-in and totalizing collection."[82]

In other words, Schwitters transferred his collecting and scavenging into a monumental, architectural scale, one which he inhabited and affected but simultaneously hoped to expose to the world. Importantly to me, the *Merzbau* carefully balanced a sense of whimsy and specific peculiarity—it had distinct galleries including "The Cathedral of Erotic Misery" and "The Cave of Deprecated Heroes"—with a sense of coherent composition. This coherency, or justifying logic, is the meeting of the chronological and spatial; the objects of his collection, however random, never cease to accumulate as time marches on, and so the space continues to evolve. The *Merzbau* was Schwitter's *Wunderkammer*, or Cabinet of Curiosities, as it was also his personal time capsule and refuge from history. Ironically, or perhaps fittingly, at twenty years into the project, the work was totally annihilated by Allied bombing, after the artist had already been forced to abandon the project in exile, and time, at least for the *Merzbau*, did stop.[83]

unfinished potential + failures are good

Step One: Unfinished Potential
Inspired by the work of Ira Progoff, from *At a Journal Workshop*, Professor Christina Bertoni, Rhode Island School of Design, designed a class titled *Form and Inspiration*. From among the many questions that she offers as reflective prompts, this is one to which I responded:

Consider a project that is unfinished in your studio—one that while put aside still holds promise. What can't you get at? What would you like to unpack again, rework, or refine?

Step Two: Failures are Good
Often failures teach more than projects that work. What is a project failure that provided a great warning or insight? Did it show you a new direction to take in your work?

What is your work not about?

Free write for 10 minutes.

repositioning the familiar

"Making strange" is an approach that takes a familiar object and through some alteration to the form undermines expectations and sets up a charged relationship between viewer and object. This repositioning creates a new framework for incubating ideas and expanding experience. It is rooted in the tradition of the Surrealist dream-like object, which brings everyday objects into opposition with the certainties of the conscious world and makes them uncannily contradictory and often erotic.

Palestinian artist Mona Hatoum uses this device of defamiliarization for many of her sculptural projects. Domestic objects, such as the commonplace welcome mat, the bed, or a kitchen utensil, are undermined so they become double-edged and often shocking at a visceral level. For example, *Prayer Mat* (1995), one of her "unheimlich" or disquieting objects, is immediately recognizable as a mat used for spiritual purposes.[84] However, the mat is constructed from myriad pins. Rather than inviting the viewer to a comfort zone, it betrays this evocation, with the paradoxical potential to inflict physical pain. Within this new framework, Hatoum leads the viewer into a physical confrontation with the deep-rooted vulnerability and anguish of exile.

Do you alter form to present a perceptual and/or conceptual framework?

What motivates you in examining the commonplace and recreating the familiar as new experience?

Free write for 5 minutes.

84 Gannit Ankori, *Palestinian Art* (London: Reaktion Books Ltd., 2006), 123–125. The uncanny, a Freudian principle, is derived from the German "unheimlich" which translates into English as "unhomely" or unfamiliar. See: Sigmund Freud, *The Uncanny* (New York: Penguin Group Inc., 2003).

85 From thesis writing exercise, Jillian Conrad, January 2004.

process

Write a paragraph about, or draw a diagram to show, the cycle of your process.

How important is it that you do something with care?

Does it have to be technically perfect?

Free write for 5 minutes.

The cycle of my process as a sculptor begins with a love of raw materials and textures. I spend a great deal of time learning how different materials respond to each other and how I can coax them to speak for me. I experiment with materials right in my hands. I stab, pile, organize, sew, and glue things together until something arises. I keep arranging and rearranging until the accumulation of materials comes together in a way that makes the whole more than the sum of the parts.[85]

JILLIAN CONRAD, SCULPTOR

a predilection to play

I still recall my delight upon seeing a video of Alexander Calder's magical *Circus* for the first time. Viewing Calder maneuver the humble, intricately crafted "wire action toys" was mesmerizing. He was totally engaged in bestowing movement, gesture, and expressive bend to each circus character: *Monsieur Loyal, Rigoulot the Ringmaster, Clown, Spear Thrower, Sword-Swallower, Exotic Dancer, Bearded Lady, Acrobat, Fire-Eater, Man on Stilts, Weight Lifter, the Lions, the Seals, the Stretcher Bearers,* and the *Charioteers*. His *Circus* stilled a center in me. It made me aware of another world—a world of play that is small, unpretentious, and imaginative.

Composer John Cage describes his music as "purposeless play. ... This play is the affirmation of life—not an attempt to bring order out of chaos, nor to suggest improvements in creation, but simply to wake up to the very life we are living, which is so excellent once one gets one's own mind and desires out of the way and lets it act of its own accord." [86]

It is hard to imagine a creative process without play. Reveling in purposeless play is improvisation at its best. It is a way of approaching things without self-consciousness. Play bypasses the intellect. Whether subverting the norm, encouraging change, or provoking discovery, play requires of us an attitude of speculation where we expand our field of action, freeing ourselves from arbitrary restrictions.

What is your perspective on play and its role in your creative process?

How do you design for play?

Free write for 5 minutes.

86 John Cage, *Silence* (Middletown, CT: Wesleyan University Press, 1973), 12.

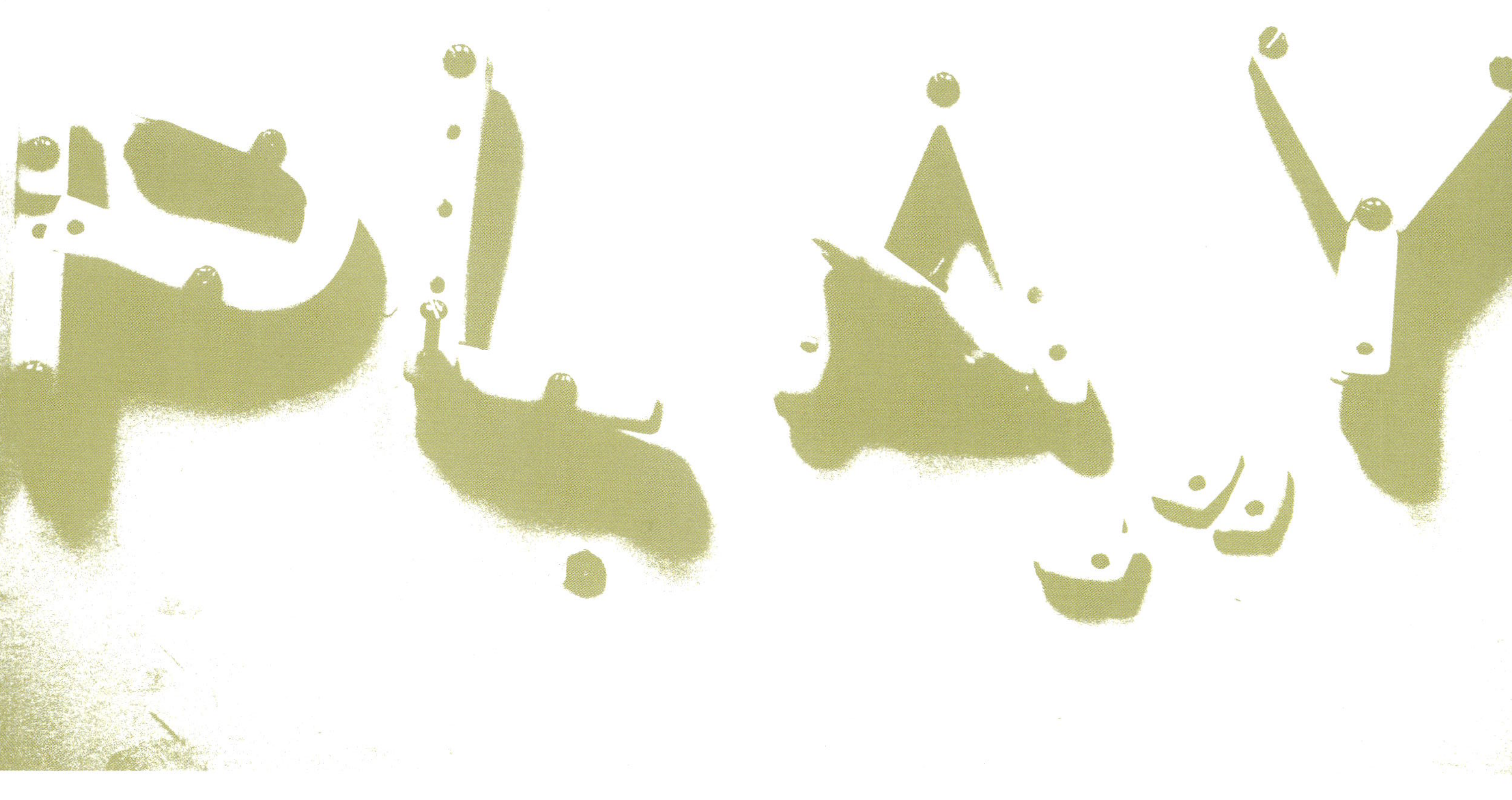

ADAPTED FROM PHOTO BY ELISE PORTER

the mundane against the fantastic

Every year during the month of March a family of ragged gypsies would set up their tents near the village, and with a great uproar of pipes and kettledrums they would display new inventions. First they brought the magnet. A heavy gypsy with an untamed beard and sparrow hands, who introduced himself as Melquiades, put on a bold public demonstration of what he himself called the eighth wonder of the learned alchemists of Macedonia. He went from house to house dragging two metal ingots and everybody was amazed to see pots, pans, tongs, and braziers tumble down from their places and beams creak from the desperation of nails and screws trying to emerge, and even objects that had been lost for a long time appeared from where they had been searched for most and went dragging along in turbulent confusion behind Melquiades' magical irons. "Things have a life of their own," the gypsy proclaimed with a harsh accent. "It's simply a matter of waking up their souls.[87] GABRIEL GARCIA-MARQUEZ

To liberate the design process, rescuing it from the merely utilitarian, esteemed industrial designer Marc Harrison advocated a method of design in which "form follows fantasy" versus form follows function.[88]

> Are your forms born from fantasy? Set loose a new story on behalf of the life and soul of your work; one that counters, spans, and even overwhelms the boundaries of the practical, the no-frills, with the wondrous and fantastical. How might you reframe your work as a catalyst for fantasy?

Think of your work as fiction, a fantastical story. Follow the tragicomic adventure of the work, the vagaries and realities of its life. Make it a legend in its own lifetime.

Free write for 10 minutes.

dream quotient

Dream and art are not a magic hoard: they link man with the life of light and darkness, with true life, with spiritual collaboration.[89] JEAN ARP

We fall asleep into deeper regions of awareness, surrendering to the pillow and to dream.

Concentrated images arising from the nocturnal world of dream hold a distinct power over the creative mind and vision. Configured differently than images informed by daylight perception, dreams unravel our familiar take on things and open a seam to deeper regions of awareness. They present new perspectives for self and the world. Once we are awake, these images, sometimes haunting or intriguing, can continue to speak back, providing the condition for a creative idea to deepen into a substantial concept.

Poet Stanley Kunitz wrote, "One function of dreams is to inform us that the boundaries of experience are definitely open and that the limits we perceive in our daily life are in themselves an illusion, that actually to be alive is to occupy territories beyond those we recognize as our physical universe. Each person's dream life is in itself a universe, a product of a single tangle of membranes and nerve centers and the rest of it. In the dream you move beyond that dominion into one where the rules have not yet been discovered and never will be."[90]

Do unconscious dream images and their symbols inform the vocabulary of your work?

What are the key dream images or objects with which you work?

How do you interpret the flux and flow of dreams and harness their potential?

Do you anticipate that dreams will draw viewers into your creative space?

Free write for 10 minutes.

87 Gabriel Garcia–Marquez, *One Hundred Years of Solitude* (New York: Cambridge University Press, 1990), 1.

88 RISD alum Jonathan Hayes (MID '95) worked in Marc Harrison's studio following graduation. He recalls seeing a note tacked to Marc's bulletin board—a 2x2" piece of yellow, torn scrap paper with Marc's cursive handwriting in lower-case letters. The note read: "form follows fantasy". Email correspondence, January 27, 2011.

89 Berger and Christie, *Cadmium Red.* John Christie sent this correspondence to John Berger on October 22, 1997.

90 Stanley Kunitz and Genine Lentine, *The Wild Braid: A Poet Reflects on a Century in the Garden* (New York: W.W. Norton & Company, 2005), 87–88.

working with physical materials

From the early 20th century onwards, many artists pushed the terms of what constitutes "materials" for art. Traditional materials such as charcoal, oil paint, and bronze were supplemented or replaced with newspaper, plastic, steel, rubber, or fat, for example, as well as "found" objects. The desire to blur the boundary between art and life instigated a more democratic spirit on behalf of art, inviting a revitalized reflection and expanded perception of how we see our world.

List the materials that you utilize in your work.

What is the character of these materials?

How important to you is the stuff something is made from?

What is the "value" of your materials?

Do you work exclusively in one medium or with a particular material?

Free write for 10 minutes.

Materials Determine Possibility

Many artists speak of being great tinkerers at an early age. They recount the endless hours of pleasure derived from picking up and experimenting with the stuff around them. In their grandfather's shops, for instance, they nailed pieces of wood together and assembled strange contraptions. Now, as mature artists, often the greatest satisfaction comes from being in the studio surrounded by random parts, industrial surplus, and other diverse objects. Using different tools and various strategies, artists explore and transform these materials and discover playful, bold paths into their art. The way they work with materials is central in shaping their ideas and responses. Finding the medium that challenges the vision and ultimately gives it expression is a joyful and felicitous discovery for any artist.

Whether approached with the spirit of the tinkerer, inventor, cultural hacker, or bricoleur, there are ways to make material reality mean something. One investigation involves playing with materials, testing the limits to find new rules for reorganizing and fashioning a given structure. Examining how objects are built, investigating their workings, taking them apart by devious means, repurposing the parts, or creating environments with what is at hand and then building new things is another possible approach.

How does working with materials shape what you do and enable you to move ideas to another level?

How do you investigate and work with a material? What happens?

What transformative processes result from your investigations?

What is the intention of the hand in your work?

Free write for 10 minutes.

Five Rules of Thumb

Your work has its own rules. List five rules of thumb for making your work. Begin with the meaning and then explain ways in which we would combine them.

Materials as Conductors of Meaning

For Joseph Beuys, one of the most celebrated avant-garde artists of the 20th century, materials were not rational, obdurate things, but conductors of meaning. As described in his "Theory of Sculpture," materials are fugitive, flowing states of thinking, feeling, and will that move between chaos and order. In his sculptures and installations—shamanic emblems to his culture's spiritual healing—he used many unconventional materials for which he had a deep affinity. They included blocks of sheep fat, fragments of felt, honey, and copper, among others. Drawing from the healing experience of his past, whether real or fictitious, these materials evoked catastrophe and radical compassion. "Similia similibus curantur: heal like with like, that is the homoeopathic healing process," wrote Beuys.[91]

Fat, a material with energetic potential, was ideal for acknowledging, exploring and demonstrating states of transformative flux between poles of chaos and order. "The flexibility of the material appealed to me particularly in its reaction to temperature changes. This flexibility is psychologically effective—people instinctively feel it relates to inner processes and feelings. The discussion I wanted was about the potential of sculpture and culture, what they mean, what language is about, what human production and creativity are about. So I took an extreme position in sculpture and a material that was very basic to life and not associated with art."[92]

How do you experience the stimuli of your materials?

What qualities of your materials come into play?

What is the intention of the hand in your work?

Latent [Latin] *lateens, latentis* (participial adjective)
Concealed, hidden. *Latere* (verb) to lie hidden

1. Present or potential but not visible or active; hidden and underdeveloped within a person. One's latent ability.
2. [Biology] Dormant but capable of normal development under the best conditions. Said of buds, spores, cocoons, etc.
3. [Psychology] Present in unconscious mind but not consciously expressed. Dormant. Quiescent. [93]

Do you believe materials possess their own latent language or inherent meaning?

How does your chosen medium help to accomplish the emergence of your material language?

Do you use materials to conduct meaning, evoke emotions, summon a quality of being, or convey ideals?

What is mediated through materials?

Examine the contrasts of materiality in your work. What are they? How do they come into play?

How does your focus on materiality lead you to engage the materiality of the world?

Free write for 15 minutes.

91 Donald Kuspit, "Beuys or Warhol?" www.griffinila.com/Portals/0/Beuys%20or%20Warhol.pdf. Accessed November 28, 2010.

92 Caroline Tisdall, *Joseph Beuys* (New York: The Solomon R. Guggenheim Museum, 1979), 72.

93 *The American Heritage Dictionary of the English Language*, 4th ed., s.v. "latent."

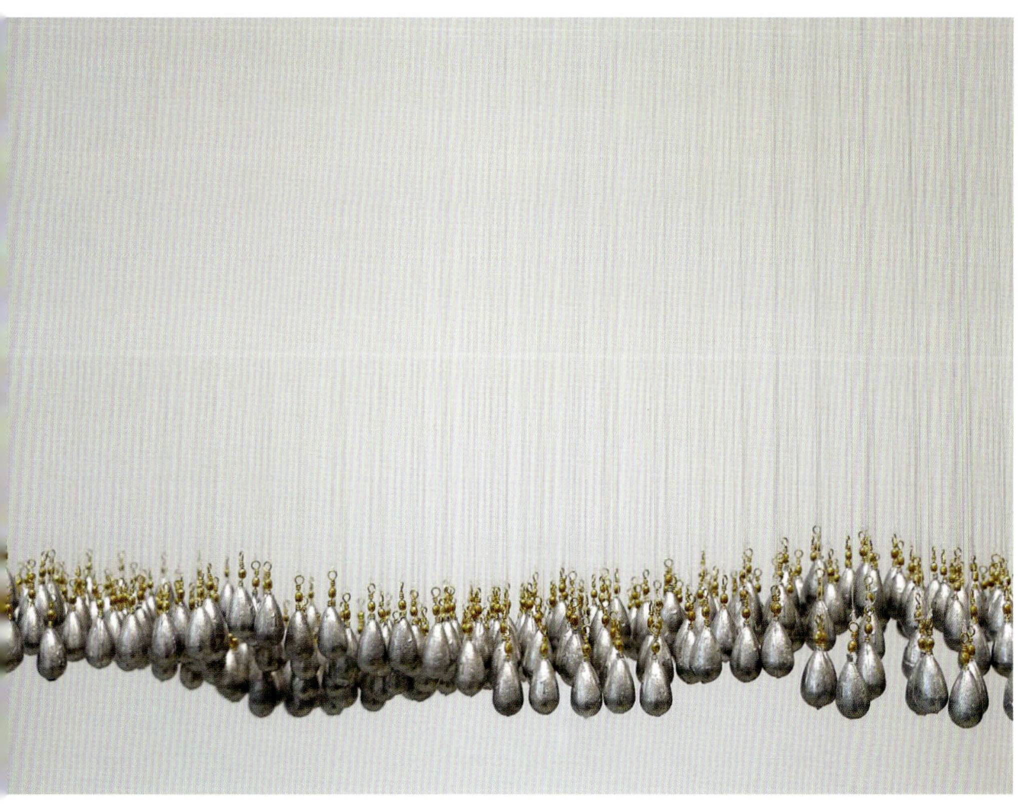

CRYSTAL ELLIS, *THE WEIGHT OF WATER*, 2009

the play of lightness + weight

In the Tao Te Ching it is said that the root of lightness is heaviness.

Consider an aspect of your work that has lightness, weightlessness. Describe it.

Consider an aspect of your work that has weight, gravity, density, and concreteness. Describe it.

Once we discover the threads that connect our making to our thinking, we begin to comprehend the intelligence of our work.

EXPLORING

map as matrix

how do you think? what do you think?

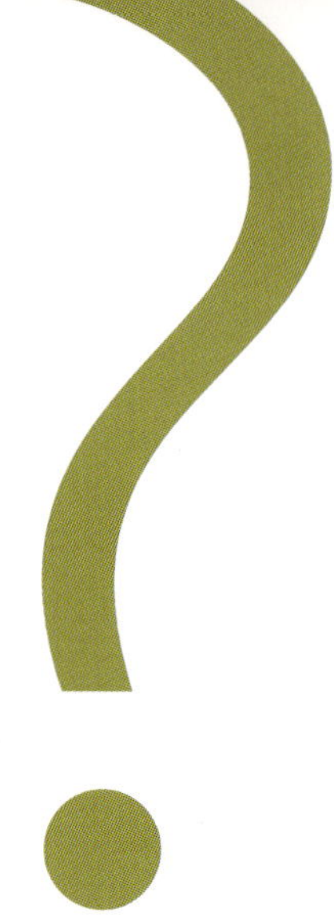

staying in the questions

Often we are working off a blueprint of creative impulses, but don't know why we make the work that we do. Find your own way of asking questions and come up with your own answers. This may help you to discern patterns in your thinking and way of working.

Free write for 10 minutes.

What are some of the questions you ask yourself as you work?

Think of your work as a question. What does it ask? What does the work do?

Log meaningful questions and comments from conversations, studio visits, or critiques.

What is the question most posed by others about your work?

marshalling reference points

You must discover the artwork that you like and realize the response you make to it. ... It is in this way that you discover your own direction and the truth about yourself.[94] AGNES MARTIN

It is the hallmark of the genuinely talented that they can reveal their reference points and not be diminished by this act of revelation. Only the terminally second rate try to conceal their reference points.[95] ADRIAN SHAUGHNESSY

Name the artists, designers, writers, thinkers, makers whom you consider to be your influences, ones who may be your predecessors or contemporaries.

If your work is informed by an art historical tradition, how does this tradition echo in your work? Elaborate on what you appreciate about this particular tradition. What have you learned from your historical predecessors?

Focusing on influential contemporary artists, what gives their work compelling stature? What in particular attracts you to their work? How do you intentionally bring forward these references?

Investigate the writings of artists whose works are relevant to yours or whom you wish to emulate. Track down monographs, autobiographies, biographies, exhibition catalogues, critical essays, and supportive journal articles about this artist.

Explain how their works relate to your thinking and artistic processes. What questions do these artists or designers pose? What problems do they set out to solve? What motivates and inspires them? Trace the roots of their inquiries.

If you discover that someone has created similar work to your own, define the places of overlap—the parallel instincts—and the areas of difference.

Free write for 15 minutes.

94 Agnes Martin, "Beauty is the Mystery of Life," in *Agnes Martin* (New York: Whitney Museum of American Art, 1992), 11.

95 Adrian Shaughnessy, "Forward," *in 136 Points of Reference*, London: Ellery/Browns, 2005, unpaginated.

your reading list

> Who are we, who is each one of us, if not a combanitoria of experiences, information, books we have read, things imagined? Each life is an encyclopedia, a library, an inventory of objects, a series of styles, and everything can be constantly shifted and reordered in every way conceivable.[96] ITALO CALVINO

In *The Book Room: Georgia O'Keeffe's Library in Abiquiu*, curator Ruth E. Fine speaks of O'Keeffe's books as the "bones of her intellectual and emotional life."[97] The contents of her library reflect intimate relationships, creative allies, and the prismatic experiences and primary interests of her life. Among many books nested are Ansel Adams' *Sierra Nevada: The John Muir Trail*, *Adventures in the Arts* by Marsden Hartley, *Fugaku hyakkei* [*One Hundred Views of Fuji*] by Hokusai, *The Ballad of Reading Gaol* by Oscar Wilde, *John Marin: The Man and His Work*, as well as periodicals and miscellaneous material. To look at her living library is to acquire magnification of her sensibility and mental climate. Whether or not we are ardent bibliophiles, we each collect and read books for many reasons. Some for comfort, renewal, enlargement, and affirmation. Some for pure fact. Some for plain enjoyment.

Notice the contents of your library. What titles surround you? How have your classified them? What are the literary genres you explore? Fairytales, myth, poetry, mysteries, short stories, literary criticism, non-fiction? If someone asked you for your reading list, what would you give him or her?

Pull ten books off your shelf that have been fundamental to your development as an artist. How have these books influenced the creation of your work? When did you first encounter these books?

If you were banished to a desert island, what single book would you take with you and why?

Which book would you re-read from childhood?

Is your work linked to a literary source? What is the nature of the allusion?

Free write for 15 minutes.

96 Italo Calvino, *Six Memos for the Next Millennium* (Cambridge: Harvard University Press, 1988), 124.

97 Ruth E. Fine "Books as Bones," in *The Book Room: Georgia O'Keeffe's Library in Abiquiu* (New York: The Georgia O'Keeffe Foundation, 1997), 11–16.

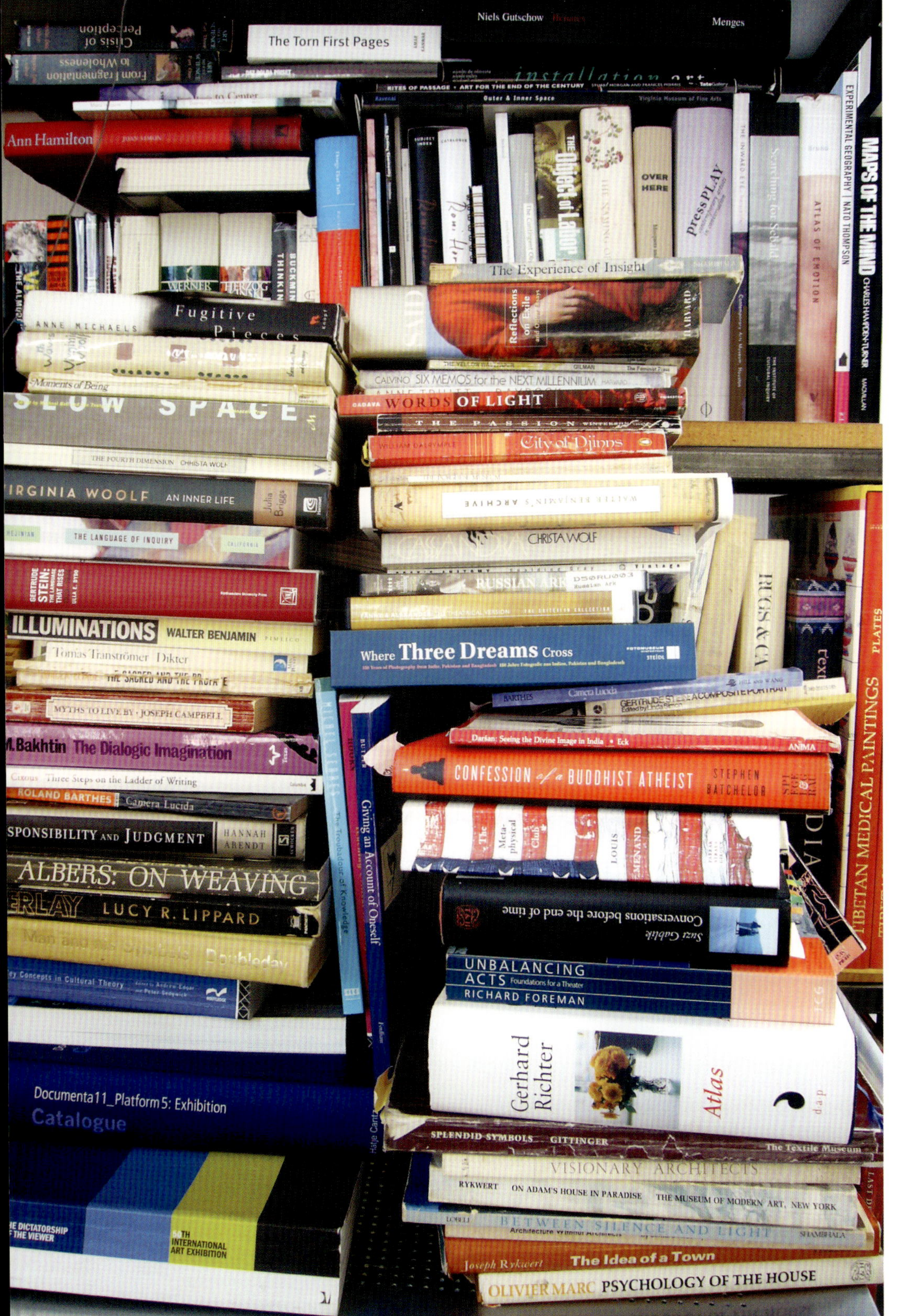

PHOTO KATARINA WESLIEN

layers of intimacy

In *A Pattern Language* (1977), the now-classic volume in architecture and planning, architect Christopher Alexander presents an array of patterns that generate a rich and subtle language for creative projects. Among them is the "intimacy gradient."[98] The intimacy gradient follows a careful progression from common, public space to private, intimate areas. Alexander identifies this pattern as fundamental to the development of spaces that illuminate public presence and inner needs. This fundamental spatial ordering principle allows us to move slowly and respectfully beyond the isolated and detached to domains of intimacy. Gradients of intimacy relate to all work, not just architecture. They encourage subtlety of interaction and offer different layers and shades of meaning.

98 Christopher Alexander, *A Pattern Language*. (New York: Oxford University Press, 1977), 610–13.

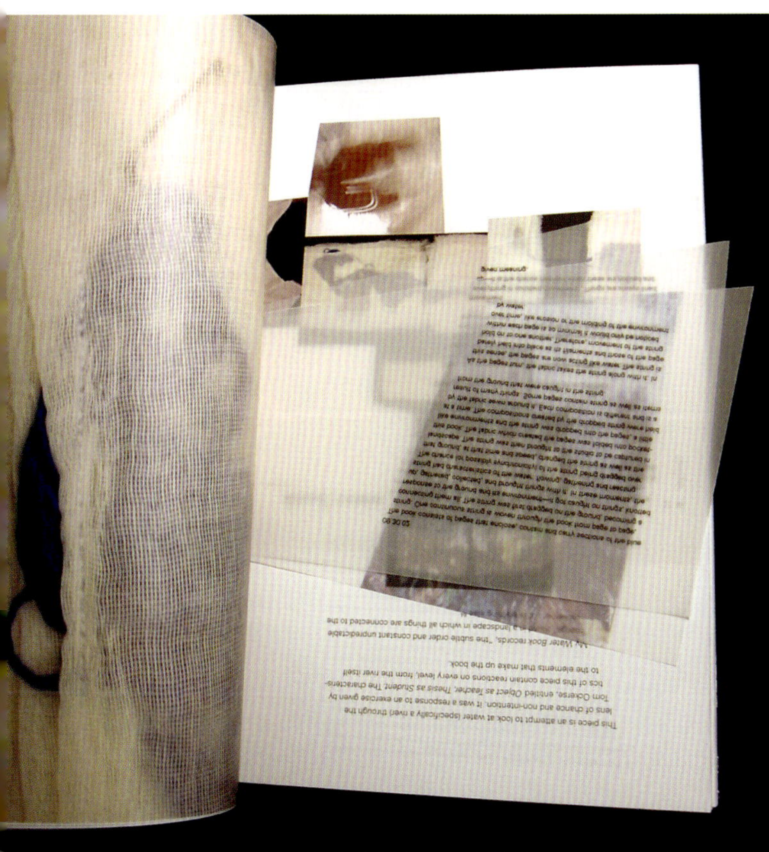

PHOTO REBECCA KLEIN GANZ

Incorporate the principle of the intimacy gradient in the construction and character of your own work. How do you allow viewers a constructive rapport that invites subtleties of interaction?

Like Russian nesting dolls, is there a well-developed progression through these layers of intimacy and intricacy?

How does one encounter each dimension from the more public to the private, all the while acquiring an appropriate intensity of awareness?

How do you work the layers of engagement between proximity and distance?

Free write for 10 minutes.

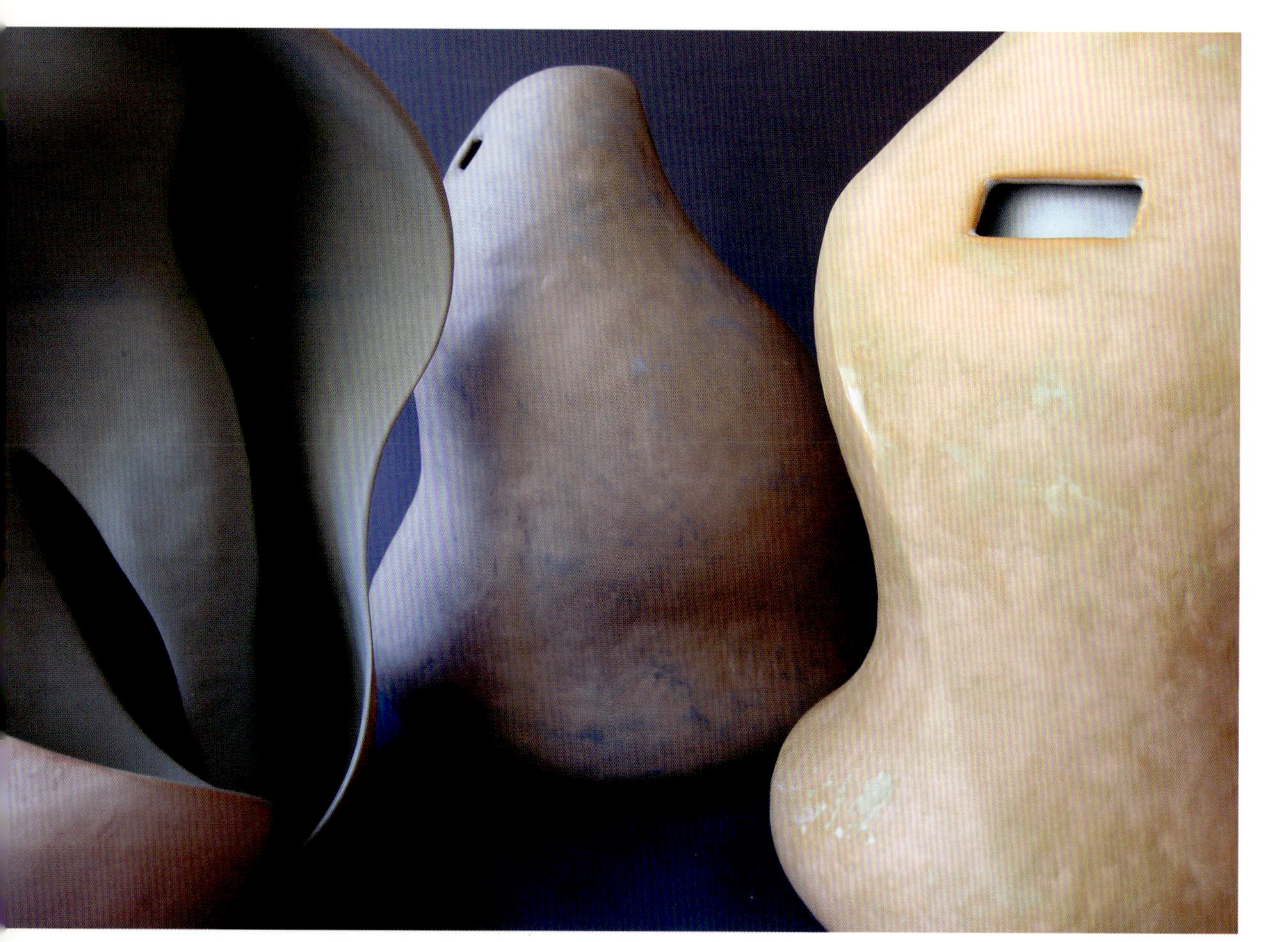

ASYA PALATOVA, *THE DANCE*, 2004

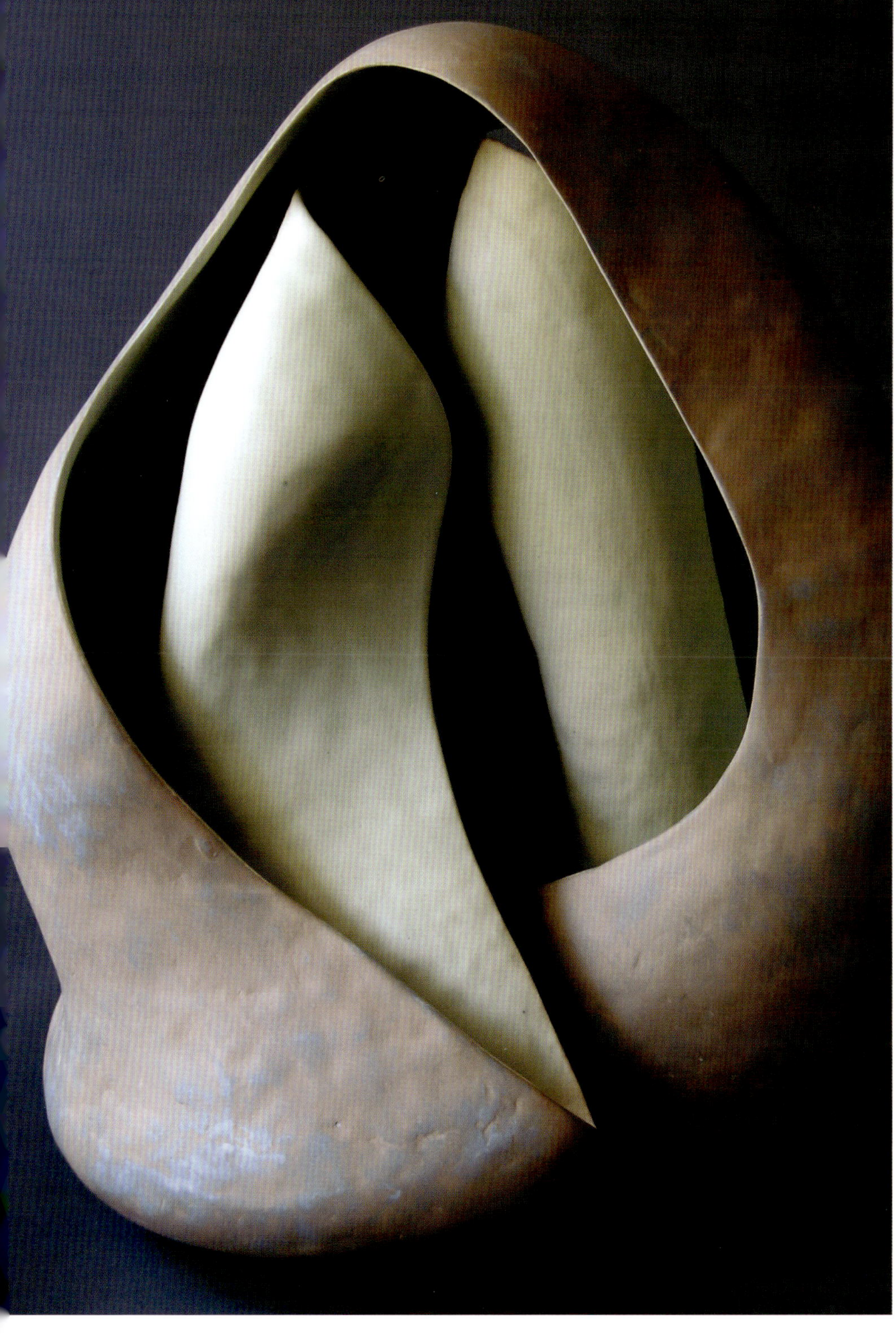

ASYA PALATOVA, *THE DANCE*, 2004

visual hopes

Art, then, is an increase of life, a sort of competition of surprises that stimulates our consciousness and keeps it from becoming somnolent.[99] GASTON BACHELARD

We hope on principle, we hope tactically and strategically, we hope because the future is dark, we hope because it's a more powerful and joyful way to live.[100] REBECCA SOLNIT

Art is "engaged" work that is tap-rooted in the circumstances and issues of our time, whether ecological, political, or spiritual. As we nurture our hopes into visual action through practices, processes, and projects we become catalysts in creating positive futures. This is compassionate, altruistic, revelatory, and transformative work. Our "visual hopes" are actions that forge enlargement in different ways. Some "actions" are quietly profound and imbued with subtlety. Some actions empower solidarity through collaborative exchange, while others address underlying misalignments through direct activism.

Consider the following questions in relation to your work and artistic presence in the world.[101]

Comment on your sense of and relationship to the world in which we live.

What are the most critical needs of the planet that are going unmet?

What are the greatest sources of pain and suffering in the world? In your community? In your country?

Who are some of the people or organizations that are addressing some of these problems?

What is the nature of your artistic "actions"? What shapes your perspective on hope?

Is it important for your work to be engaged with the critical needs of our times?

Free write for 15 minutes.

99 Bachelard, *Poetics of Space*, xxxiii.

100 Rebecca Solnit, *Acts of Hope: Challenging Empire on the World Stage*. Web exclusive to the January/February 2004 issue of *Orion* magazine, 1.

101 Adapted from an exercise in *Learning Through the Real World (LTI), Interest Inventory #3, Big Picture Advisor Guide, Section 2: 10, Big Picture Learning*. Adapted from Lawrence G. Boldt, *Zen and the Art of Making a Living: A Practical Guide to Creative Career Design* (1993).

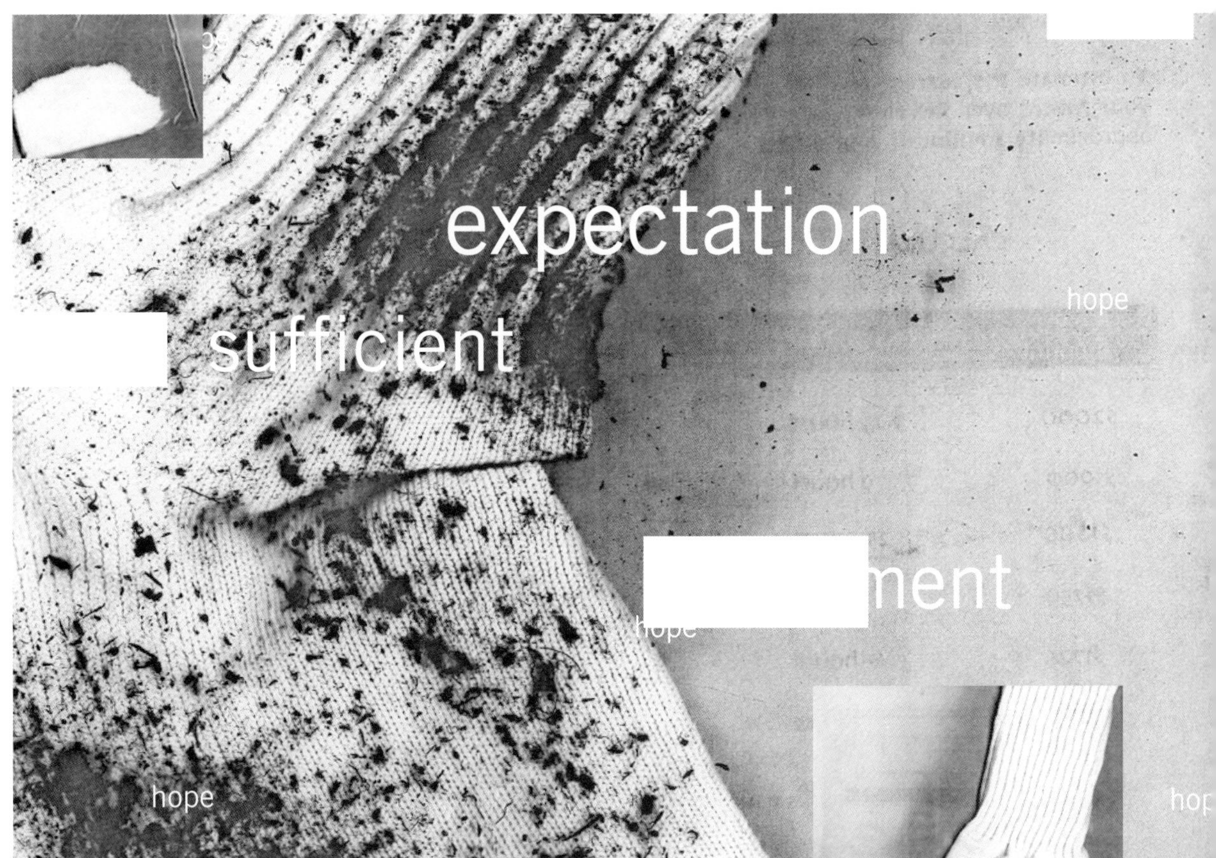

DARYL SMITH, *HOPE AND WATER*, 2002

before the "beginning was the word"

Imagine an eye unruled by man-made laws of perspective, an eye unprejudiced by compositional logic, an eye which does not respond to the name of everything but which must know each object encountered in life through an adventure of perception. How many colors are there in a field of grass to the crawling baby unaware of 'Green'? How many rainbows can light create for the untutored eye? ... Imagine a world before the "beginning was the word."[102] STAN BRAKHAGE

To suspend or recast our regular habits of viewing and to have fresh contact with a subject, we must invent new lenses, new ways of responding, new vocabularies. The question is, how do we open our perceptual framework as a means to free ourselves from constraints, from rigidity? How do we get back to before the beginning was the word?

To interrupt our dominant ways of thinking we need to place ourselves in a state of fresh discovery. Philosopher Paul Valéry suggests that this means breaking from the containment of our preconceptions, our labels, is to "forget the name of the thing one sees."[103]

102 Stan Brakhage, *Metaphors on Vision* (New York: Anthology Film Archives, 1976), 1.

103 Paul Valéry, as quoted in Lawrence Weschler, *Seeing is Forgetting the Name of the Thing One Sees* (Berkeley: University of California Press, 1982), 203.

Project

Take a small object – anything that can be held in the hand. Play with it as though it were alive. Hear it before seeing it. Record the sensory aspects without getting into its functional aspects. Sniff it out for clues. Taste it. Physically handle it. Move it. Check its underside. Without naming the thing itself, describe it to someone who is blindfolded.

To encourage a fresh, more dimensional reading, replace this object with one of your works. Again, imagine someone is walking in blindfolded. The idea is to add depth, variation, and nuance to your description. Describe what she or he would experience.

the gap that drives the work

In all our voluntary thinking there is some topic or subject about which all the members of the thought revolve. Half the time this topic is a problem, a gap we cannot yet fill with a definite picture, word, or phrase, but which. ... Influences us in an intensely active and determinate psychic way. Whatever may be the images and phrases that pass before us, we feel their relation to this aching gap. To fill it up is our thoughts' destiny. Some bring us nearer to that consummation. Some the gap negates as quite irrelevant. Each swims in a felt fringe of relations of which the aforesaid gap is the term.[104] WILLIAM JAMES

The unscripted gap is a tension point, a vital zone for inquiry, inspiration, and translation.

Where is the topic that defines the gap in your work?

How do you acknowledge, encourage, and invite the gap to come into play in your work and working process?

What is the language you use to define an understanding of this zone?

Free write for 10 minutes.

There has been much speculation, scientific and philosophical, on the causes and processes of the triggering of nerve firings in the brain that recreate patterns of past sensations, finally evoking a memory. Central to the brain's operation is the fact that all of its neurons are physically disconnected from each other, and begin and end in a tiny gap of empty space. The flickering pattern evoked by the tiny sparks of thought bridging these gaps becomes the actual form and substance of our ideas. All of our thoughts have at their center this small point of nothingness.[105] BILL VIOLA

104 From William James, *The Principles of Psychology*, Vol. 1 (New York: Henry Holt), 1890, as quoted in Laing, Katherine Knight, 259.

105 Bill Viola on his video/sound installation "The Theater of Memory," in *Bill Viola*, eds. David A. Ross and Peter Sellers (New York: Whitney Museum of American Art, 1997), 83.

106 From thesis writing exercise, Naomi Kaly, RISD, Fall 2005.

I was born and raised in Israel. I am Israeli.

I live in Japan.

I hear Japanese. I read English. I write English. I think Hebrew. I am Israeli.

I hear Japanese. I speak Japanese. I read English. Japanese. I write English. Japanese.

I think Hebrew. English. Japanese. I dream Hebrew. I am Israeli.

I live in America.

I hear English. I speak English. I read English. I write English. I think English. Hebrew.

I dream Japanese. Hebrew. I forget. I remember. I miss Japanese. I am Israeli.

Space is an opening—an interval—an opportunity for the unexpected to happen, for the hidden to be revealed and for the silence to be heard. As an alien, space for me is a gap—what I do not understand, what is said without being meant, or meant without being said. Western languages often associate space with void or emptiness, which suggest a lack, a shortage of something. Eastern cultures, however, consider space as a whole, a sensory space, which combines physical space as well as space in time (*Ikebana*, Japanese flower arrangement, emphasizes the space between the flowers rather than the flower itself). In my work, I use space to explore textual and linguistic aspects of identity and culture.[106]

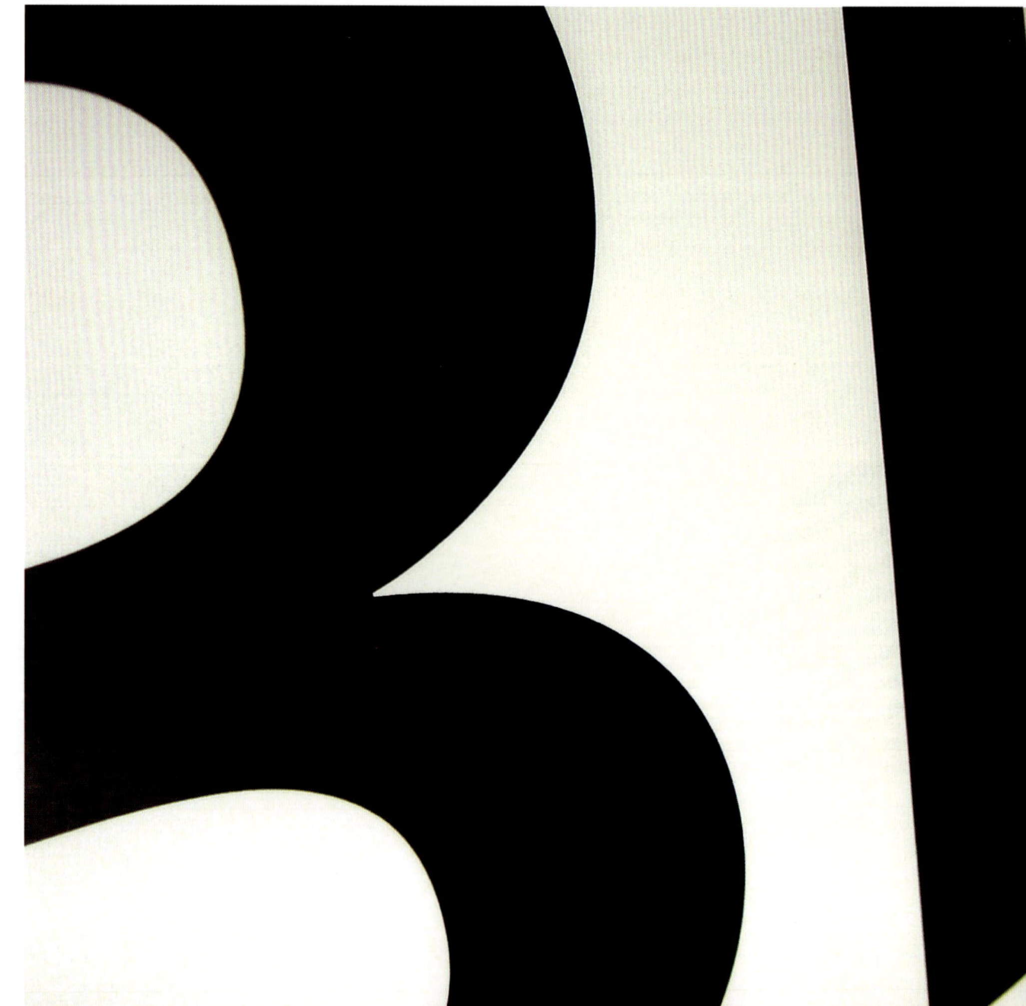

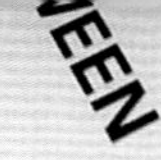

REBECCA KLEIN GANZ, *BALANCING IN THE BETWEEN*, 2003

becoming threshold without a map

> One must go further; one must make the encounter with relations penetrate and corrupt everything, undermine being, make it topple.[107]
> GILLES DELEUZE + CLAIRE PARNET

> He is closer to the world when he carries chaos in himself. Our work is to metamorphose the chaos.[108] ELIAS CANETTI

As we explore the idea of mapping, we must also turn our attention to moments that take us away from the map, when our creative process is unclear. Suddenly we are on unfamiliar ground. Ambiguity surfaces and we experience art angst.

Confronted with doubt, uncertainty, and the fact that we simply don't know, we are stalled in a time between work and non work, as artist Eva Hesse refers to it.[100] Something has clearly become dislodged. On this threshold of defamiliarization, we hover eerily in what seems a perpetual present tense between non-connection and hyper connection, between presence and absence.

The threshold is a place of threshing + holding.[109]

Within the process of creation, "becoming threshold" is a rich and important zone of imagination and mind. While there might be dissolution of clarity, there is also much potential to be unlocked. Since this is an active place of flux and shifting energy, it is a time when metamorphoses occur. Perception expands and we see things in new ways. This frame of mind shapes our relationship with the world on different terms.

Negotiating the threshold is fundamental to all becoming. "Concrete metamorphosis makes the world," says Bulgarian-born novelist and fiction writer Elias Canetti.[110] Canetti, thinks of the artist as a "dichter"—the one who carries this chaos within but works it consciously. We are asked to be fluent with the chaos in order to widen perception, to learn a new language. This requires great diligence, concentration, and attention. As one design student states, it is a "process of finding and losing, seeing and not seeing, pulling, stretching, and reflecting."[111] Constantly the boundaries of awareness alter as the chains of familiar responses evaporate. A path of discovery is inaugurated which awakens potency for the new. Shifts in ontological awareness occur. Sensibility deepens. Consciousness is heightened.

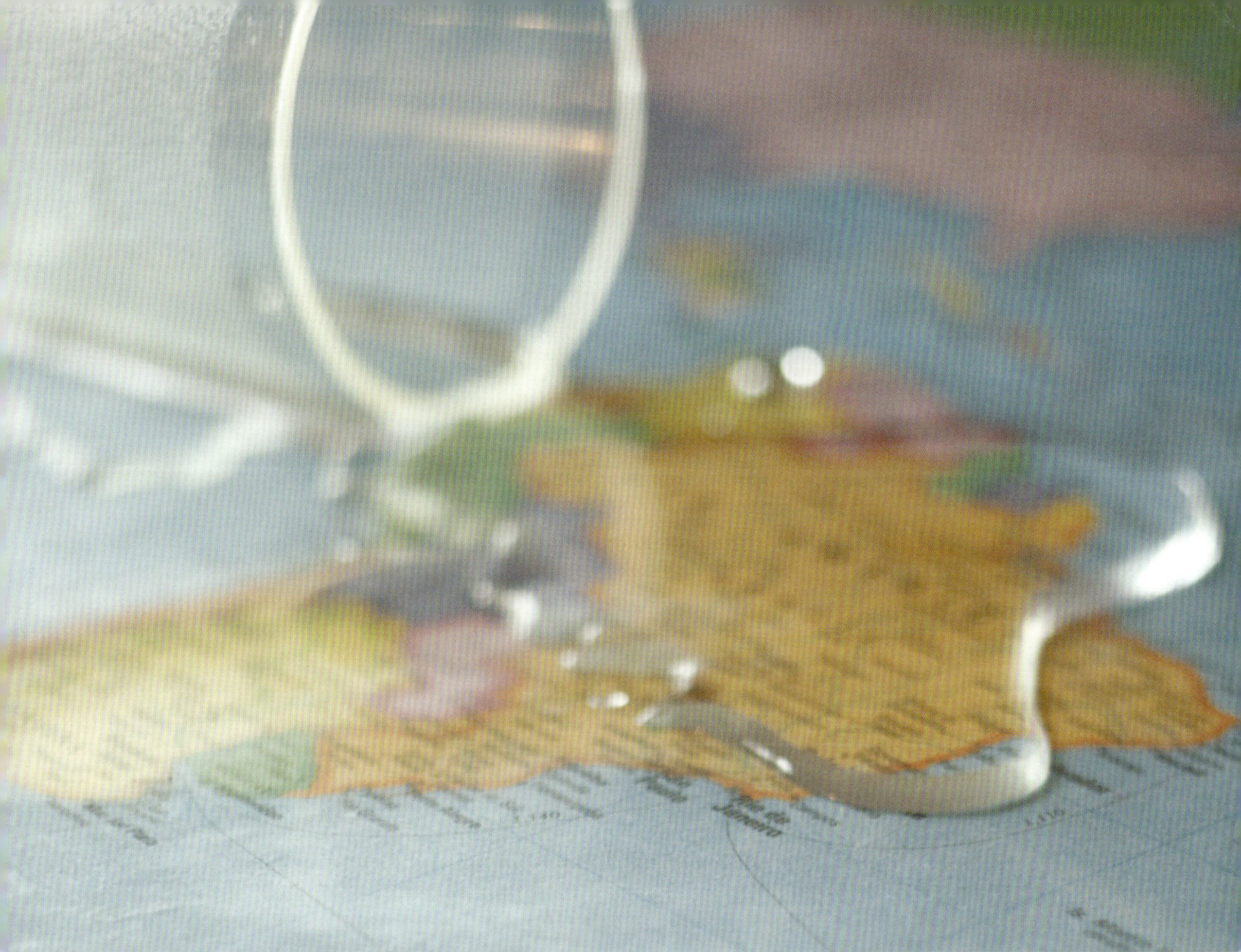

PHOTO BRADLEY SLADE, *SEEING THE EVERYDAY* MAGAZINE, 2011

How do you understand this state of becoming threshold?

How does the threshold inform your work as an artist and the nature of the work you produce?

How has your working process opened you, surprised you, refreshed you, perhaps even frightened you, wherein you found something new?

Free write for 10 minutes.

106 Gilles Deleuze and Claire Parnet, *Dialogues II*, (New York: Continuum, 2006), 47.

107 Elias Canetti, *The Conscience of Words & Earwitness*, trans. Joachim Neugroschel (London: Pan Books, 1987), 157–67.

108 Eva Hesse, In *Eva Hesse: A Retrospective*, edited by Lesley K. Baier, Maurice Berger, and Helen A. Cooper (New Haven, CT: Yale University Press, 1992), 102.

109 Anjali Srinivasan, "Particle Activism," MFA thesis in Glass, Rhode Island School of Design, 2007, x.

110 Canetti, *The Conscience of Words*, 157–67.

111 Gunta Kaza, "Muse. Mute. Mutiny.," MFA in Graphic Design thesis, Rhode Island School of Design, 2001, Signature #4.

in the collective sphere

Take the deeply personal relationship with your work to a broader readership. This is an opportunity for you to consider your message, the form, and the means of distributing the message. As you do so, you will address the question of audience and how you might enter into a more complex structure of agency and engagement.

Project: A Mock Two-page Article for a Magazine of Your Choice.

Spend some time with the current periodicals at a local bookstore or library with a generous magazine rack and select a journal that suits your work and point of view.

Carefully study and understand the format of the magazine. Consider the nature of the articles and how they are presented.

Develop a two-page article for this magazine of choice. This article could be a review, a feature, an interview, etc.

Clearly communicate your concept into a textual and visual arrangement that coheres with the design character of the magazine.

Broadway-Lafayette St

CITY LITERATE

Weird things are happening in New York. Weird literary things. After a long night out Saturday, I said goodbye to my friend Glori on Houston Street. She was going North and I was heading Southbound back to Brooklyn. We parted ways at the stairwell. Then I proceeded to wait 45 minutes standing directly across from my friend. While we were waiting something unusual happened. There was text projected onto Glori and the whole platform around her. Words made of light moving across the space. "What are we waiting for?" The words spilled onto the floor; the platform had become like a stage.

s the story?

entino checks out some strange things popping up around the city.

rojecting on my
m also, but it was
ead. I'm sure they
the other side. I
out I was pretty
ogue from *Waiting*
e waiting. They
ange.

g. On my Metro-
ally says "*Swipe*
t said "*I thought*
it to be locked out;"
y card through the
little screen that
" continued the
hought how it is worse,
d in." Cool. But I
e line. And I was

in the elevator. I
teries to my editor
g. First I talked
r Annette Dorothy.
n reading and
aid.

o the texts that
cting us, selling
en a textual voice
more poetic or
edge our time
more likely to pay
tive and engag
the audience to
ically, socially or
reate design
re more memo-
and educational."

cademic for our
Out. So I went
d some regular folks
osite page).

tside Barnes and
says "*Great bod-*
er responsible for
n read it from my
ople didn't notice
over it. But for the
e the time to read
treet, the pedestri-
mers.

picture? Is this part
where we are all
s? Let's keep on
ore.

MetroCard

(((I thought how unpleasant it is to be locked out;

Are you talking to me?
The Metrocard in question. It woke me from the blind stupor of my daily commute, and gave me a story to tell my cubicle mates when I got to work. We all admitted we need to read more. Then we caught up on last night's *American Idol*.

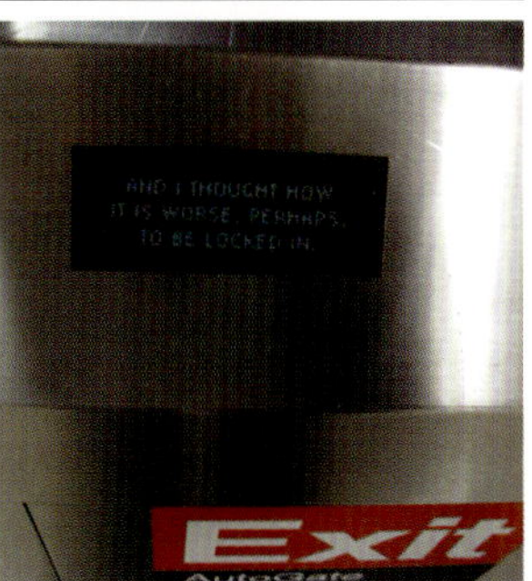

Curious?

Who's behind it all? Do you think it's just another advertising campaign? What's the last book your read? We asked a few New Yorkers these questions and more.

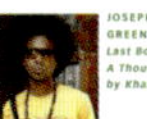

JOSEPH, 24, ARTIST
GREENPOINT
Last Book Read:
A Thousand Splendid Suns by Khaled Hosseini

"I don't bother reading this stuff. I am sure it's some kind of guerilla marketing thing. I wonder who will own up to it eventually."

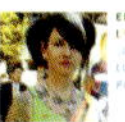

EDN[illegible] 29, STUDENT
L[illegible] EAST SIDE
[illegible] Book Read:
Lush Life by Richard Prince

"Now that you mention it, I think I saw some Shakespeare on a construction sign near Central Park South yesterday? It reminded me of all the bizarre, unexpected things happening in this city."

"I was walking my dog in Central Park yesterday and I think I saw some Shakespeare on a construction sign."

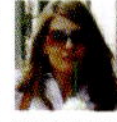

JENNY, 32, PR ASSOCIATE
CHELSEA
Last Book Read:
Harry Potter and the Deathly Hallows by J.K. Rowling

"I saw the subway projections too. I was having my weekly Monday morning existential crisis about hating my job and what I'm going to do with my life, and there it was. Writing on the wall! "It'll pass the time" it said. "We'll be back tomorrow and the day after." Something like that. Sometimes living in New York I feel like I live in a movie, and this was one of those days."

PHOTO MARY-JO VALENTINO

seeing the doubleness of the work

night / day

moist / dry

fresh / decayed

cold / warm

soft / hard

entry / escape

oblivion / emergence

oppression / liberation

bright / dark

active / passive

permanence / change

order / chaos

gaseous / solid

precious / cheap

natural / synthetic

open / hidden

inside / outside

complex / simple

strange / familiar

attract / repel

confusion / clarification

real / meretricious

According to French cultural anthropologist Claude Levi-Strauss, things that matter happen along binary lines.[112]

112 Claude Levi–Strauss, *The Raw and the Cooked*, trans. John and Doreen Weightman (New York: Harper & Row, 1969). Levi–Strauss extended the ideas of binary pairings to anthropology, in such oppositions as nature/culture, raw/cooked, inedible/edible.

seeing the doubleness of the work

night / day

moist / dry

fresh / decayed

cold / warm

soft / hard

entry / escape

oblivion / emergence

oppression / liberation

bright / dark

active / passive

permanence / change

order / chaos

gaseous / solid

precious / cheap

natural / synthetic

open / hidden

inside / outside

complex / simple

strange / familiar

attract / repel

confusion / clarification

real / meretricious

According to French cultural anthropologist Claude Levi-Strauss, things that matter happen along binary lines.[112]

112 Claude Levi-Strauss, *The Raw and the Cooked*, trans. John and Doreen Weightman (New York: Harper & Row, 1969). Levi-Strauss extended the ideas of binary pairings to anthropology, in such oppositions as nature/culture, raw/cooked, inedible/edible.

Do you agree with Levi-Strauss?

Record the binary pairings that appear in your work. What are the tensions or opposing qualities?

Do opposites attract?

How are differences configured?

Does duality clarify definition?

Free write for 15 minutes.

Counterpoint In music, the pattern that results from combining melodies. The composer creates a balance between the rhythmic and melodic independence of several lines to combine and set each other off to form the greater whole.

Symbolic Duality In his poetry, William Blake juxtaposes opposites such as the tyger and the lamb, the clod and the pebble, the cankerworm and the rose, and through the interplay of dualities seeks clarification.

Tension Dialogue Stillness

Contrast Are the words / objects / concepts distinct and in contrast to one another, a strife of opposites that are separate, repellant, and in conflict?

If they are, why and where is the unrest or collision between the two? How do you explore this interplay of tensions or contradictions? How do you establish the boundaries?

Complement If you juxtapose two thoughts or ideas in an essential play of energies, how do they correlate or correspond as a dialogue of co-present, parallel activities? How do you translate the space between them?

Harmonize Are there instances when the separation, the polarity of the twosome intermix, dissolve, blend, conjoin, and harmonize so that they come to coexist as vital paradox?

Multiply Are there instances when they split, divide, and mutate, breaking out into a hybrid of something more?

"All things," said Hegel, "are in themselves contradictory, and it is this principle, more than any other which expresses the truth, the very essence of things."[113]

How are these played out in a discernible visual language that speaks from both sides?

What is the imaginary line in the language of the double?

113 As quoted in *Art Without Boundaries*, eds. Philip Thompson, John Williams, and Gerald Woods (New York: Praeger, 1974), 13, 16.

ambidextrous word play

Words and their meaning ride on the vagaries of the human voice. Words carry different weights depending on the tone of voice, the accent, the emphasis, the syntax, and the context.

Cadence, rhythm, and breathing shift our point of view from the micro to the macro. Volume also adjusts according to the scale of a space. We do not say the same thing in a small room as we say in a large room.

Step One: Word Play

On a note-sized sheet of paper, with the hand opposite to your writing hand, print small, subtle words. List words that conjure up lightness, diminutive action, sensitive nuance, privacy, invisibility, latency, or gestures of minor significance.

With a jumbo crayon on a large sheet of newsprint using your dominant writing hand, print large, commanding words. List words that suggest power, substance, weight. These may be declarations, pronouncements, shouts, or large gestures. They may also be categories or subject areas.

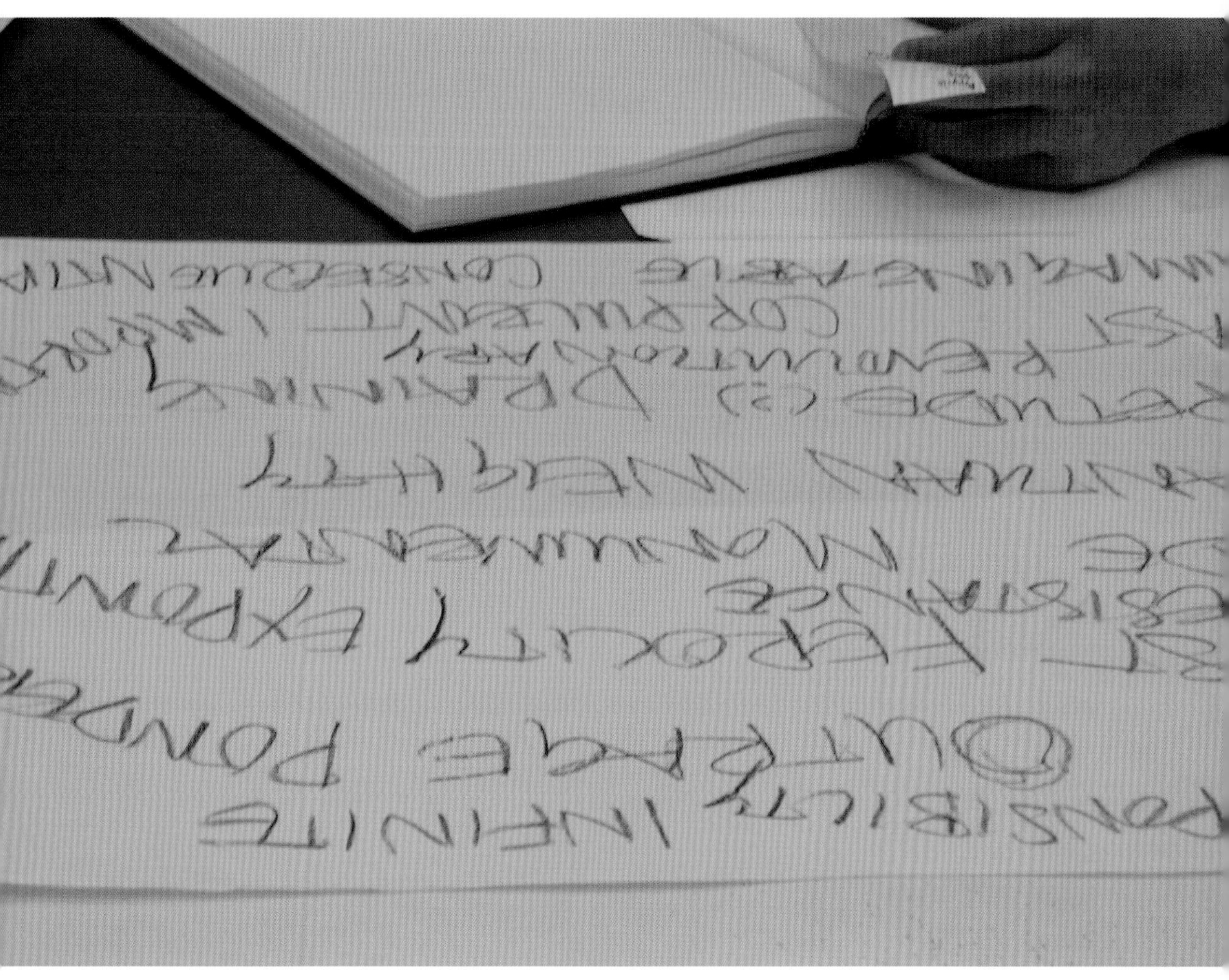

PHOTO ANNE WEST

Step Two: Meld Opposites

Place the two lists in front of you. Take a word from one list and link it with a word from the other list. In doing so, consider the fact that all things exist in relationship to their opposites and are indeed defined by them. Create three different pairings. Meld them together. Work the antonyms. Hold the paradox of paired opposites.

Step Three: Project Descriptions

Write three short project descriptions. For the first, use words from your list of subtle words, in the second build your description from your list of commanding words, and in the third, combine your list of words.

Do you insist or question? Murmur or shout?

114 From thesis writing exercise, Jessica Roundy, RISD, Fall 2010.

subtle words	COMMANDING WORDS
grayscale	DYNAMIC
path	CONNECTIONS
growth	SYSTEMS
gentle	CAPTURE
perception	RELEASE
gradation	LIVE/LIVING
	FLUX
	EVOLVE
	FILTER
	REVEAL
	CONSTANT

Subtle Project Description:
As a gentle way of progression through the site, an elevated path extends across a salt marsh. The success of the project is based on whether or not growth occurs under the walkway and whether or not people perceive the subtle changes of plant communities they pass through. The changing species give a gradation to the site and illuminate the existing water conditions.

Commanding Project Description:
A path extends across a salt marsh, filtering light through it and people along it. The path connects people to place by revealing systems at work. The construction is lightweight and transparent in order to be fully functional as an integrated part of the site.

Combined Project Description:
An elevated path extends across a salt marsh, filtering light through it and people along it. The path connects culture and ecology by capturing views into the systems active on the site. Across the site plant species change. These changes reveal water conditions and give a gradation to the journey through the marsh. In order to function as an integrated part of a dynamic site, the construction of the path is lightweight and transparent. It sweeps through the upper reaches of Spartina while bisecting the height of Phyragmites. The flux of the height of the grasses reveals a new living topography.[114]

Using the metaphor of the early Turkish carpet, architect Christopher Alexander shows that the degree of wholeness which a carpet has is directly correlated to the number of centers in the carpet. These centers are the building blocks that give the work a sense of the whole. The more centers it has the more powerful and deep in its degree of wholeness. As artists, we can draw upon Alexander's analogy, as we probe core elements of our work to find the deeper ideas that inform it.[115]

EXPLORING
map as matrix

mapping the multiple centers alive in the work

key words

Create a list of key words.

Begin by pulling out key words from your writing. Key words hold the scent of our work. They are the word base for our writing, allowing us to build upon them as we generate open word maps.

Read through all of your writings. With a highlighter, illuminate key words, and then write these key words on a separate sheet of paper. You may wish to separate them as verbs, nouns, and adjectives.

To encourage familiarity with your key words, write each word on a Post-it™ note. Then using these Post-it™ notes build a compositional board where your images and words live side by side. Freely move them around as you explore meaningful groupings.

115 Christopher Alexander, *A Foreshadowing of the 21st Century Art: The Color and Geometry of Very Early Turkish Carpets.* (New York: Oxford University Press, 1993), 31–51.

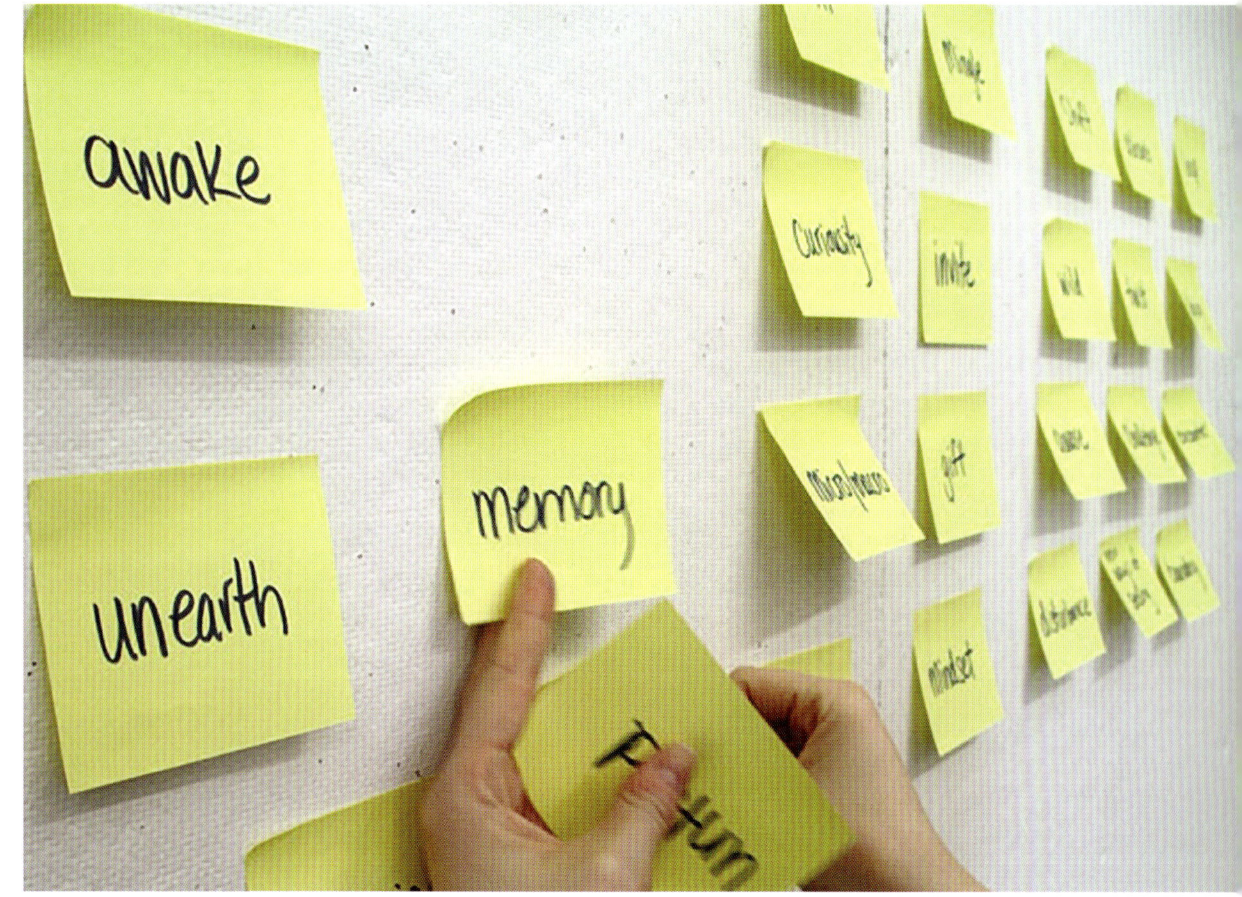

PHOTO STEPHANIE GREY

your thinking + working process

This is a preliminary mapping exercise leading to the next step—the creation of a matrix map.

Here three artists map their processes, allowing them to look closely at how their minds work, as well as offering insights into a way of working and presenting their ideas.

Sculptor Jake Beckman uses rolls of paper and Sharpies™ to map his process, which involves responding to questions and figuring out definitions. Beginning on the right side of the roll, to avoid its curl, he starts with a question posed to him during a critique. This question leads to another. Terms are dismantled. New ideas for work arise. Random thoughts ignite unexpected pathways, sometimes leading down a rabbit hole. He circles. Jumps around. Creates bubble diagrams. Over two days of immersion, a rich array of non-linear connections come to the surface.

Graphic Designer Megan Feehan builds compositional boards where images and words live side by side. For one board she allows initial points of thought, influence, visual interests, and potential ideas to exist in meaningful groupings in one space. Another stage is an attempt for more structure. A bulletin board is divided into project ideas, influences, quotations, and readings. In the last stage she synthesizes and edits down the pieces.

Ceramist Lee Johnson uses a large sheet of paper mounted on a wall to display his thinking and working process. Since his work deals with considerable content, this format allows him to tackle massive amounts of information and to be messy. Within this format he tracks two trains of thought simultaneously. Around the perimeter, and tied to a grid, are quotations and articles pinned to the surface. In the center, are his ideas—explorations in flux. He is dogged about tracking his thinking and working process because he enjoys the sheer exploration of the human mind. He is eager to find lines between his works and to discover a framework for how he has been thinking. This system of mapping allows him to work with information that is not only pertinent to now, but which is part of an overall journey, lasting a number of years. By containing it on one surface, he sees the resources at hand, and establishes a more synthetic perspective.

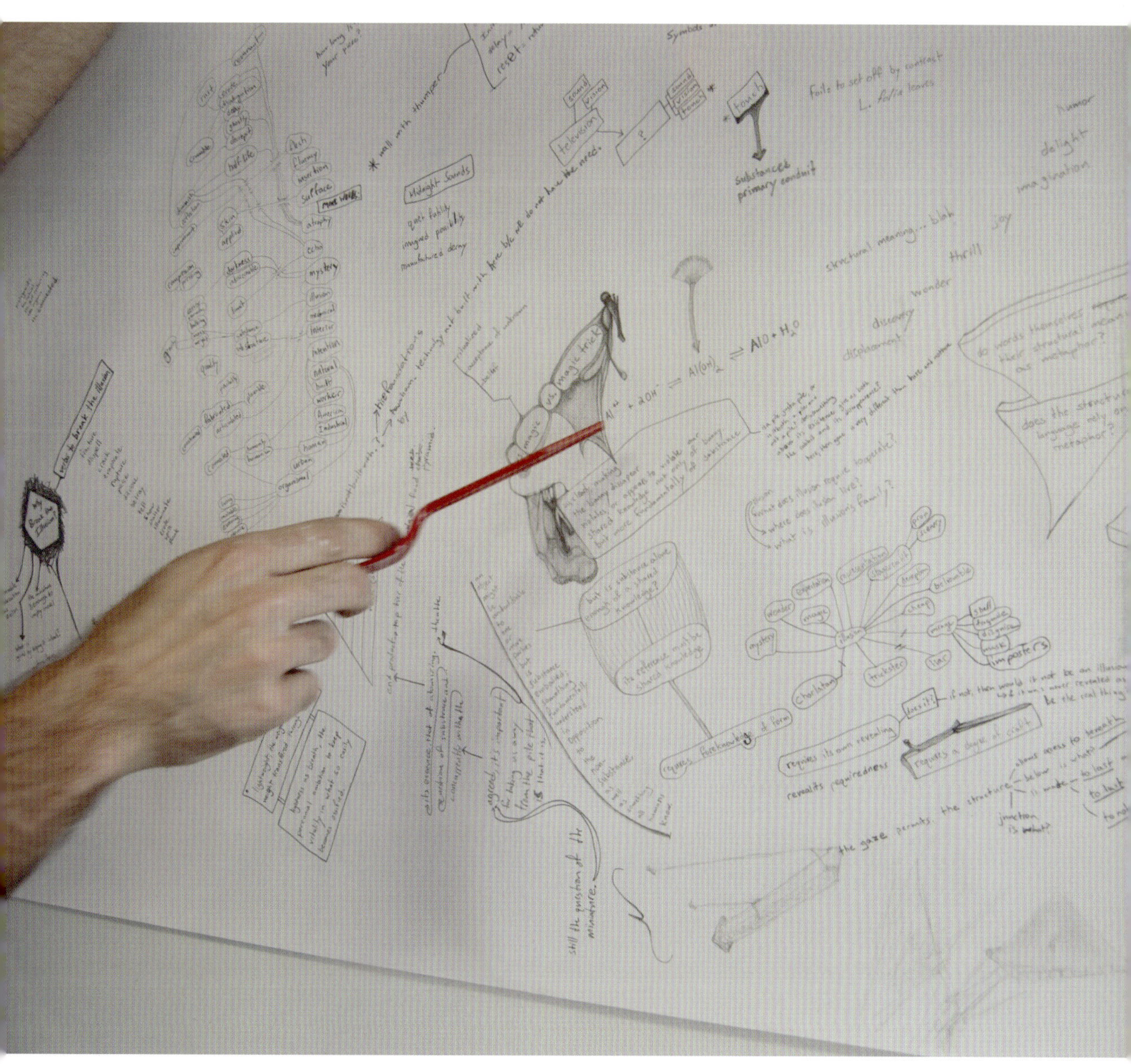

JAKE BECKMAN, *MAPPING EXERCISE*, 2010 PHOTO ADAM LUCAS

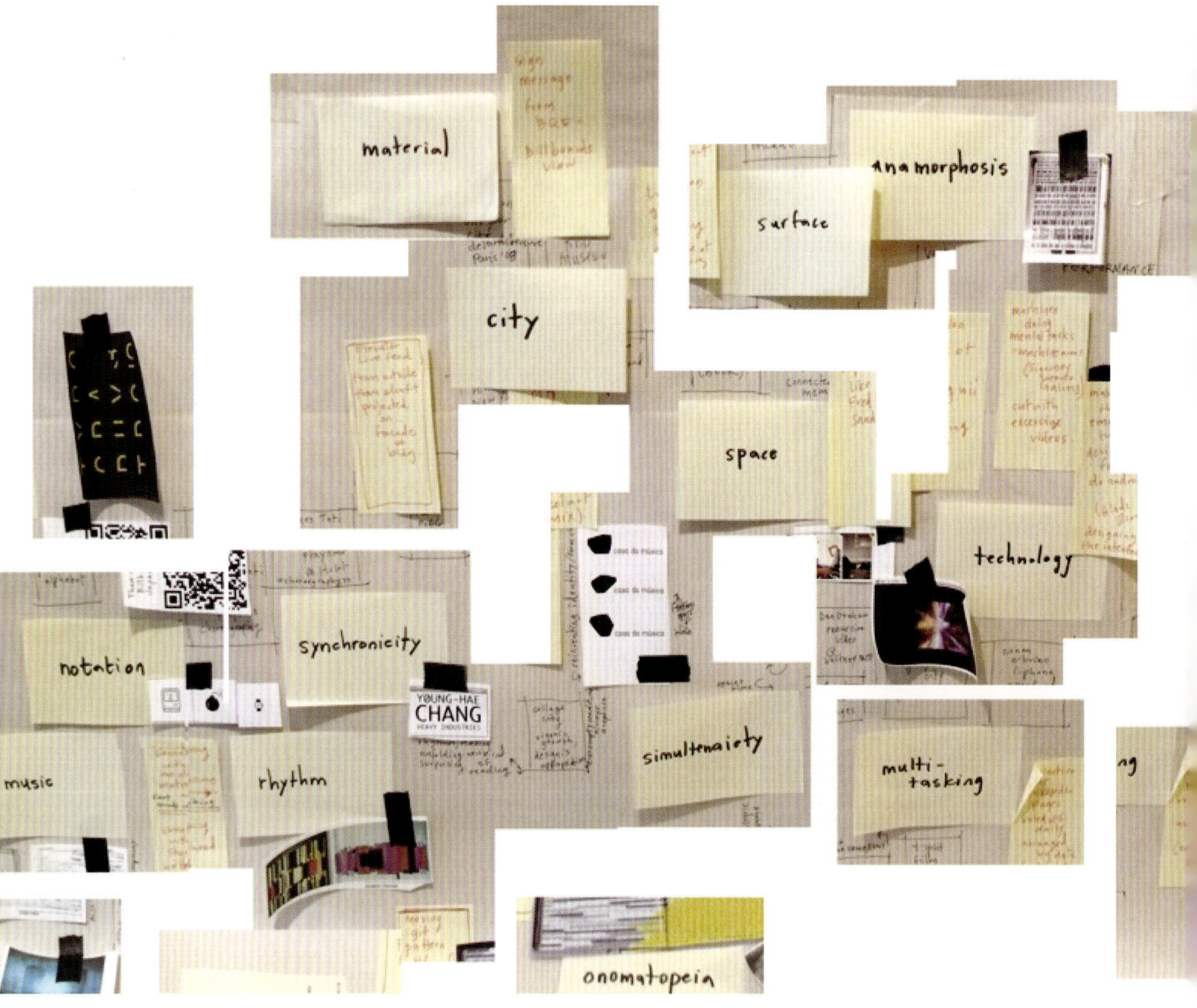

MEGAN FEEHAN, *MAPPING EXERCISE*, 2009

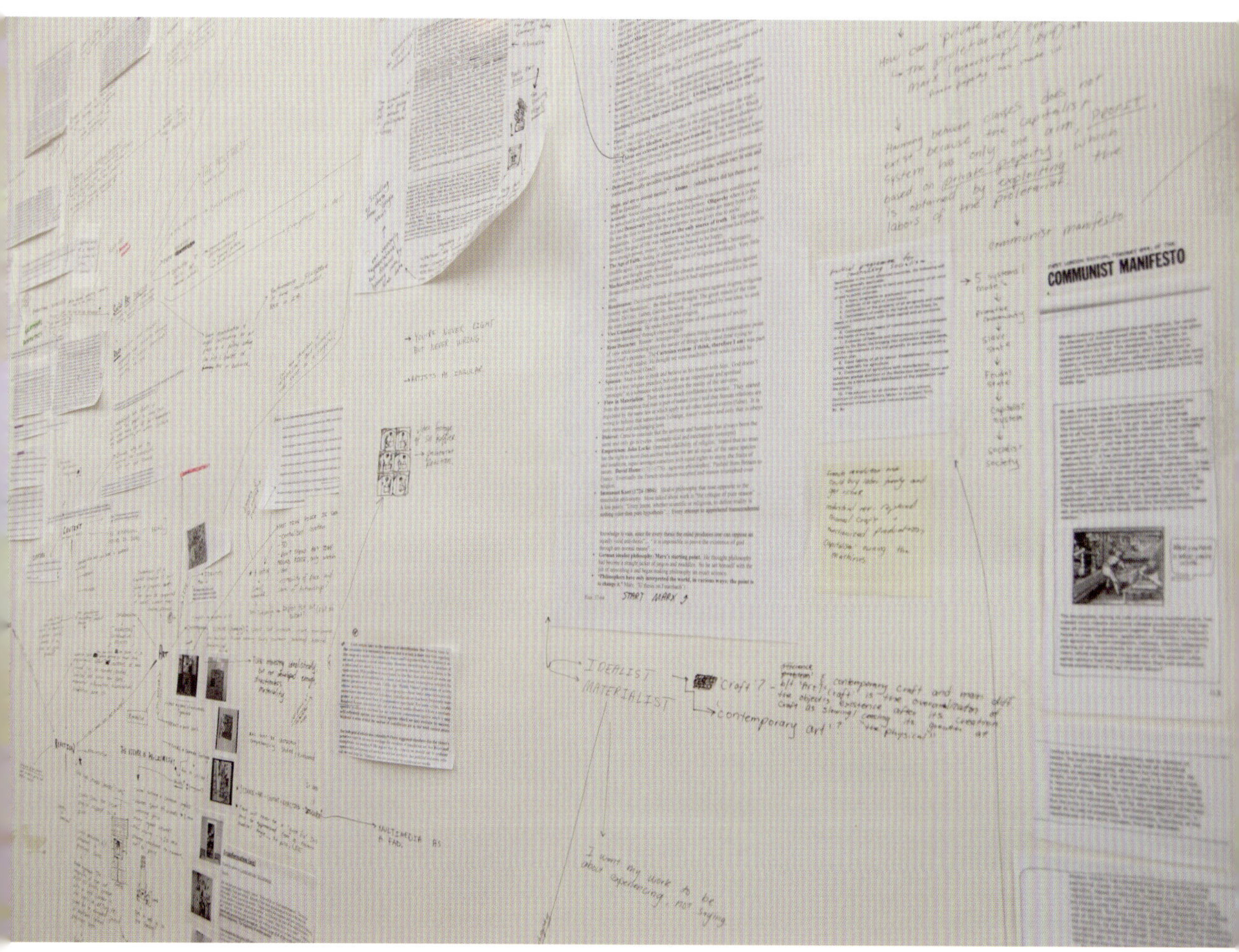

LEE JOHNSON, *MAPPING EXERCISE*, 2010 PHOTO ADAM LUCAS

matrix map

Creating a matrix map gives tangible representation to our vision field.

Matrix, derived from the Latin word for "womb" is an embryonic or generative non-linear space. It is the sub-soil or substrate that underlies and buoys our work. When conceived as a mapping system, it is the space where we allow a perspective of our work to grow subtly, with no pressure to make logical sense of it all. In the early stage of developing understanding, we use this space as a first level dumping ground. We put it all out in a stream-of-consciousness approach. This gives us a chance to begin to see what we think and to note the language we use, sketched in broad outline. We begin to find the dots, so to speak.

I liken the creation of a matrix map to the process of "ground truthing." To "ground truth," a term borrowed from field biology, is to go into the field and correlate remotely sensed visual data with what is found on the ground. A field biologist maps trees and crops. As artists, we wade through the multiple dimensions of our visual search—intuitions, sense impressions, memories, perceptions, salient interests, and research—in order to get to the ground of our work. The process of creating a matrix map requires patient attention as we gather before us the particulars of what matters.

Create a Matrix Map

Approach the creation of your matrix map as if you are tracing the workings of a living system. You are beginning a process of assembling an organic body of knowledge. Keep in mind the words, "organic," "familiar," "whole," "interconnection," and "relationship." Allow this mapping process to be generous, flexible, and cumulative.

There are many ways of visualizing data. Here are two ways: There is a dynamic, hyper-space approach using mapping software, such as, *Mind Node* or *Mind X*. Or there is a tactile approach that involves connecting to physical matter and ideas. I like the hands-on approach. I sit on the floor with a large sheet of paper, colored markers, scissors, scraps of paper and/or Post-it™ notes. Then I cut and paste.

Enter your key words as ground coordinates or anchors. Start in the middle of a large sheet of paper. Allow each key word to announce a category of thought and then permit paths, branches, or associational connections to radiate out. They can also become a means for splintering into other paths of interest. Small notions will connect into a larger whole. At first these do not need to be logical interrelations. Meaning can circulate around the words but not be fixed by them.

As you begin to see the terrain you are describing, start noticing connections, analogies, symmetries, and confrontations. Allow thought fields to organize into meaningful groupings. Diagram relationships. Draw lines where you think things connect. Plot thematic patterns. Try to render the dynamic interaction of the whole thing as a systems drawing. Allow various perspectives or partial perspectives of the whole to be simultaneously present. Think in terms of layers, penetrating fields, different angles of vision, and multiplicity.

In the end, matrix maps usually look like thought paths, meandering trails, word trees, unfolding scrolls, flow charts, webs, or knots. Hopefully you come to some epiphany about how things fit together.

As you conceptualize new work, place it on the matrix map.

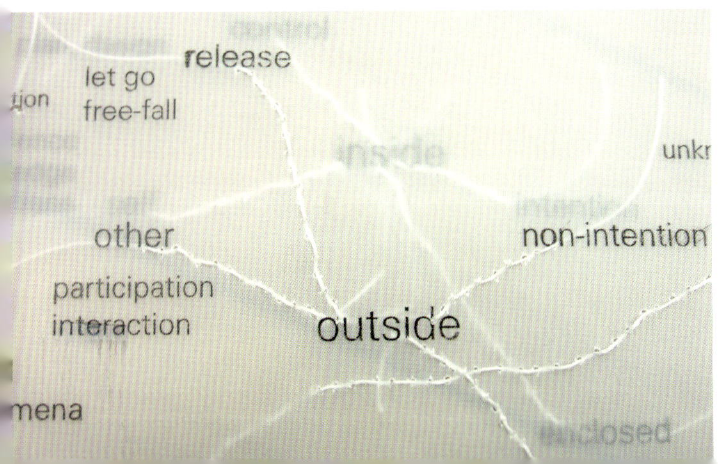

REBECCA KLEIN GANZ, GRAPHIC DESIGNER
MATRIX MAP, 2003

>>

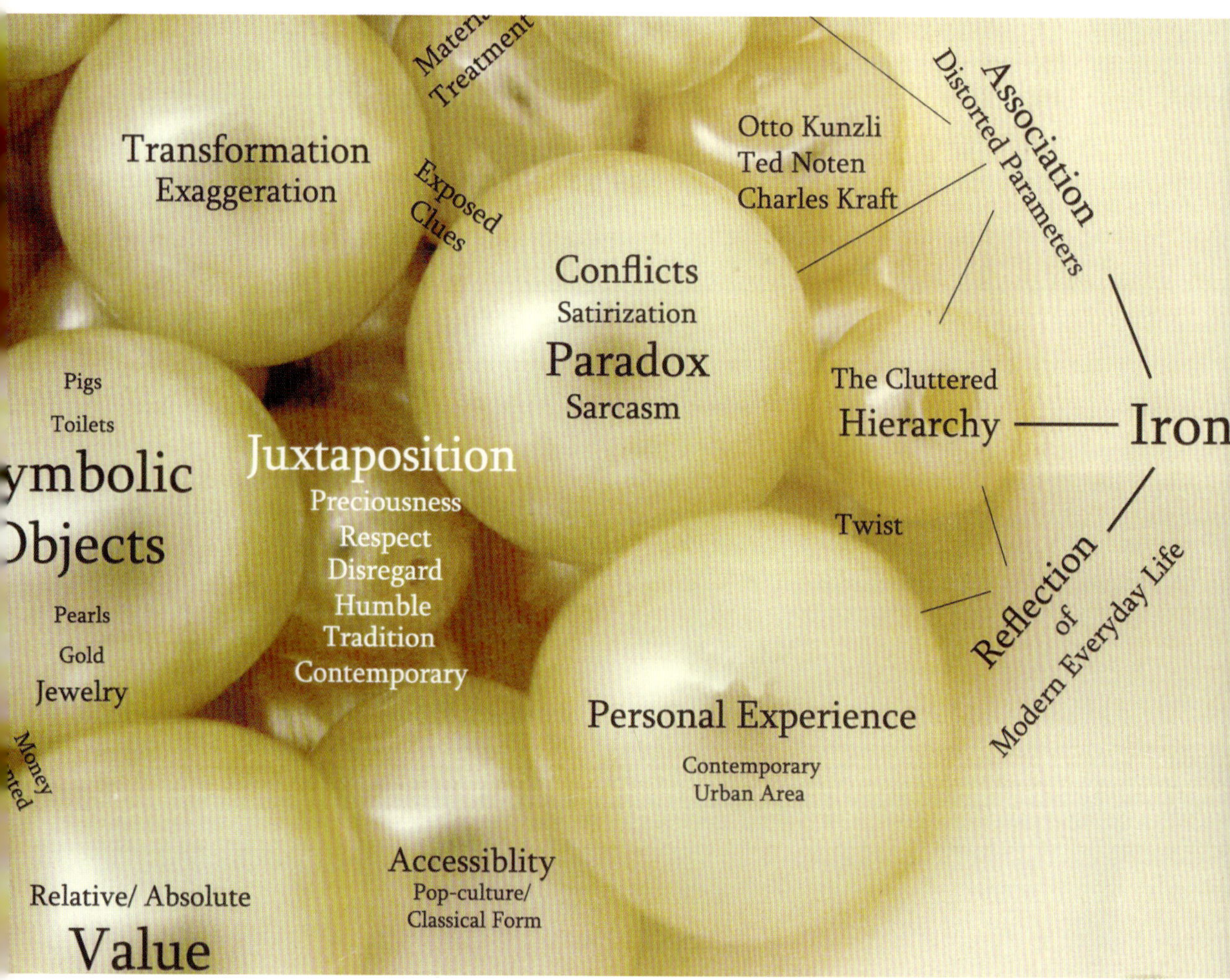

JIMIN PARK, JEWELRY DESIGNER
MATRIX MAP, 2006

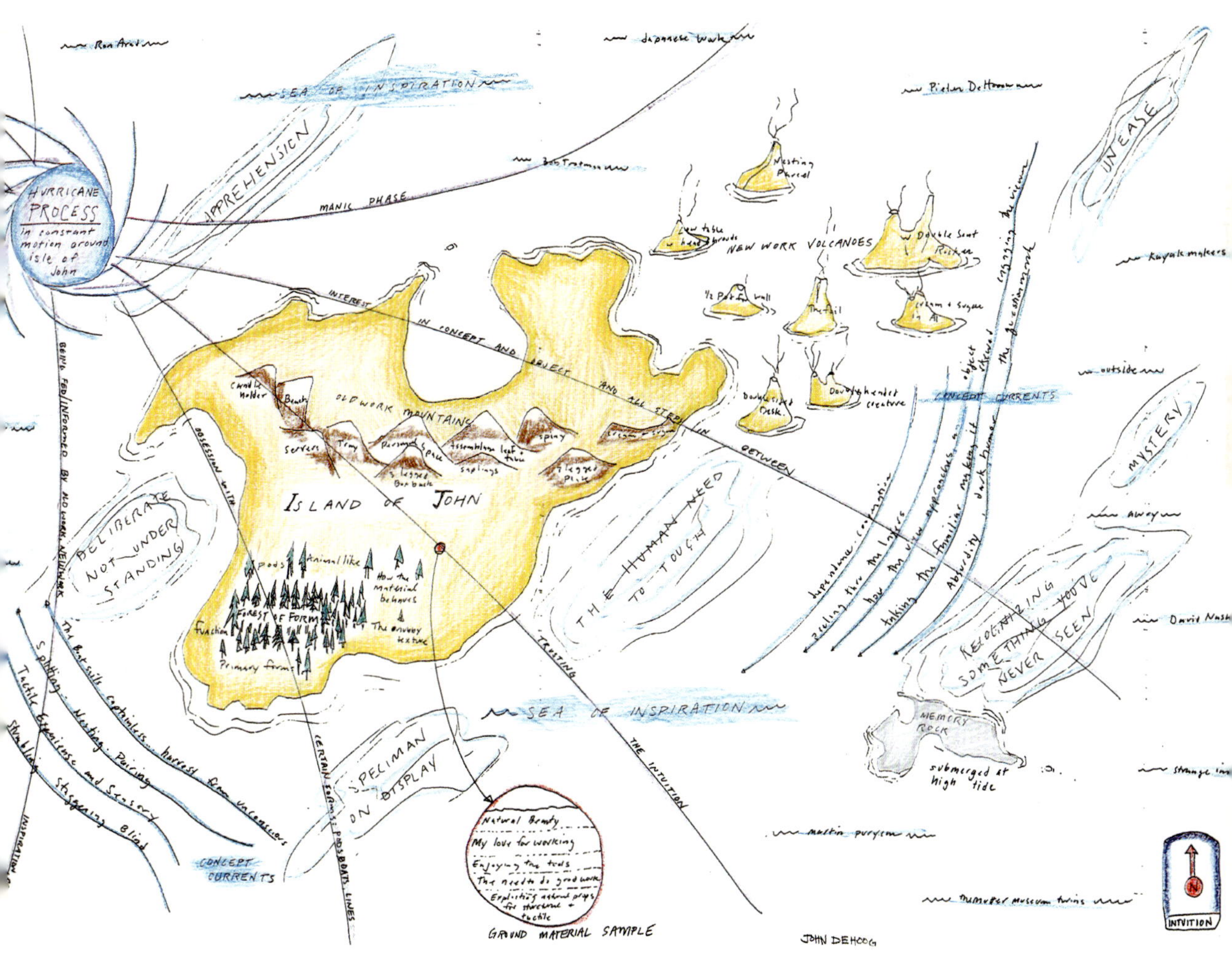

JOHN DEHOOG, FURNITURE DESIGNER
MATRIX MAP, 1999

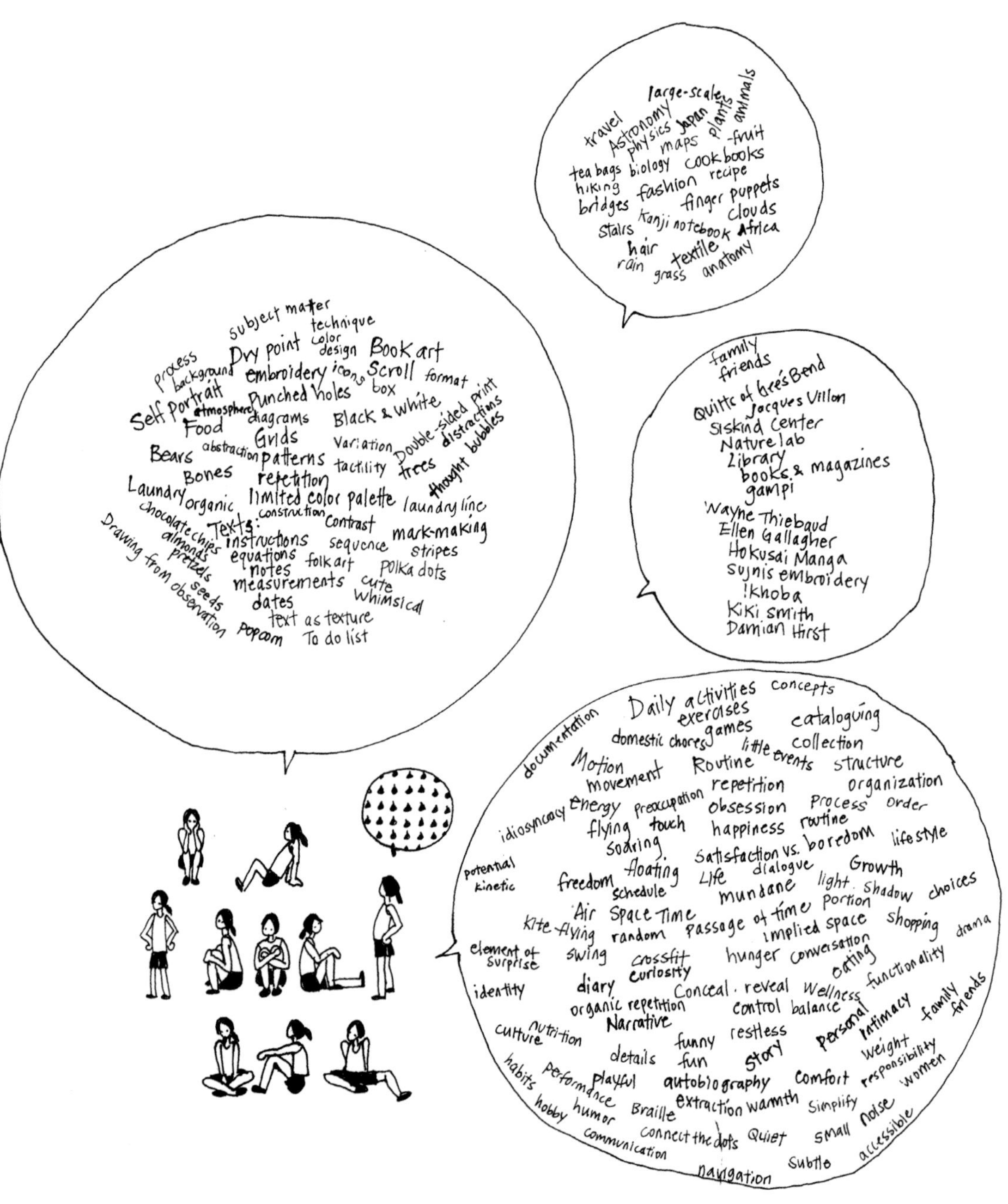

MIE YOSHINAGA, PRINTMAKER
MATRIX MAP, 2006

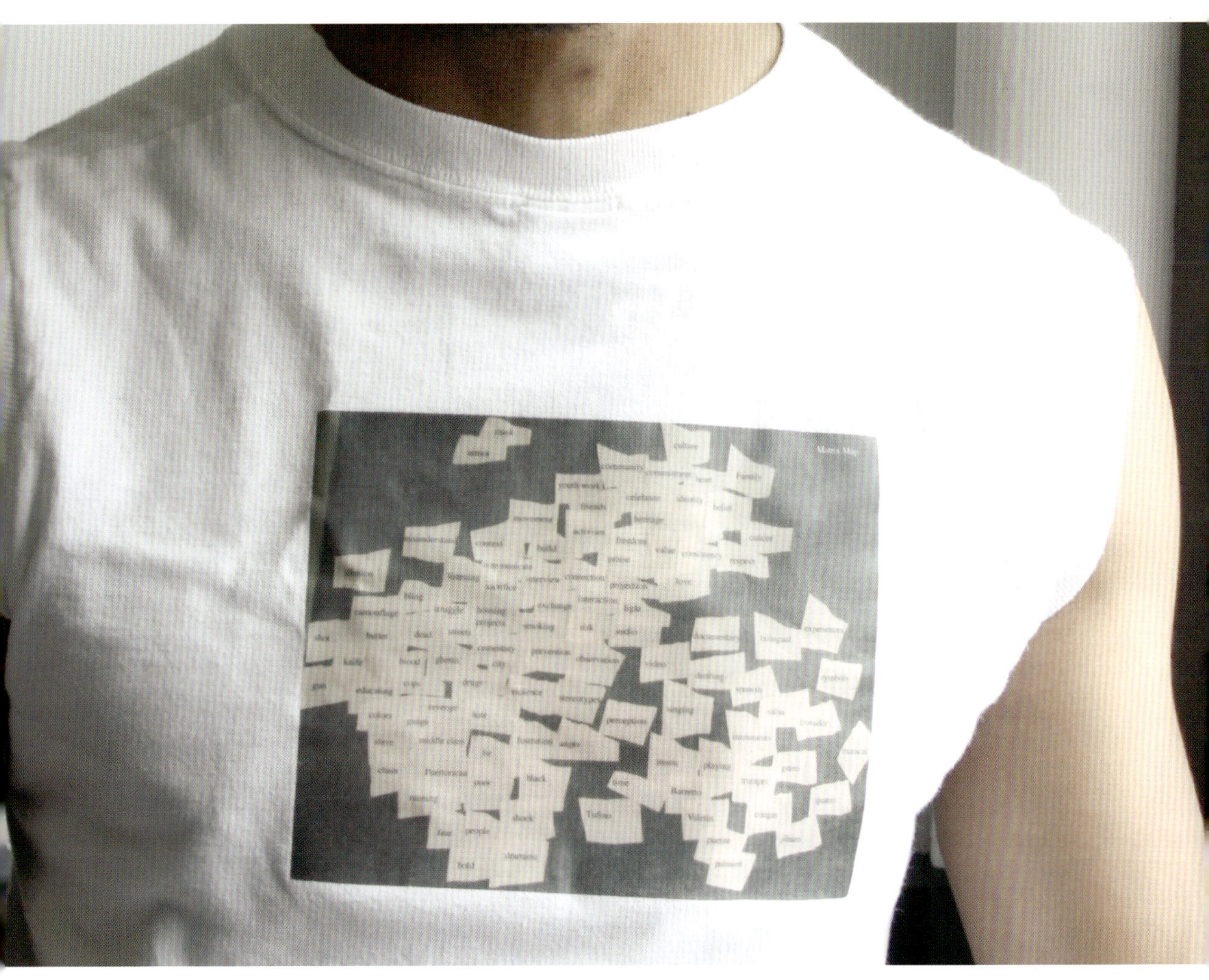

VICTOR PACHECO, SCULPTOR   PHOTO PATRIZIA PILOSI
MATRIX MAP, 2006

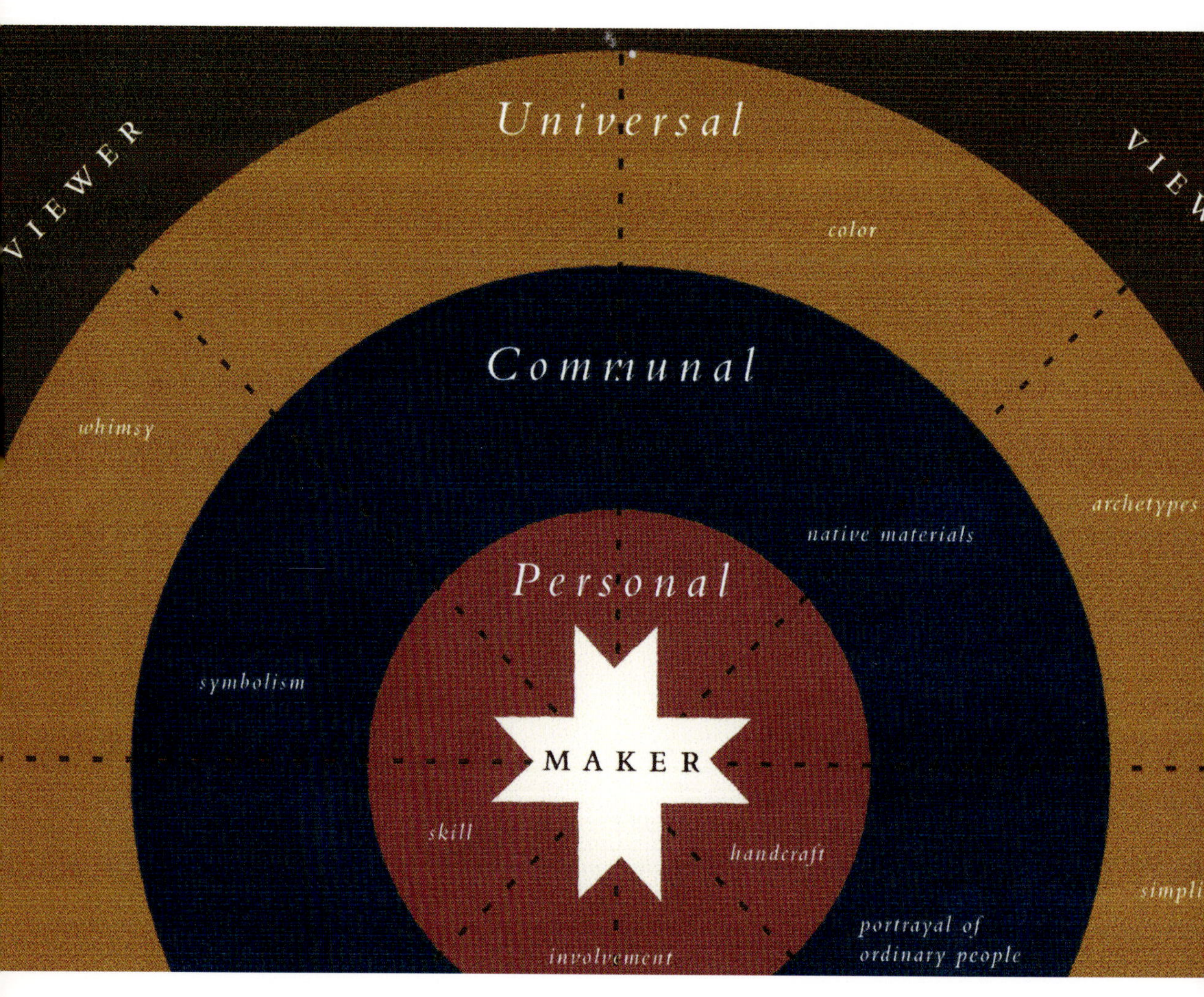

KRISHNA JOSHI, GRAPHIC DESIGNER
MATRIX MAP, 1999

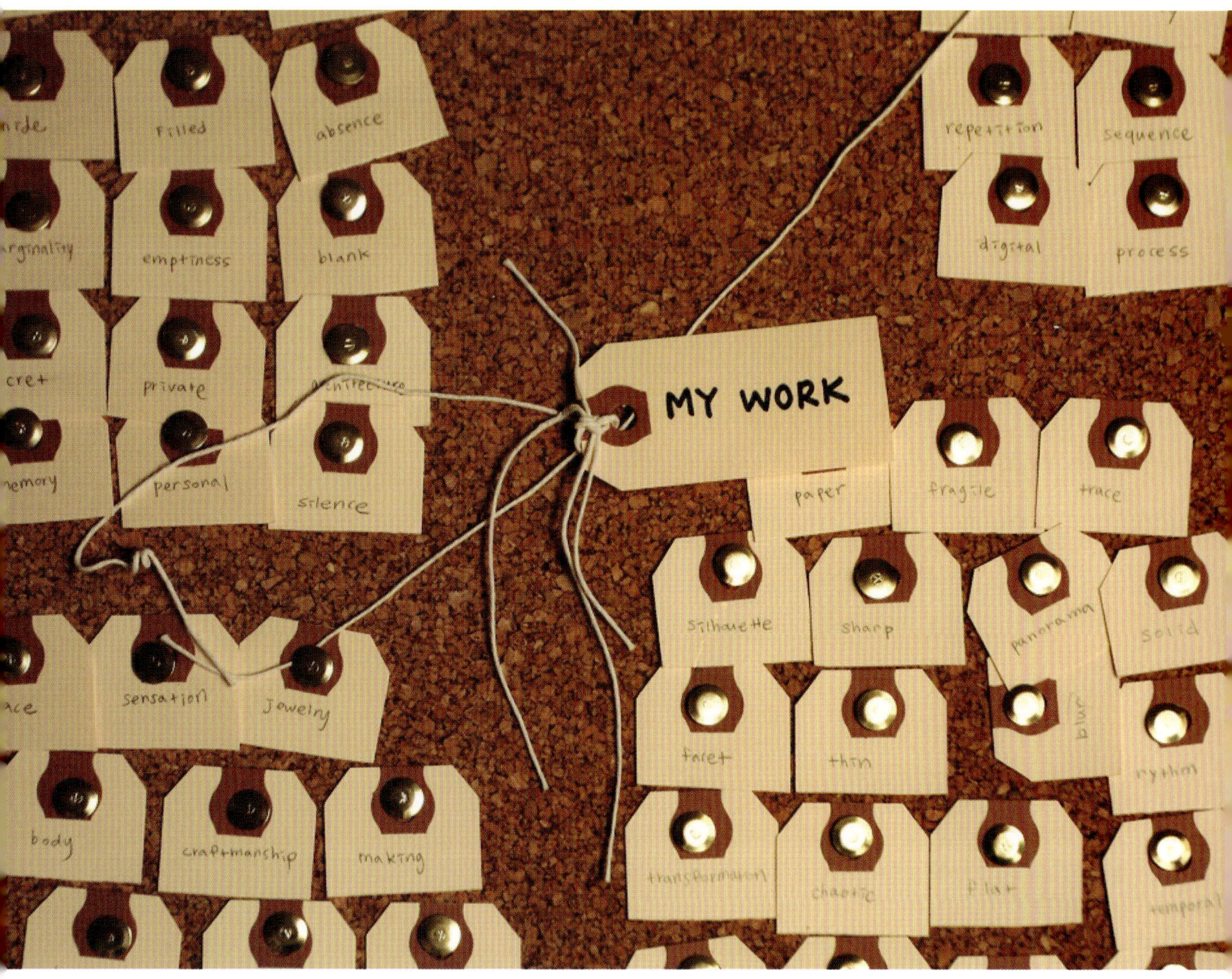

SOOYEON KIM, JEWELRY DESIGNER
MATRIX MAP, 2010

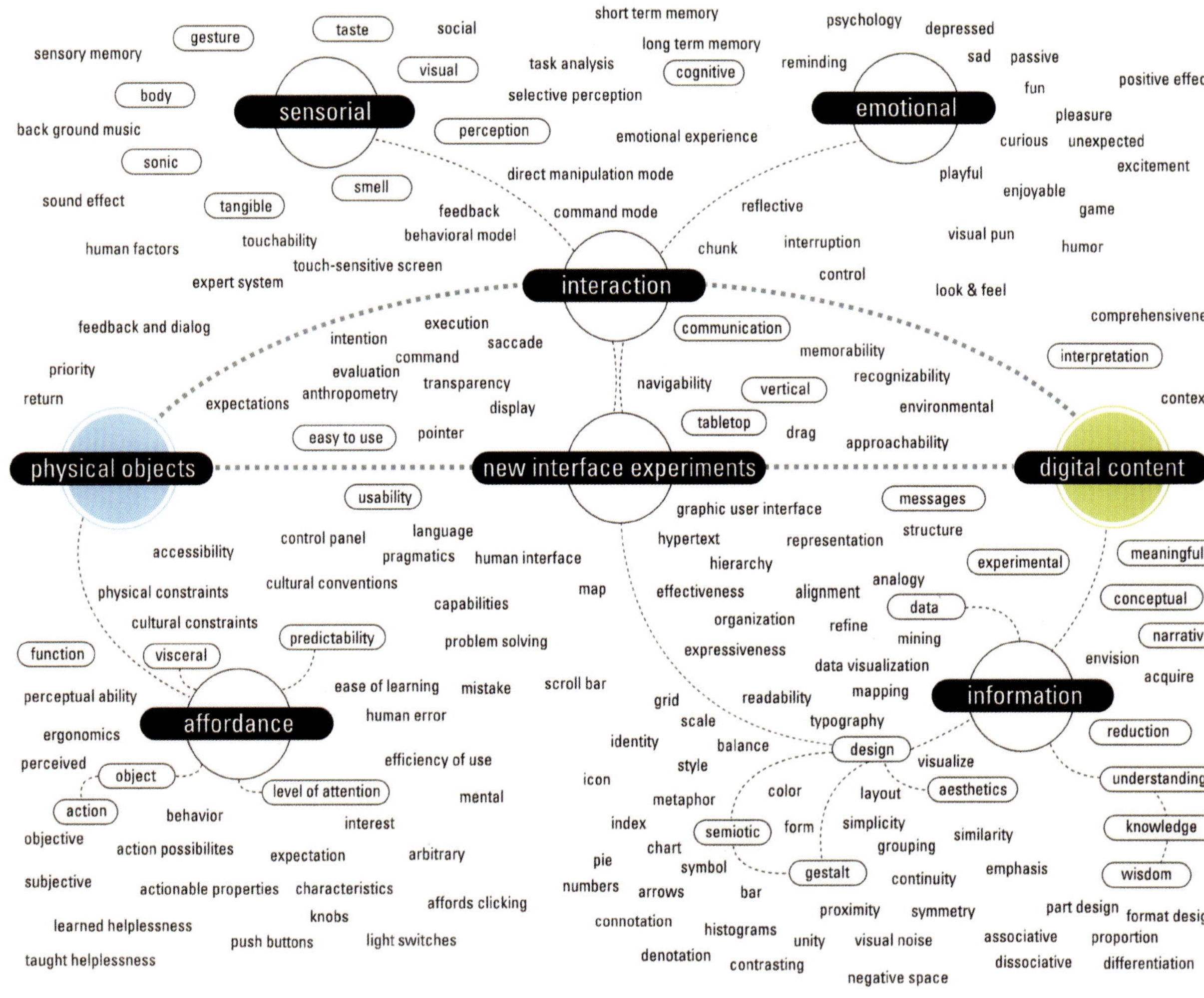

GEON DONG KIM, NEW MEDIA ARTIST
MATRIX MAP, 2006

Mine is a landscape of unpredictable transformations and connections deeply imbued with nature and life processes. There are no fixed places on my map. I have added words and images yet I can move them around, try them in different locations, see how they blend, compete, and contrast.

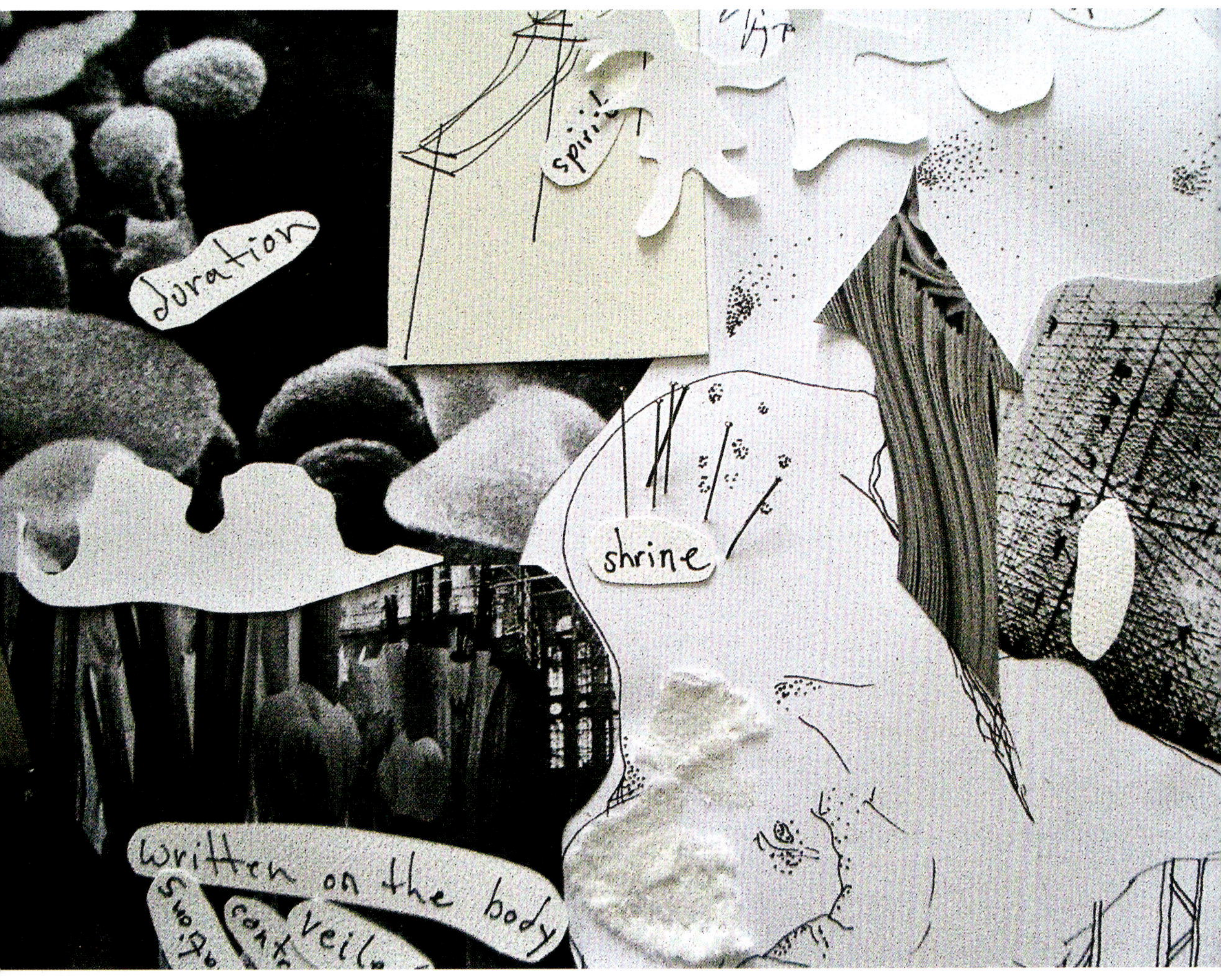

KIMBERLY JONES, SCULPTOR
MATRIX MAP, 2011

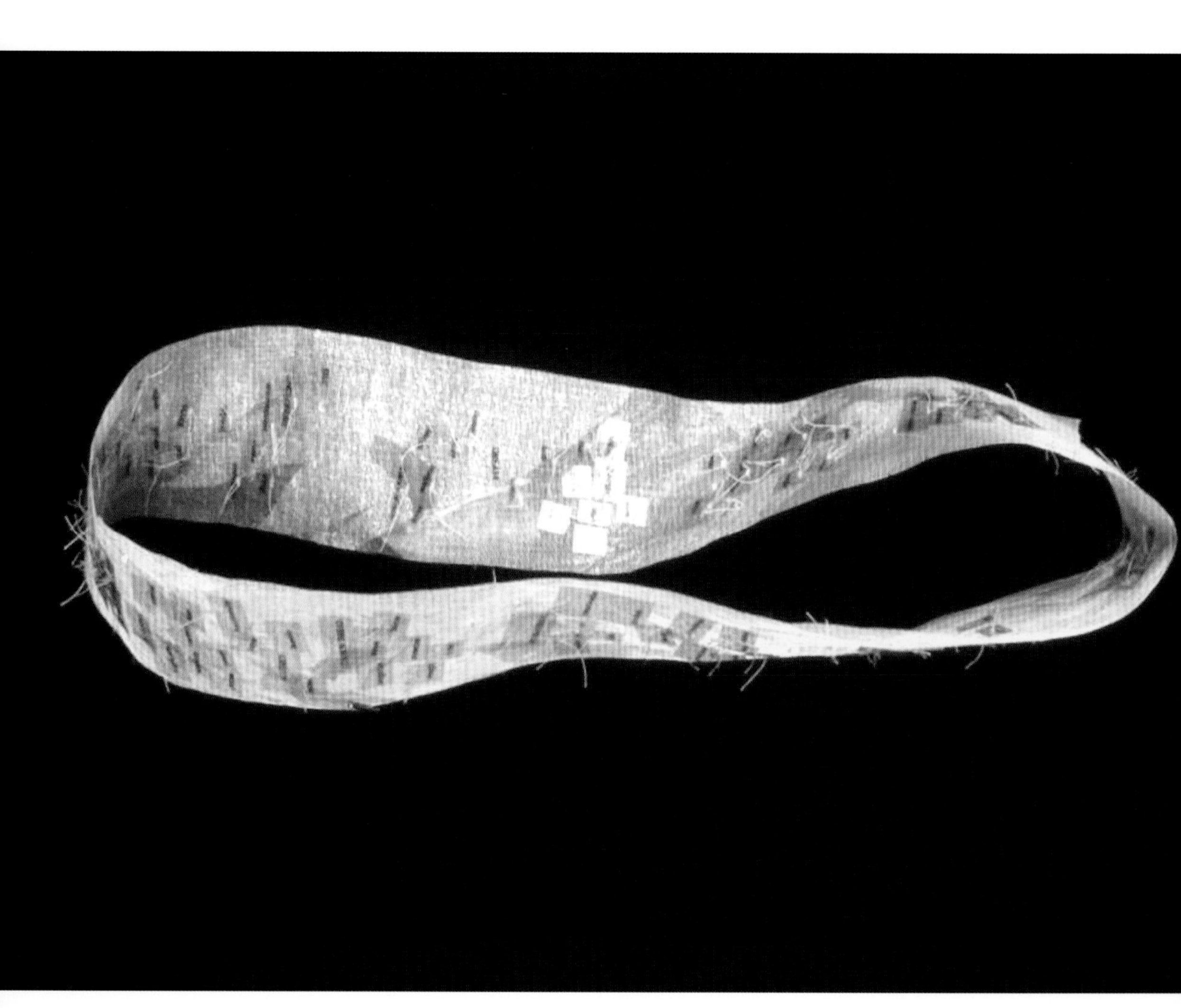

JANE SISCO, TEXTILE DESIGNER
MATRIX MAP, 2000

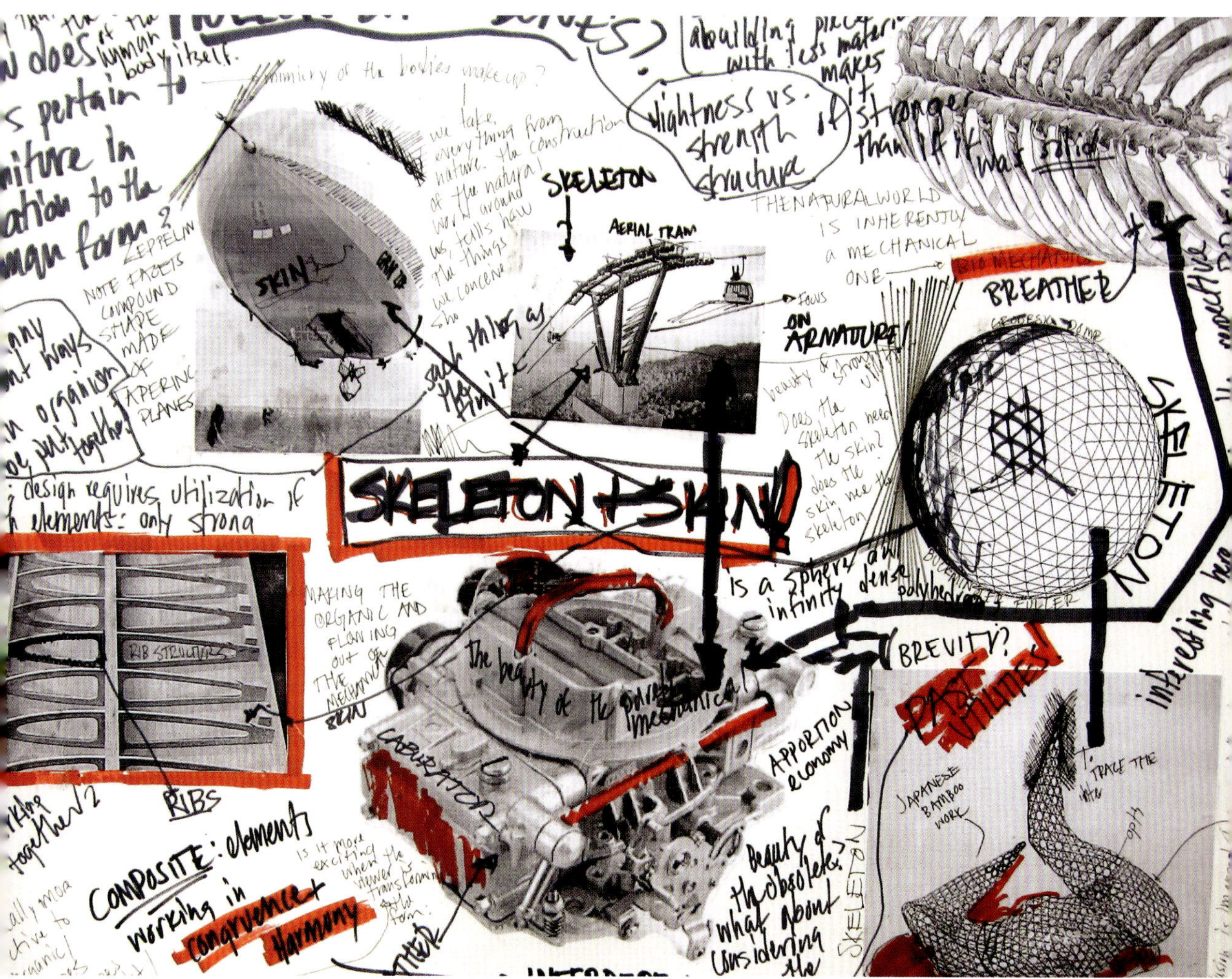

PETER HEDSTROM, FURNITURE DESIGNER
MATRIX MAP, 2009

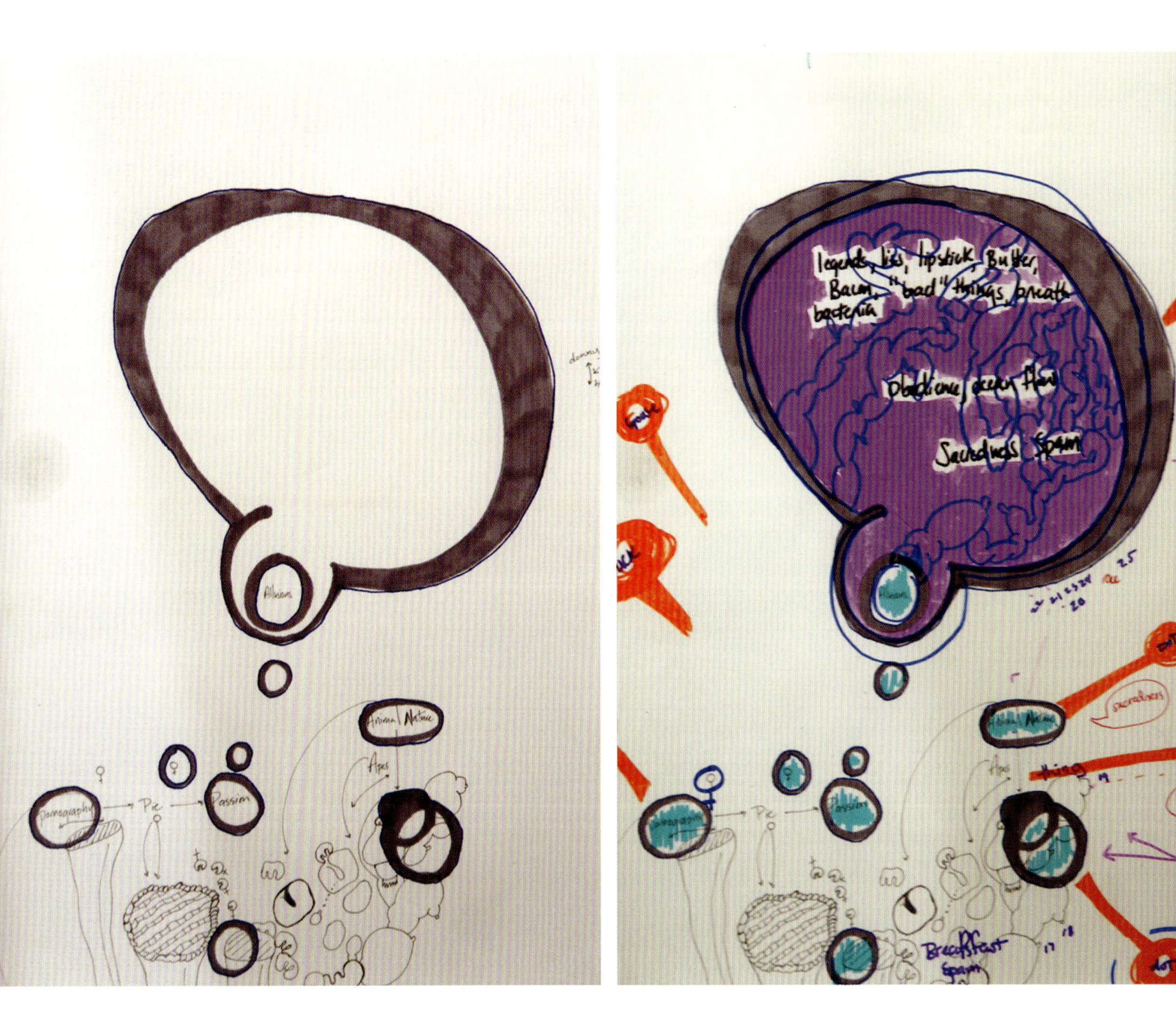
Allusions
Animal Nature
Apes
Pornography
Pie
Passion
legends, lies, lipstick, Butter,
Bacon, "bad" things, breath
bacteria
Obedience, ocean flow
Sardines Spam
sardines
Breakfast
Spam

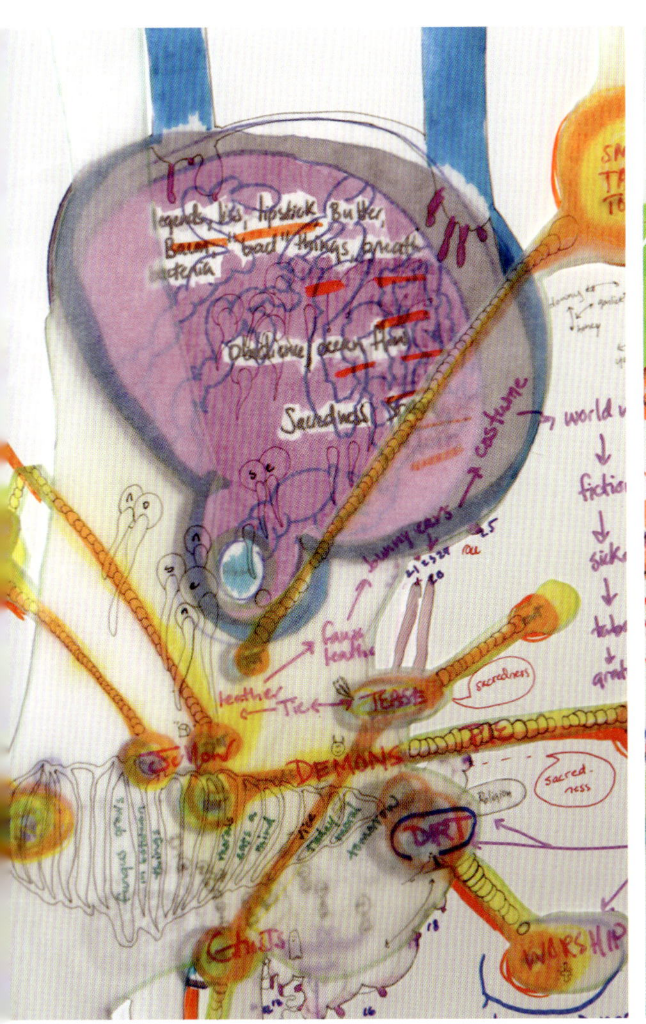

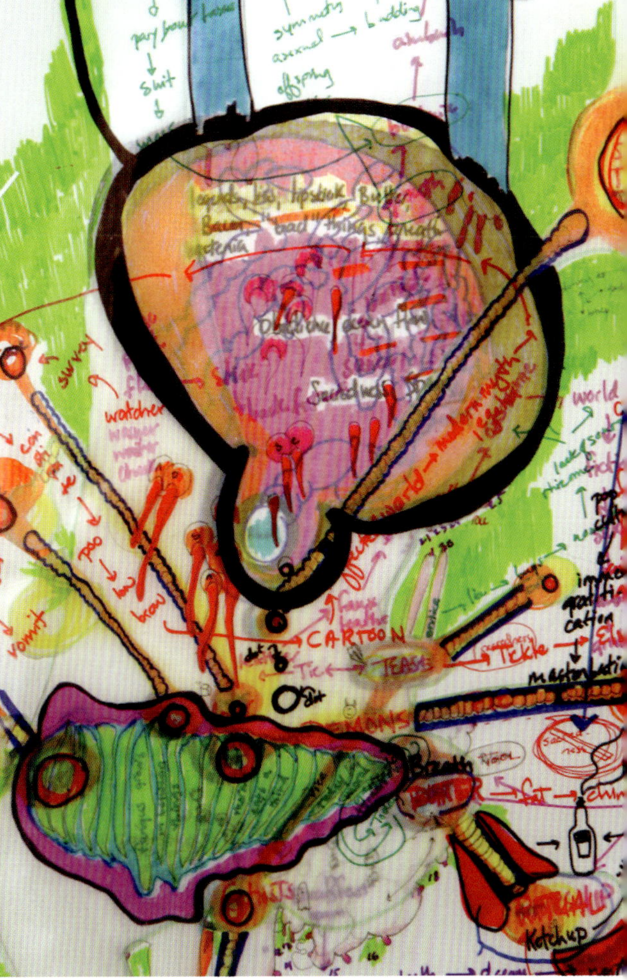

STEPHANIE WILLIAMS, SCULPTOR
MATRIX MAP, 2006

artist statement as origin point

An artist statement isn't written, it is built. It is built from a sustained inquiry. As we show up for the various pressures of investigation, the statement can serve as our origin point. We can return to it countless times, each time in attempt to set a clear priority and focus for our work.

Think of your statement as a divergent process—that is, as an active place to sort and shift around ideas until they assume "face."

Using your key words and matrix map as backdrop, write a one-page artist statement. Consider this the first round of many.

The progression of my art has reflected the arc of my life. Along the way, my impulse has been singular—to give expression to the mystery of life's contrasting forces—the joy of new life, new beginnings, and the wonder of growth; the complexities of dying and the mystery of death; the lifelong process of grief. Through visual language, I have sought to understand, and ultimately to accept, both the beauty and the cruelty inhering in the cycles of nature.

The persistent touchstones in my work have always been nature and natural forms. I am drawn to these subjects first on the level of a purely sensuous aesthetic, but also and of equal importance, on a level of meaning. Nature is for me the palpable manifestation of the divine; I am fascinated with its seamless harmonies and troubled by what I see as the nascent rupture of humanity from it. Dialectically, I aspire to the potential for reconciliation of people with the earth from which they've sprung, a potential intuited in my artwork.

The creative process begins for me with an epiphany, a spark or flicker, in the fog of my artistic search for meaning in form. The act of making marks, whether pencil to paper, crayon to lithographic stone, or carving tool to wood or clay, becomes the passionate response to the very moments when ordinary perception links to the extraordinary—it is an act of reverence.

Translated into visual metaphors for life experiences, illuminated for a time, such seemingly insignificant perceptions can deepen into moments of radiance, of clarity—jewels for the memory—offering a glimpse of the essence of a thing.[116]

116 Artist Statement written for exhibition, *Arc of Intent: Claudia R. Fieo, Selected Works 1988–2008*, Beard and Well Galleries, September 4–October 19, 2008, Wheaton College, Norton, Massachusetts.

Who but an artist fierce to know–
not fierce to seem to know–
would suppose that a live image possessed a secret?

The artist is willing to give all his or her strength
and life to probing with blunt instruments
those same secrets no one can describe
in any way but with those instruments' faint tracks.[117]

ANNIE DILLARD

117 Annie Dillard, *A Glimpse of the Writing Life* (New York: Harper & Row, 1989), 78.

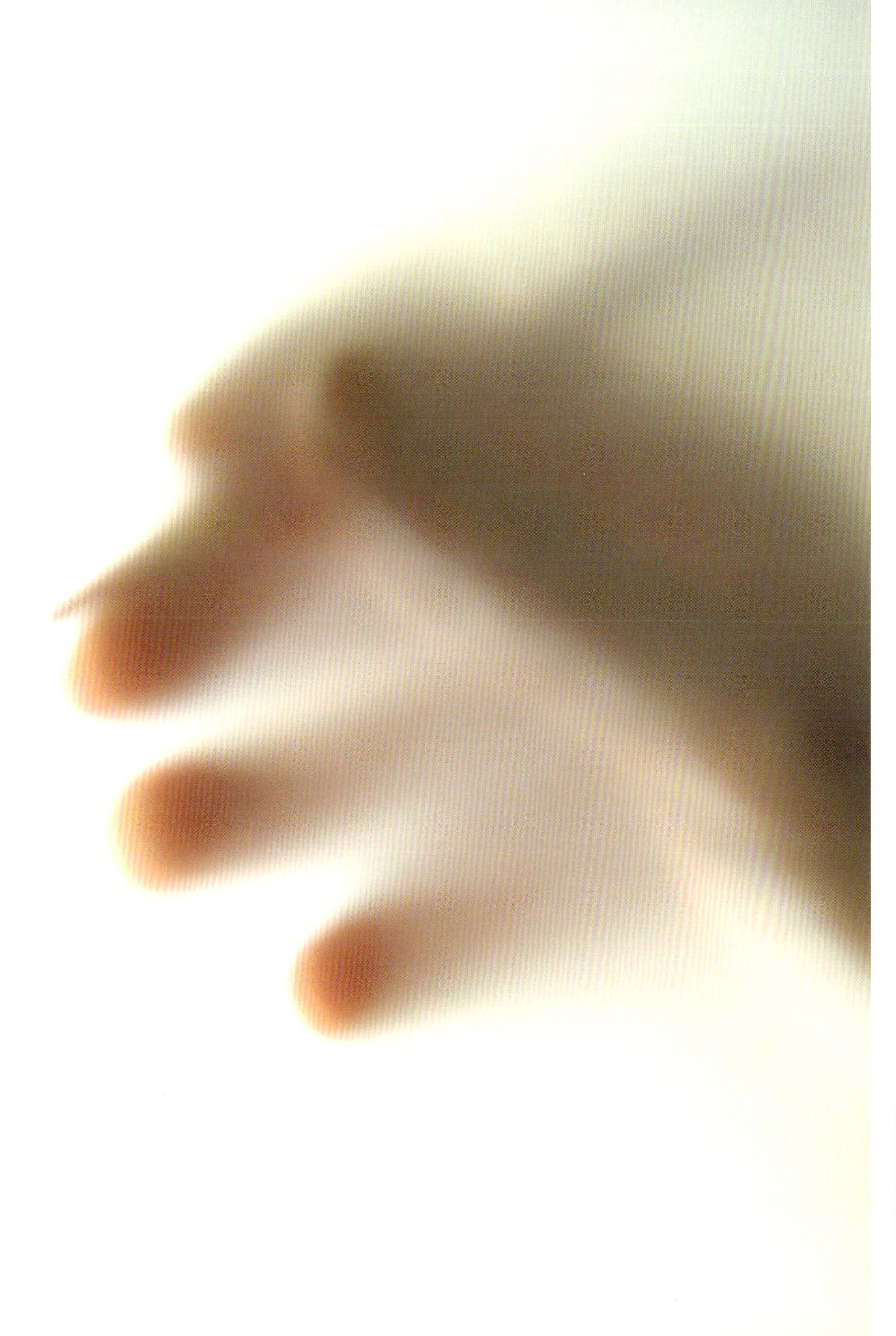

PHOTO NANCY SKOLOS

CHARTING

map as pattern

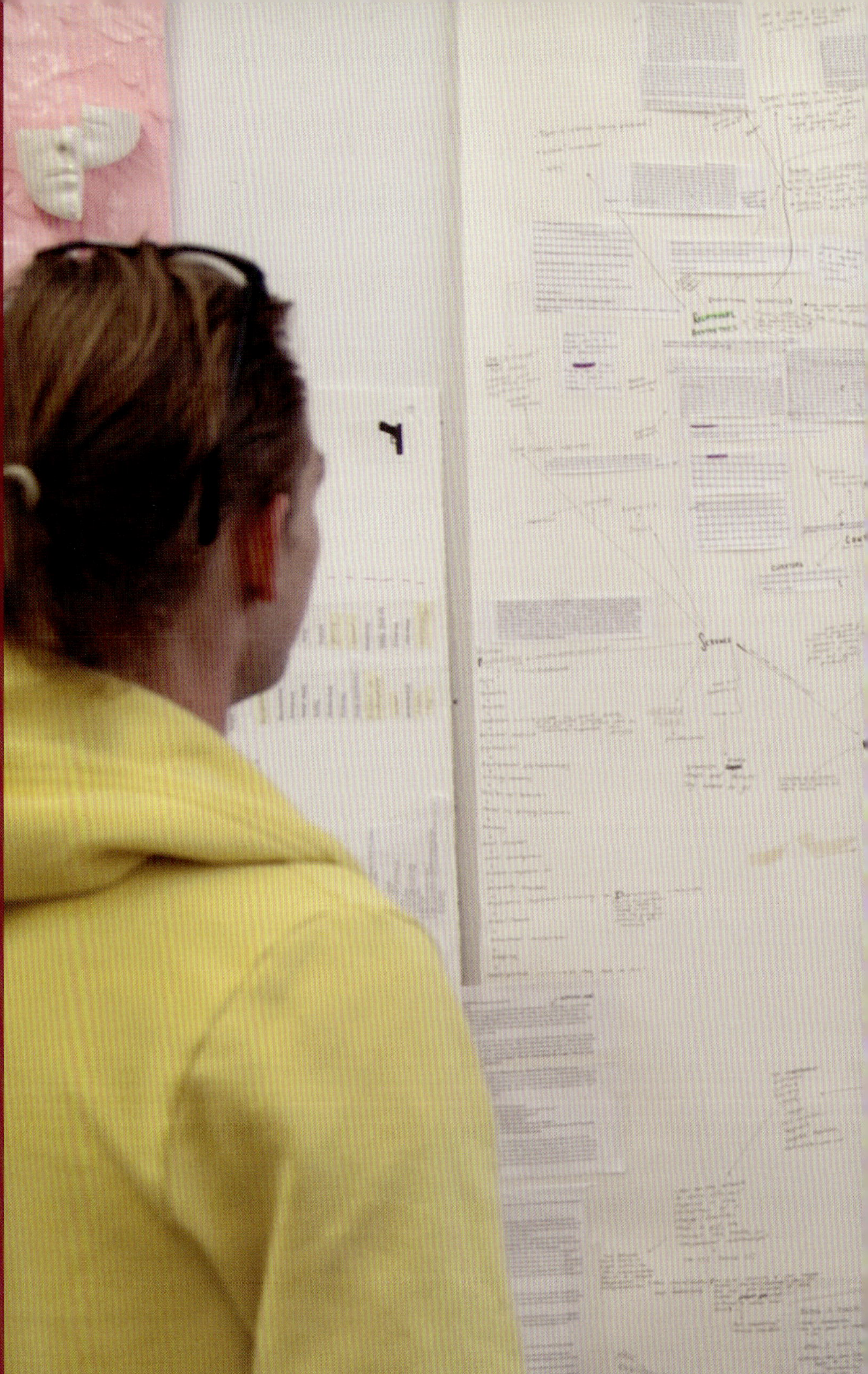

LEE JOHNSON, *MAPPING EXERCISE*, 2010 PHOTO ADAM LUCAS

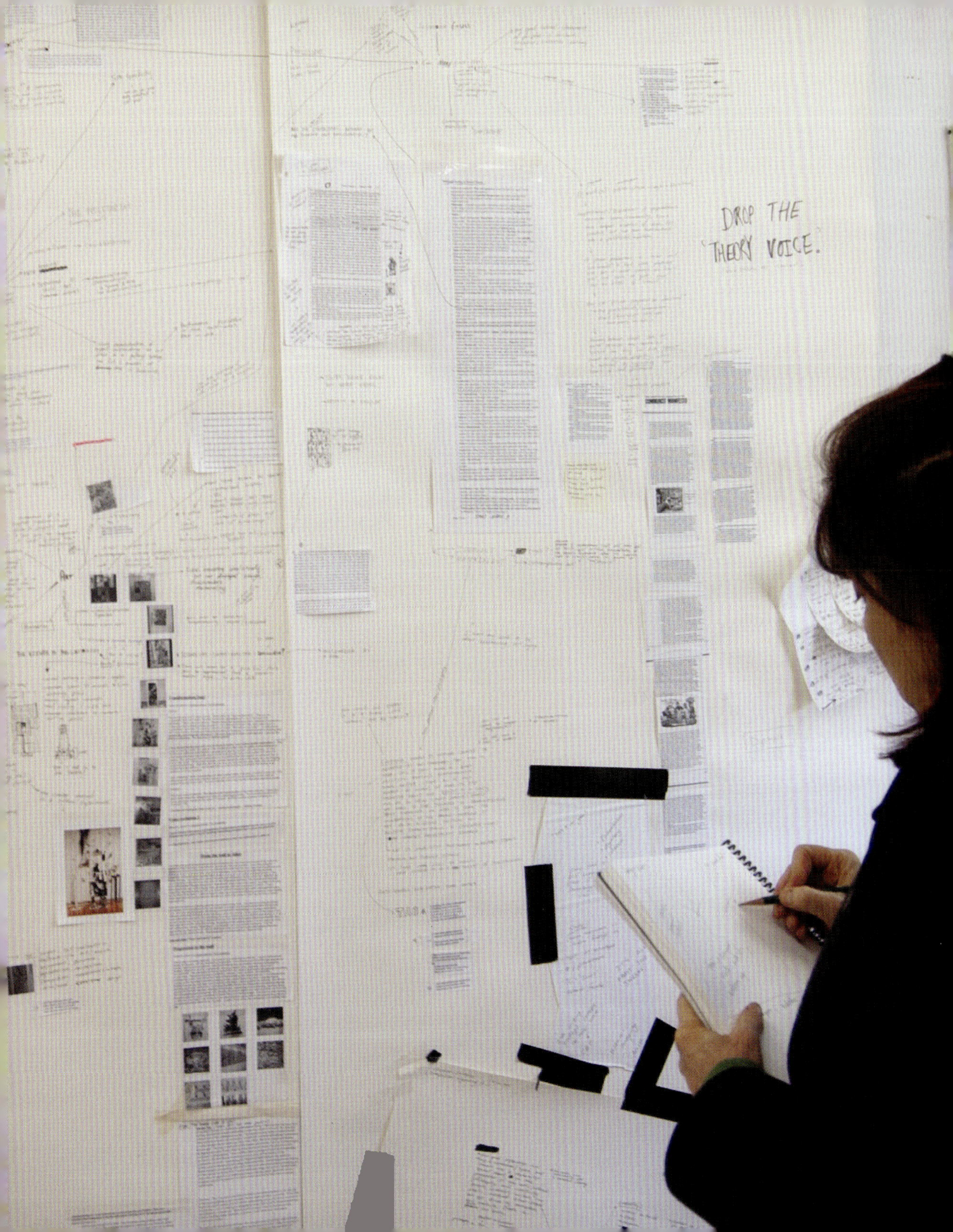
DROP THE
'THEORY VOICE.'

CHARTING
map as pattern

We now move from having identified a rich field of seemingly unrelated points of inspiration to a consolidation that yields patterns of interconnected meaning. The exploring stage has surfaced much raw material that is pregnant with texture, feeling, images, and fact. Now we need to see into these events of inspiration and find inherent order.

Essentially this is an exercise of synthesis—finding the whole among the parts. The image that comes to mind is one of gradually backing away from a bird's nest. At very close range we see twigs, pieces of bark, and unrelated organic matter. Slowly as we add distance a unifying form emerges, one that ties together the fruits of our gathering. We are offered what Italo Calvino calls "a connecting thread, an inner rule, a perspective, a discourse."[118] Discovering our nest is like coming home to the intelligence of our work.

Charting brings the previous material from the Exploring section into full view. It is the meeting ground where the independent elements come together and we are able to portray meaningful relationships. We compile, scrutinize, select, make legible, subdivide, organize, create links, combine, and recombine, all in an effort to comprehend and understand what we have come to see through the activities of interrogative reflection.

What we get from this process.

We activate our pattern-seeking capacity of mind as we identify the bold fragments of the puzzle. We prioritize, organize, select, sort, frame, and consolidate. We look at our ideas in a different way within a broader conversation and discourse. We gather this together in a composite map that stimulates meaningful conceptual links.

118 Italo Calvino, *Invisible Cities* (New York: Mariner Books, 1978), 44.

IN THIS SECTION

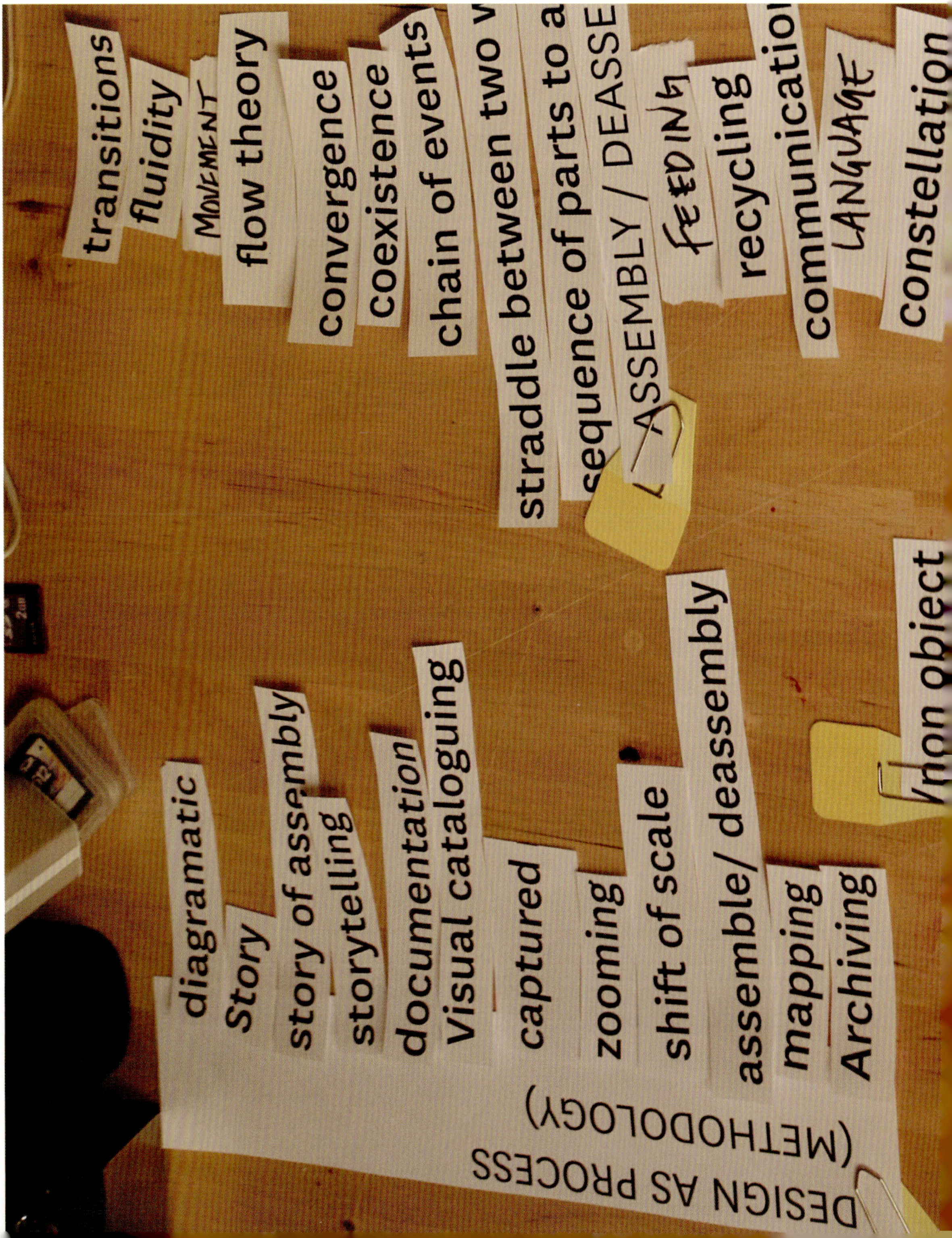

DESIGN AS PROCESS
(METHODOLOGY)

diagramatic
Story
story of assembly
storytelling
documentation
Visual cataloguing
captured
zooming
shift of scale
assemble/ deassembly
mapping
Archiving

/non object

transitions
fluidity
MOVEMENT
flow theory
convergence
coexistence
chain of events
straddle between two w
sequence of parts to a
ASSEMBLY / DEASSE
FEEDING
recycling
communicatio
LANGUAGE
constellation

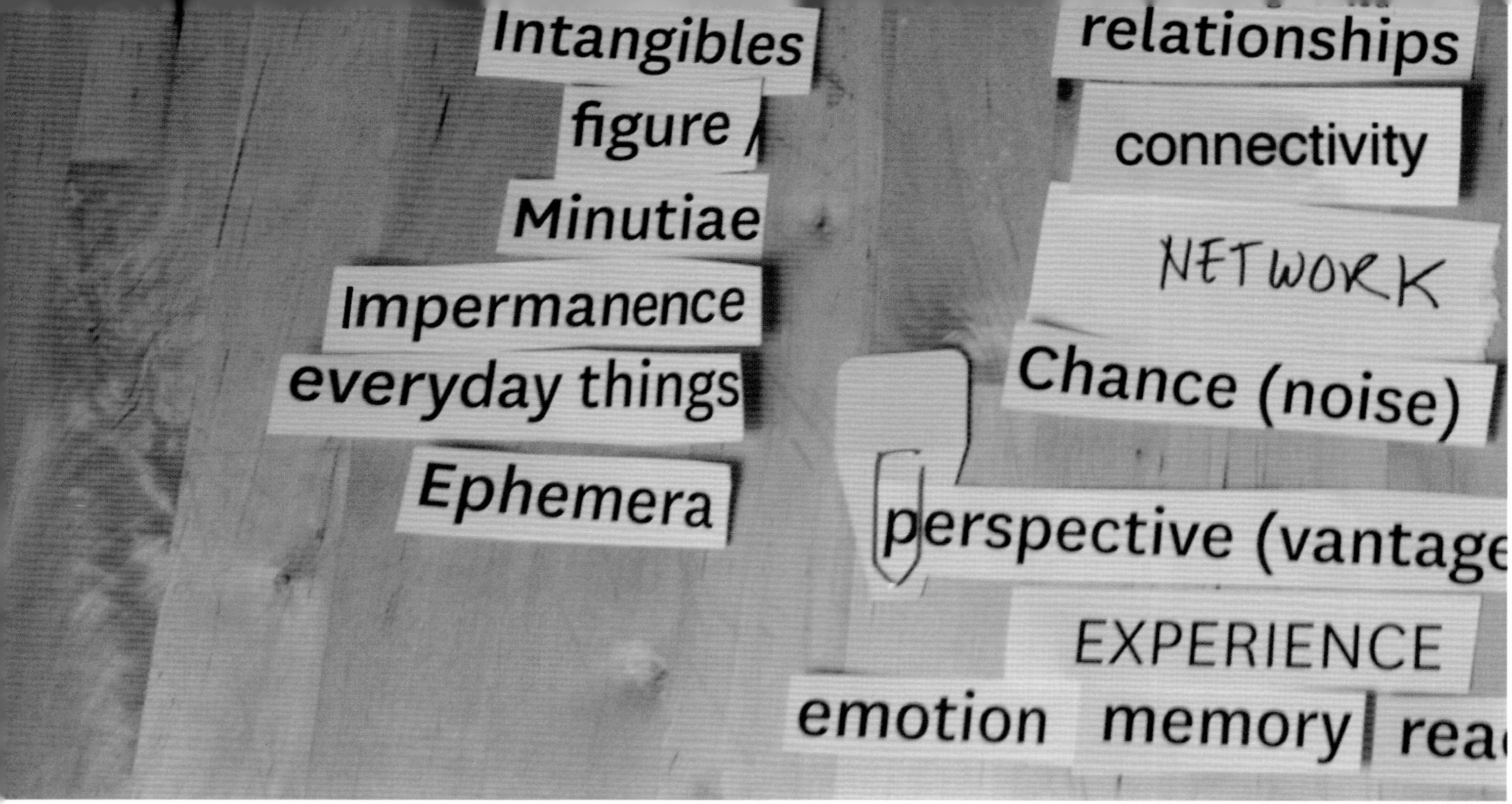

ELISE PORTER, *COMPOSITE MAP*, 2009

alphabetical list as inventory

Three lists of words I came upon around the same time inspire this exercise.[119] John Baldessari's "My List of Movie Stills" indexes the raw materials he uses in creating his photo-based montages. Rebecca Horn's word bank gives the reader an overview of leitmotifs and favorite words that recur in her sculptures, performances, and films.[120] Alan Wood lists visual thoughts that inform Peter Greenaway's cinematic vocabulary.[121] These lists strive for order, simplicity, and comprehensiveness without needing to be conclusive or hierarchical. These lists are shorthand artist statements: materials, images, subject matter, and recurrent themes are structured either within alphabetical categories or arranged in thought clusters, offering an overview of a corpus of work.

Create a List

Review your key words, matrix map, and collection of writings. With an objective eye, create a story of your work alphabetically. Execute an alphabetical registry or archive of materials, themes, precedents, and references. An arbitrary order gives new perspective.

Note: **www. Alphabetizer.com** may help to put your list in order.

119 John Baldessari, "My Files of Movie Stills," in *Blasted Allegories: An Anthology of Writings by Contemporary Artists*, ed. Brian Wallis (Cambridge, MA: MIT Press, 100–03.

120 Brice Curiger, "Rebecca Horn" (Zurich: Kunsthaus, 1983), 9.

121 Alan Woods, *Being Naked Playing Dead: The Art of Peter Greenaway* (Manchester: Manchester University Press, 1996), 191–95.

Absence	Immemorial
Abstraction	Inhabit
Alteration	Insider
Balance	Journey
Barrier	Kaleidoscope
Belonging	Light
Blind	Linger
Boundary	Materiality
Bridge	Memory
Building	Mind
Caroussel	Monochrome
Cinematic	Motion
Claustrophobic	Motionless
Connection	Navigate
Continuity	Negative
Cultural	Object
Childhood	Observer
Daydream	Outsider
Dejà Vu	Pause
Deconstruction	Perceptible
Defragmentation	Perception
Delusion	Personal
Depict	Perspective
Depth	Physical
Dimension	Place
Disjuncture	Possibility
Displacement	Presence
Door	Protection
Domain	Psychological
Dreams	Quality
Dwell	Reality
Elasticity	Reconstruction
Ellipsis	Relive
Emotion	Remote
Emptiness	Rethink
Ephemeral	Reveal
Escape	Revisit
Exile	Rupture
Experience	Senses
Extended	Sequence
Extension	Shadows
Extract	Shell
Eye	Sight
Familiarity	Space
Fear	Stereoscope
Fixations	Structure
Flow	Subject
Fragility	Subtle
Fragment	Strangeness
Frame	Syntax
Gaze	Threshold
Glimpse	Transit
Ground	Unfamiliar
Hiatus	Unreal
History	Viewer
Home	Virtuality
House	Whole

PHOTO: MARTA LABAD

etymology

The etymologist finds the deadest word to have been once a brilliant picture. Language is fossil poetry.[122] RALPH WALDO EMERSON

This exercise will help you to discover a deeper understanding of your work through etymology. Etymology traces words back to their earliest forms and meanings. The etymology of the word itself comes from the Greek "*etymos*–true meaning" and "*logos*–word."

Using an etymological dictionary, look up your key words and write down their etymology.

Etymology allows for a connection to the original images preserved in the sensuous roots of language. By going to the root of your key words, you discover vivid images that help establish significant mental connections to your work. As German philosopher Johann Gottlieb Fichte makes clear, too often language is taken for dead and closed off from the whole sphere of imagery. Etymology allows us access to the vision of language. Abstract words, which may appear in their abstraction as flat or opaque, come to life when traced back to their root sources in language.[123]

122 Ralph Waldo Emerson, "The Poet," in *The Second Series* (New York: J. Munroe and Co., 1844).

123 I thank Walter Wright, Professor, Department of Philosophy, Clark University, for leading me to Fichte and the English version of his Fourth Address, which speaks to the issue of "living language" and origins. See: J.G. Fichte, *Addresses to the German Nation*, trans. R.F. Jones and G.H. Turnbull, ed. George Armstrong Kelly (New York: Harper and Row, 1968).

124 *The American Heritage Dictionary of the English Language*, 4TH ed., s.v. "deru."

In *The American Heritage Dictionary of the English Language,* there is an appendix of Indo-European roots that enables us to trace and understand the etymologies of certain English words. The words, "tree, truth and mark," for instance, are ones that we associate with durability. These words share the same root, "*deru*" which means "firm, solid, steadfast."[124] The word earth is derived from the Indo-European root "*dghem*," thus the words human, humanity, humus (soil), humility, humane, and humiliation.

History of use also enlivens words. Each time a word is used throughout time by different people they bring to it a different vision. For example, consider the word "muse." In Greek "muse" implicated nine figures, each of whom held a separate portfolio and presided over a different art or science. A muse dwelt among us on the physical plane. In the Middle Ages the muse was reduced to a single guiding spirit, who was both abstract and disembodied.

dghem

human

humanity

humus

humility

humane

humiliation

pairing words + images

This is an opportunity to see your words in relation to your images and your images in relation to your words.

Make three word/image pairs that draw out and bring to light core ideas in your work.

While improvisational in nature, these must be considered expressions. You might design page layouts, exhibition invitations, or actual works of art and design. Think about the size, typeface, and weight of your text, as well as the scale and clarity of your images.

Select three words from your list of key words, as well as three images from your collection of images (photographs of actual work, inspirational images from your working repertory, or found images from a picture file).

In one pair make a harmonious relationship between the image and word.

In another create an image/word relationship that is a collision, a rupture.

In the third, combine word and image to realize a state of ambiguity or some conundrum.

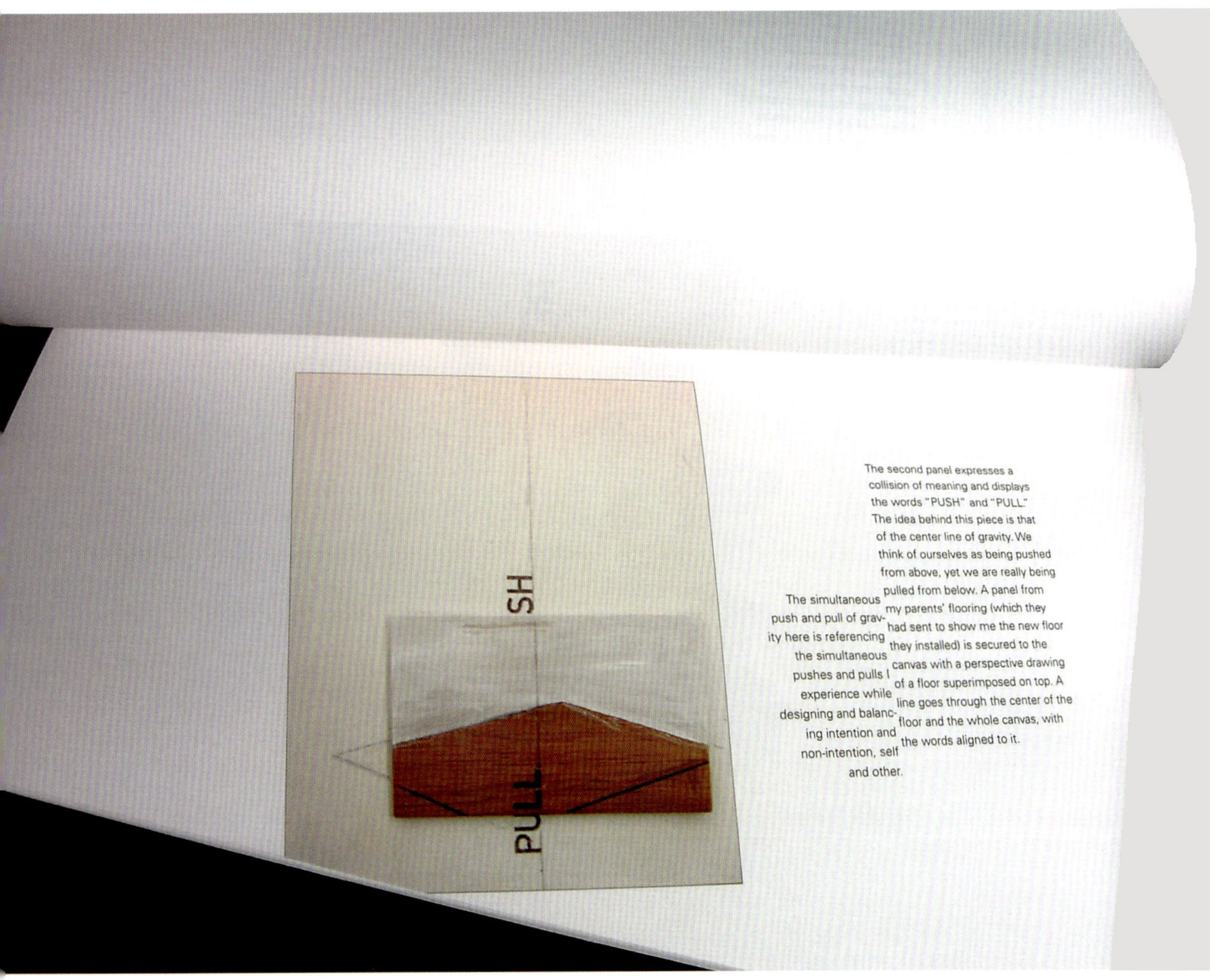

The second panel expresses a collision of meaning and displays the words "PUSH" and "PULL." The idea behind this piece is that of the center line of gravity. We think of ourselves as being pushed from above, yet we are really being pulled from below. A panel from my parents' flooring (which they had sent to show me the new floor they installed) is secured to the canvas with a perspective drawing of a floor superimposed on top. A line goes through the center of the floor and the whole canvas, with the words aligned to it.

The simultaneous push and pull of gravity here is referencing the simultaneous pushes and pulls I experience while designing and balancing intention and non-intention, self and other.

PHOTO REBECCA KLEIN GANZ

object-writing

Object-writing is what we do as artists. Our visible forms are a type of correspondence, a fully expressive language designed to connect with others. Like messages in a bottle that are released into the ocean, they will ideally reach someone who is willing to unpack the sealed contents.

In this exercise, adapted from Hans Jensen's description of a letter sent by a Yoruba man to his wife, we adopt a perspective on what it means to share art objects as sympathetic communication.[125] The feeling life of another is expressed anonymously and exclusively through objects.

Imagine a package arrives at your doorstep from an anonymous sender. In the package are the following: a black stone, pieces of charcoal, pepper, a large withered leaf, and a shearling buffer pad. These objects are a form of writing—object-writing. A sender has carefully assembled them to tell you about his or her life situation. As you study these objects, what impressions come to you about this individual? Allow a portrait to shape itself in your mind. Write a short passage telling this person's story as revealed through these objects.

In the spirit of imaginative exchange, assemble a return package. What objects would you send to this person? Endeavor to tell the person something about you and your sensibility as an artist. What would you send from your world?

125 Hans Jensen, *Sign, Symbol and Script: An Account of Man's Effort to Write*, trans. George Unwin (New York: G.P. Putnam's Sons, 1969), 24–31. Thanks to Sandra Brownlee for this reference.

126 From thesis writing exercise, Lisa Olson-Wong, RISD, Fall 1997.

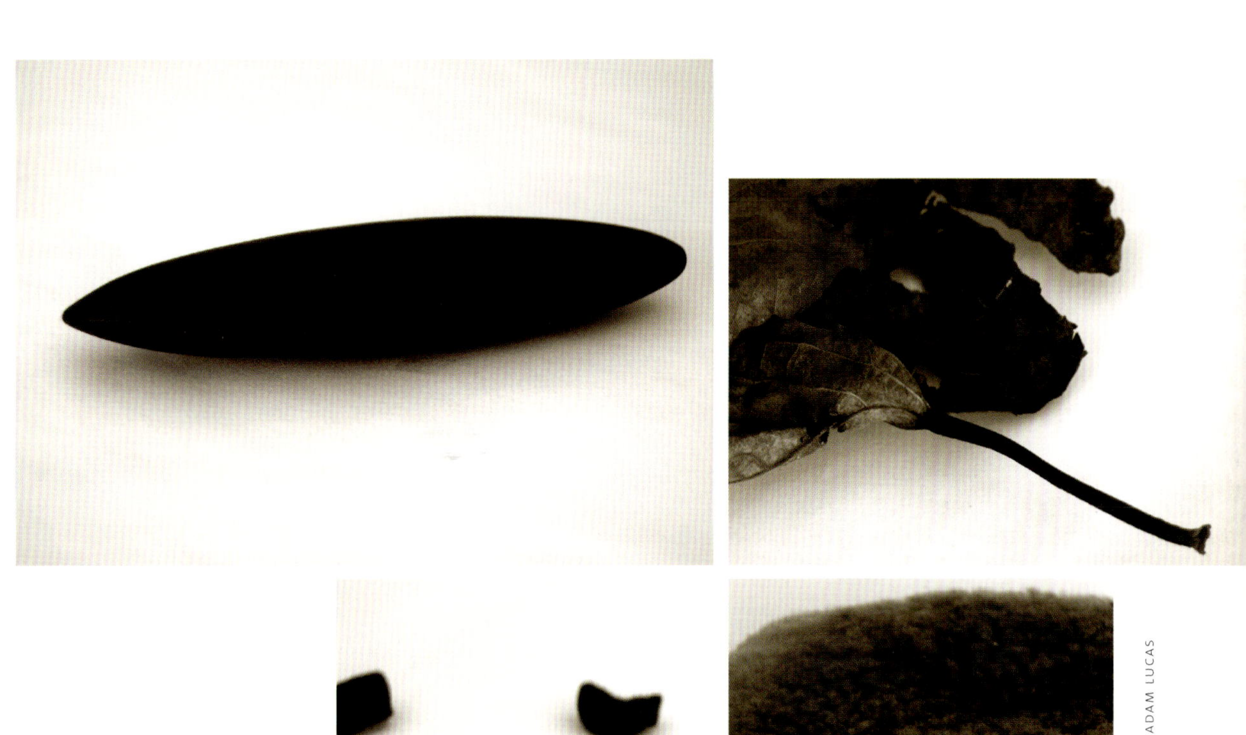

PHOTO ADAM LUCAS

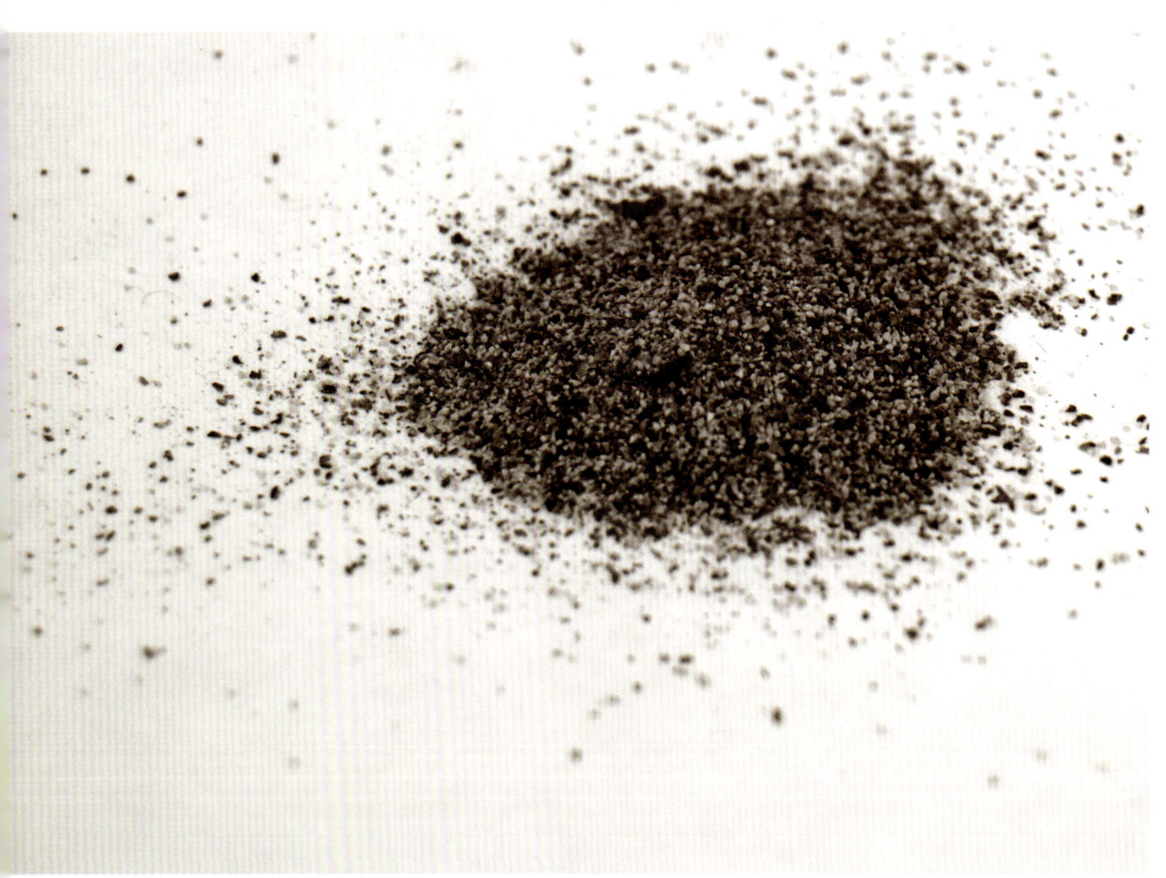

PHOTO ADAM LUCAS

When I look at these objects, I get an overwhelming sense of a lack of life, dryness, a feeling of a desolate place. The person who has sent the package is caught in a place of death, where life is missing. There is no thriving organic green life in this place. For some reason it seems like this person is living in either the distant future or the distant past. It is as though something has happened to cause such a place to lose all of its life and this person is stuck there. This person's world is very dry and always a slight cold uncomfortable temperature. He is thirsty.

Why these objects? Perhaps they are the only way to describe this person's world. Or maybe they represent a cycle. The stone is intact and hard, the charcoal crumbling, the pepper pulverized, the leaf long dead and fragile and ready to crumble back into the earth, and the polishing pad aches to polish something in a world where everything is withered and disintegrated. It sits there in a pathetic attempt to smooth a world that only turns to dust. The most beautiful object is the deep, black charcoal. It is the only object with any depth of color and richness. It is priceless and he has tenderly kept it for many years. Perhaps it has even been passed from generation to generation. He has sent it to me as a plea. He wants a way out of this world and so has offered up the most valuable thing he has. It has taken a great deal of hope and courage to send it and it is heartbreaking that it is of no real value in my world. I cannot bear to tell him and am deeply touched with sadness but also immense respect for his life. Although I have never met this person, I feel a deep connection with his humanity for some reason. I cannot help him, as he would wish. It isn't possible for me to travel there or for him to come here.

So, I decide to send him a package, one that contains objects that represent this world and the place he can only imagine. I will send him symbols of the beauty of life, captured in objects that he can look at again and again. Perhaps looking at this collection of objects will sustain him. The abstraction of the beauty of this life can become part of his world and in his mind he can imagine everything.

I will send something that looks like water and the sky, wet, fresh and vast; something of the most rich and clear color red, delicious and pure; the finest piece of silk satin, smooth and sumptuous in a rich green blue because I think that the objects that he sent become beautiful when placed on this color. And finally I will send him something to polish, a smooth marble stone of the milkiest white color.

Although I feel this story is sentimental, it brought to light some of the issues that are of importance to me: the shared experience, the collecting of experiences of beauty, how noticing beauty can sustain us, the idea of capturing the character of different experiences in objects (communication through objects), pausing to experience something and to further imagine beyond what we see; the issue of hope and the sensual triggering of imagination or memory.[126]

A butterfly
poised on a tender orchid
how sweetly the incense
burns on its wings

MATSUO BASHO, JAPAN (1644–94)

the drip

echoes
unknown
before

the cave[127]

WILLIAM J. HIGGINSON,
UNITED STATES (1938–2005)

As I dig for wild orchids
in the autumn fields
it is the deeply bedded root
that I admire
not the flower

IZUMI SHIKBU, JAPAN (974–1034)

haiku sketches

Haiku is an ancient Japanese form of verse that employs the seventeen syllabic pattern of 5–7–5 in its rhythmic structure. Often called the "shallow art," these miniature poetic etchings are an exercise of spontaneity and parsimony. Haiku speaks in an unpretentious way to the substance and essence of experience. Like a Giacometti sculpture that is pared to the marrow, or a gesture drawing with its expressive, minimal line, haiku gets to the essential character of a subject. According to A.C. Missias, "Haiku is more than a form of poetry; it is a way of seeing the world. Each haiku captures a moment of experience; an instant when the ordinary suddenly reveals its inner nature and makes us take a second look at the event, at human nature, at life."[128]

In this exercise, we use the poetic form of haiku to re-ignite our senses and to deepen artistic understanding. This exercise invites a group of artists to meet and to write haiku sketches inspired by each other's works of art. Through the lens of the haiku practice, we experience the concrete resonance of each work of art—the "aha moment"—and then bring words into play to capture, with sensory directness, the essence of the visual form. In the spirit of gift exchange, each participant comes away with a collection of haiku about his or her work of art.

Haiku Exchange

Poet-wanderers visited inspirational sites known as *ute makura* (poetic pillows) to write.[129] Treat this exercise as a poetic pillow.

You will need a video projector, one still image, or short video of a current work from each participant, small sheets of paper, envelopes, and a writing tool.

Ask each participant to bring an image or video for projection. Gather the images into one file. Distribute a collection of small sheets of paper to everyone. The number of sheets is equivalent to the number of participants in the group. With the projection of each image allow enough time for each member to compose a haiku response. Assign one person to project the images and to collect the haiku in small numbered envelopes, to be returned to the artists in order of the projection sequence.

Here are some guidelines on writing haiku:

1. Typical Japanese haiku are written in one line vertically and have a total of seventeen syllables or sounds divided accordingly in 5–7–5 phrases. Since the Japanese writing system is very different in its grammar and method of counting sounds and syllables, we can be flexible with the form, yet respecting the discipline of simplicity. Our intention is to get as close to the form and yet be spontaneous.
2. Imagine you are gesture drawing with words. Respond to what appears directly before your eyes. Provide a clear-cut picture of what you experience. With breath going out, write one line of five syllables.
3. With the same minimal gesture, get closer to the essential character of the image. What strikes you in this image? What gives it freedom and energy? Establish a vivid juxtaposition—a comparison with another concrete image—that gives resonance, depth, and unity to the images. Write a line of seven syllables.
4. Conclude your haiku by writing the third line (five syllables). With the flowing out of spirit, choose a thought that is the culminating *ahhh*—the moment of clarification and intense awareness.

Compose your artist statement as a collection of fifteen haiku. These can be your own haiku or those of others strung together in a meaningful order.

127 William J. Higginson, with Penny Harter, *The Haiku Handbook* (New York: Kodansha International, Inc.), 1985, 131.

128 A.C. Missias, *Contemporary Haiku: Origins and Directions*, http://webdesol.com/Perihelion/acmarticle.htm.

129 Matsuo Basho, *Narrow Road to the Interior: And Other Writings*, trans. Sam Hamill (Boston: Shambhala Publications, 1998), 18.

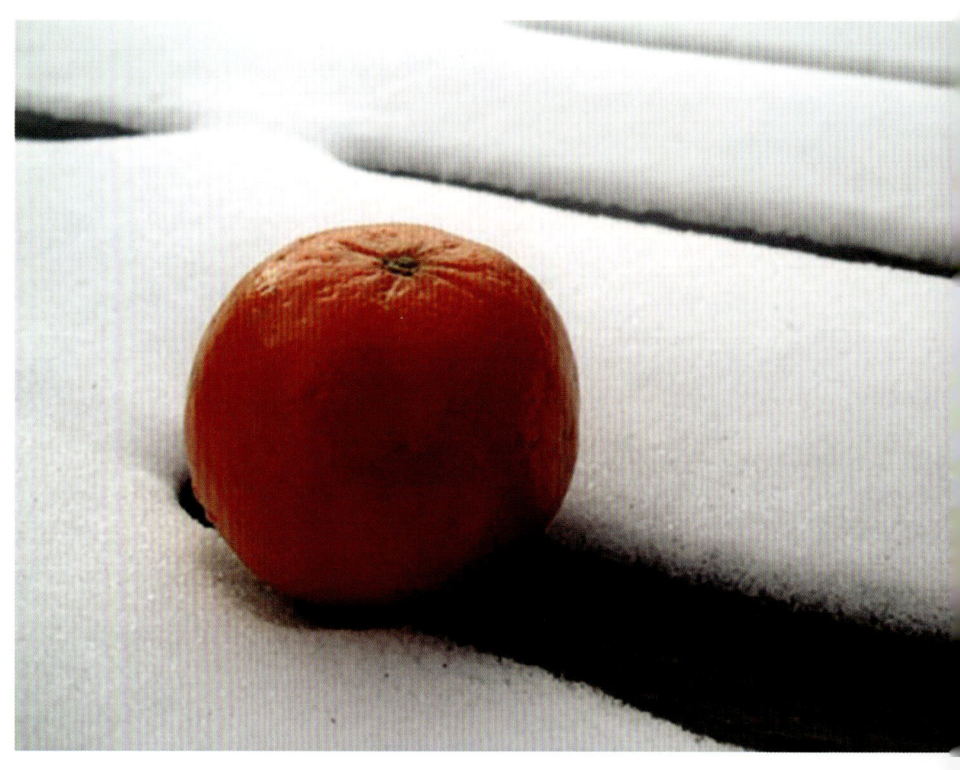

PHOTO STEPHANIE GREY

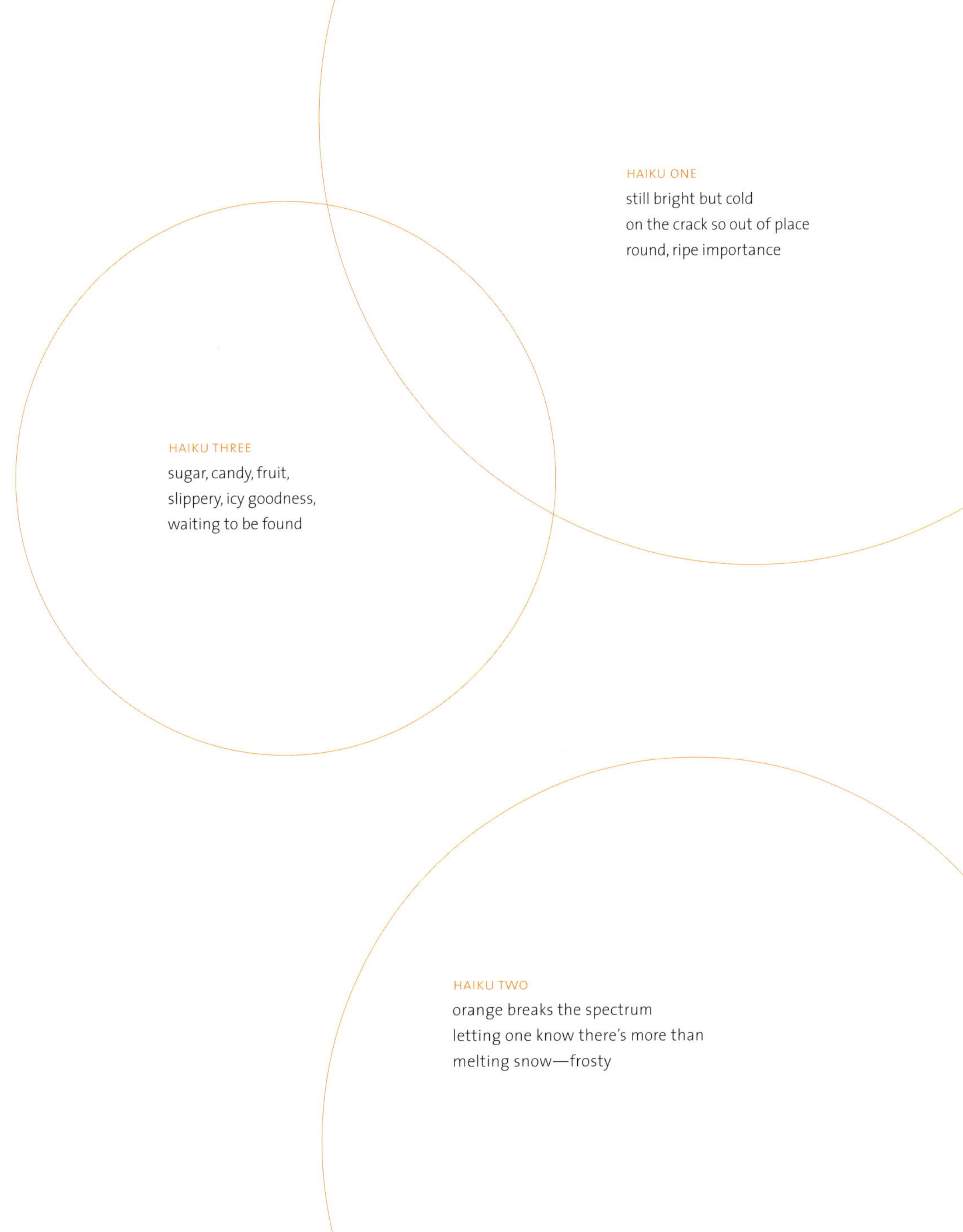

HAIKU ONE

still bright but cold
on the crack so out of place
round, ripe importance

HAIKU THREE

sugar, candy, fruit,
slippery, icy goodness,
waiting to be found

HAIKU TWO

orange breaks the spectrum
letting one know there's more than
melting snow—frosty

research sprees

There must be a systole and diastole in all inquiry.[130]
GEORGE ELIOT

One of my students told me that for him the acquisition of external knowledge required careful artistic navigation. Though he informed himself about historical and contemporary art, he also maintained a measured distance in order to achieve "true uncontrived meaning" in his work.[131] He, like George Eliot, saw that a diastole (the dilation or opening to receive within) had to be alternated with a systole (the contraction or forcing outward) in order to sustain vital, creative inquiry. Cautious of influence, I suppose he was consciously walking the wisdom line between the unpremeditated "now" of direct creative experience and the ground of understanding offered by art criticism, history, and tradition.

The habits and joys of dedicated research, one of the many skills we must develop on behalf of our work, represent the diastole of creative commitment. To research is to learn our place, to imbue us in context. It is a means of coming into community with other people and ideas and adding our voice to a larger, constantly evolving conversation about art and the human experience. It asks that we think about the intent of our work within a larger cultural and historical continuum and about how our work calls others to participate. What we ultimately want from this arm of inquiry is a well-grounded point of view, a point of view built through self-criticism and external comparison, and through connections of reference and association.

130 George Eliot, *Middlemarch* (New York: Harper and Brothers, 1873), 221.

131 In conversation with painter Robert Nadeau, RISD, October 1998.

132 Malcolm Gladwell, *The Tipping Point: How Little Things Can Make a Big Difference* (New York: Little, Brown and Company, 2002), 88–132. Many thanks to Anjali Srinivasan, one of the most research-savvy students with whom I have worked. Anjali likens the experience of research to visiting a spice market in India. It was Anjali who suggested that I read *The Tipping Point*.

Research triggers exploration. Exploration pushes a new perspective.

Research is an act of faith through which we discover intent and perspective. Author Malcolm Gladwell writes in *The Tipping Point,* about how ideas become memorable and move us to action. One characteristic of a successful idea is that it needs to be "sticky."[132] It needs to make an impression that leads to deeper levels of connectivity. Following the "stickiness factor" is a necessary step in cultivating and maturing our instincts. What makes something stick, according to Gladwell, is that it is practical and personally important. In the unearthing of this sticky quality, we define what is important and determine the essence of the work.

Allow yourself time for several research sprees. Consider the importance and difference of virtual research versus on-site research.

Give yourself time for an hour of on-line research. Also, visit the library. Be a trusting browser. Walk the aisles of the library. Glance through the shelves. Peruse books that cater to your interests. Establish connections with other thinkers and makers. Rummage. Read. View. Revitalize!

Step One

Put together your to-do reading list. What do you plan on researching?

Step Two

Develop a visual bibliography.

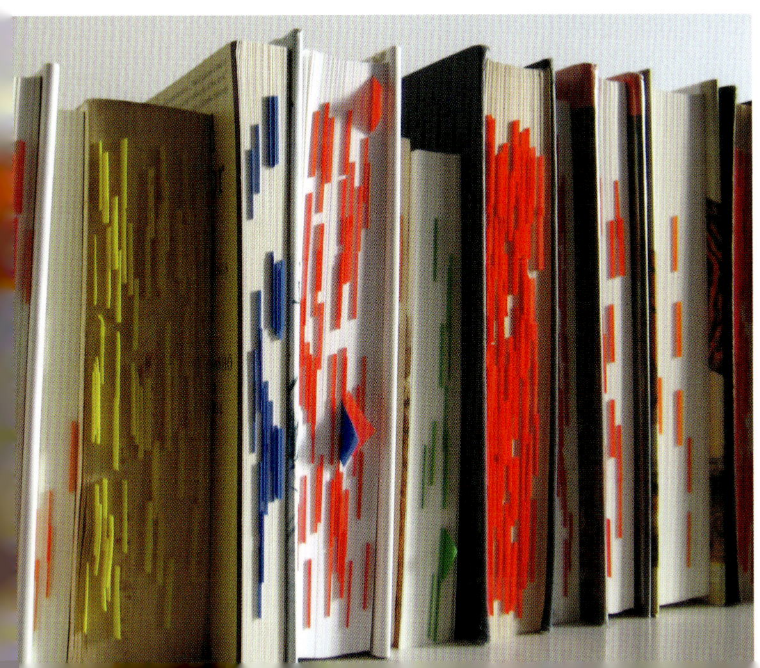

PHOTO DAN MARSH

>>

GLASS ARTIST ANJALI SRINIVASAN OFFERS HER THOUGHTS ON THE IMPORTANCE OF A VISUAL BIBLIOGRAPHY IN DOCUMENTING HER RESEARCH

As I walk along the stacks in a library, I—as many other people—find books that catch my attention. Sometimes, it is the spine of a book; sometimes, it is the words on the spine; sometimes, it is the color. And I stop to explore the title, read an article, contemplate the writer's perspective, be inspired by an image. Over the past few years, I have come to realize that these brief strays or diversions from what would otherwise be a focused, topical research jaunt at the library, are, in fact, an integral part of my process of making. What I am attracted to in the books I choose to leaf through, actually reveals patterns in my thinking, in a manner that no conscious effort could. A tool that has helped me unravel the sometimes seemingly scattered threads of interest in my mind is a visual bibliography. A visual bibliography is nothing but a digital collection of book pages, scanned or shot with a camera. Each "entry" includes the cover or title page and the pages I wish to keep. I use several systems to organize entries:

- a pdf file or folder of images for each book (which can get tedious and lengthy while searching for small and specific bits of information but serves memory well in an encyclopedic way),
- pdf files bundled by interest (which I personally find limiting since interests change all the time and establishing themes can rigidize the mind's lens),
- links from mindmaps through keywords, which was most useful in connecting details of information while keeping individual pdf book entries intact.

No matter which system you devise, the first step is to simply maintain an image archive in a way that is most accessible and easy to manipulate as needed (images in iphoto versus on disk). Admittedly, the process of scanning or clicking pictures of a book's contents consumes time, but not as much as one would imagine. Many libraries have fast and painless overhead scanners that either save to a flash drive (on which folders can be named suitably) or email the images to a specific address (where the subject line of the email may be used to track the entry later). I found myself devoting 20 minutes to the process of documenting my research (of say, 10 books, with perhaps 15–20 Post-it™ notes marking page ranges whose information I wished to retain) before checking books back in to the library. At times, I scan books instead of checking them out in the first place. On occasions when I am unable to spare time at the library, I take pictures using a digital camera in my studio. No matter which way I record the information, I do so at a high enough resolution that offers me greater flexibility of use later.

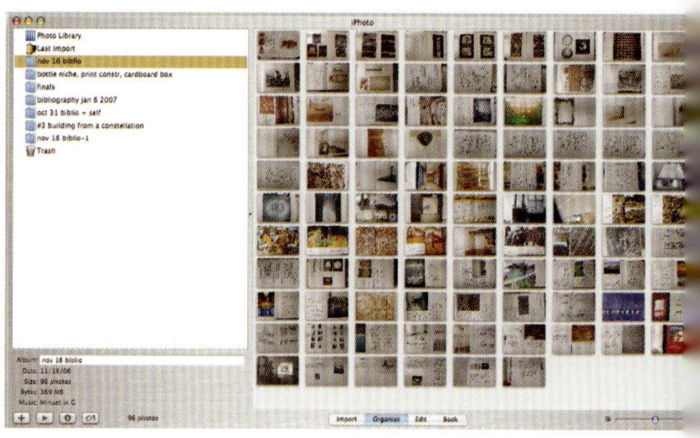

PHOTO ANJALI SRINIVASAN

The advantages to this method of collection are many:

- Accurate citations, quotes, images, and credit information become easy to pull for papers, presentations, and discussions without rummaging through notes or photocopies.
- You now have images of high quality to print in articles or theses instead of having to scramble for a high resolution scan.
- Posterity. Books that I only skimmed through at one point, I am able to go back into and rediscover the wealth of information or connections that drew me to the source.
- If you participate actively in the discourse or critique of art practice—perhaps as a visiting artist, a curator or a faculty member—having research leads to send off to galleries or students at short notice is most useful. Several students I emailed images/articles to in their moments of creative block were able to use the information constructively. It does not hurt to keep a personal database of the contemporary dialogues you are interested in.
- And in my mind, the most important contribution: the process of linking seemingly random points of curiosity in one's studio practice, creating a clearer, richer and far more interesting mental space for work to be inspired by.

The main disadvantage of maintaining a visual bibliography—and I will discount the time invested in recording information—is that the archive can become large and unwieldy with time, especially if you are a bookworm and "mapper" like myself, or if you tend to get inundated or overwhelmed easily with information, or, if your memory struggles to trace files across the collection. I would argue that the problem there lies in management, not method of the bibliography. My most recent solution is to build web-like maps of keywords that allow me to "locate" the visual data side-by-side to allows a distillation of information (pattern recognition rather than pre-determined agenda). Having said that, each artist will have to determine how to best manage her or his sets of data.

To keep any kind of a bibliography is a good idea, but to keep it visual is an even better one! For a simple reason: As a visual artist, I trust my intuitive inclination to track visual data. I know and respond to a strong image when I see one, even when the image is created in my mind's eye upon reading a phrase of text. If I am attracted to it—an image, text, title—I need to keep it, even if I cannot explain why exactly. I need to be able to conjure up the same at a later point in the creative process when the connection between my interests becomes clearer. While conventional bibliography listings may remind me of materials reviewed, they do not accommodate the above process of linking research to the studio. A visual bibliography does.

research as material for the studio[133]

So what I did simply as a way of getting myself out of the dilemma I was in, was that I said I would go anywhere, anytime, for anybody, for anything. I made myself very available—and I made it for free. ... I was and continue to be available in response.[134] ROBERT IRWIN

Allowing something new to be part of your inspiration.

Research is about wanting a larger perspective for our work. We do this by extending the frame in order to arrive at certain positions. Close examination of a subject is one option. Another is to crack open a comfort zone.

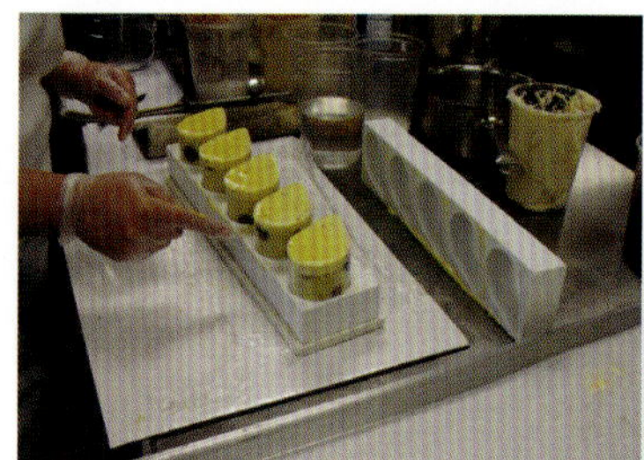

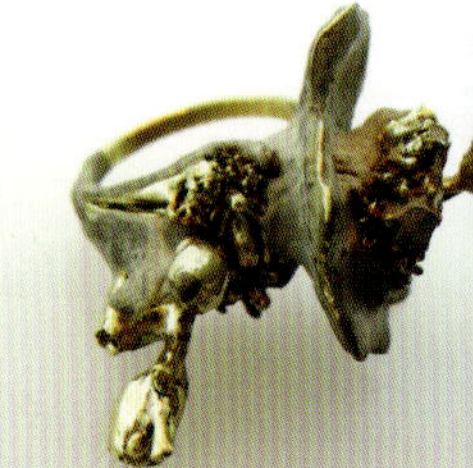

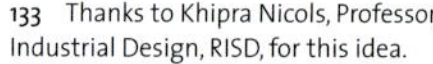
133 Thanks to Khipra Nicols, Professor, Industrial Design, RISD, for this idea.

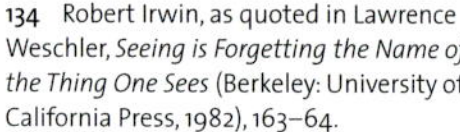
134 Robert Irwin, as quoted in Lawrence Weschler, *Seeing is Forgetting the Name of the Thing One Sees* (Berkeley: University of California Press, 1982), 163–64.

Project: A Field Trip

Leave your studio and embark on a field trip. What does your work need? What will widen the language of the work? What will move the work to a place of pleasure through some understanding of a new subject or new context?

Screen films. Explore the Special Collections of local libraries. Go outside your discipline. Visit the local landfill. Bleach out any naïveté in your thinking by conversing with or interviewing an expert in your field. Take a workshop.

Challenge yourself to be moved and informed by something more or something else.

Step One

Write a 500-word text that explains why you chose this orientation and summarize your findings. How has this trip added to your studio practice?

Step Two

Present a brief (10–15 minute) workshop that reveals to others how this field trip enriched your studio interests.

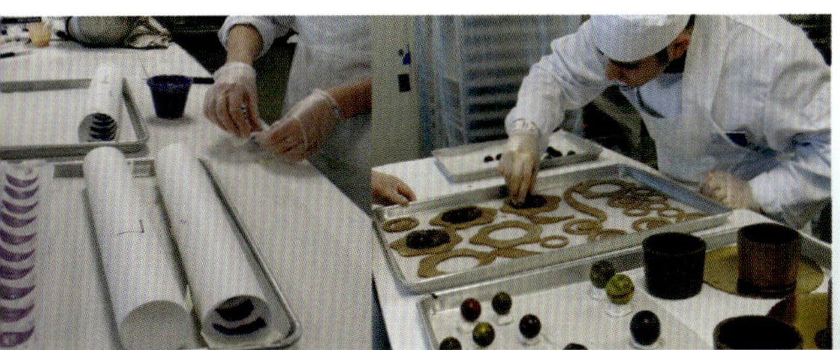

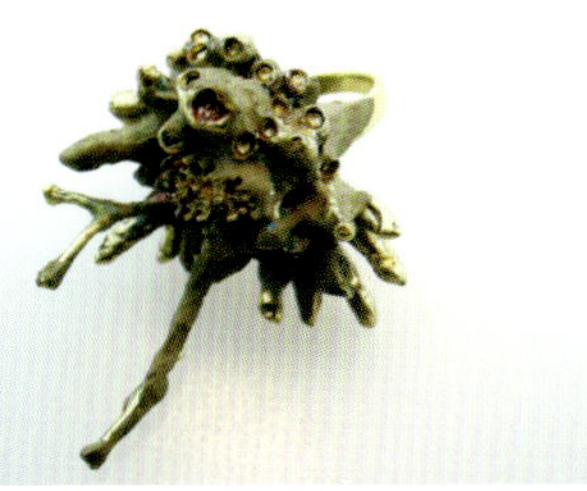

Jewelry Designer Ruth Reifen visits Baking & Pastry Deparment at Johnson & Wales College of Culinary Arts

PHOTO RUTH REIFEN

understanding your processes of understanding

There is a delicate form of the empirical which identifies itself so intimately with its object it thereby becomes a theory.[135]
JOHANN WOLFGANG VON GOETHE

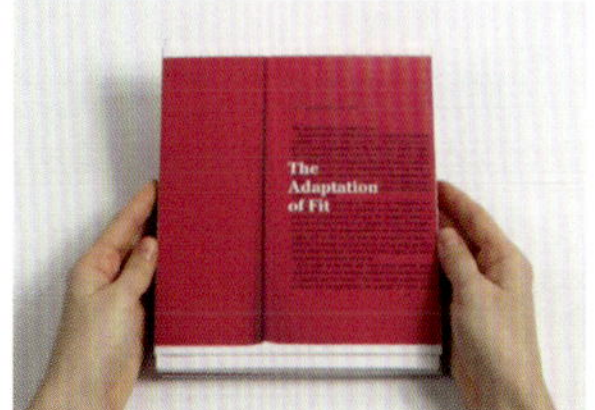

PHOTO JENNIFER MAGATHAN

Project

Select a text—an article, chapter, interview, essay, or book—that you consider highly informative to the way in which you think about your work.

Rework the existing text: Deconstruct. Redact. Delete. Re-type. Re-write. Reconstruct. Discover new overlaps. Analyze. Look for new possibilities of interpretation. Peel back taken-for-granted conceptions. Transform. See for the first time. See again.

Re-present this existing text in an expressive, interpretive form that engages and reveals your unique reading of it. The reconstructed text could be a signature article for a current art or design journal, a photo essay, CD liner notes, or a broadsheet for an exhibition. Show how you read this text through the lens of your concerns. Make the process more important than the aesthetic outcome.

135 http://www.arch.ksu.edu/seamon/book%20chapters/goethe_intro.htm

In the composition of this "publication" think about how a reader moves interpretively between your writing, the images, and the original text. In the end, you should reveal a theoretical position. To paraphrase Goethe, we are making theory *(theoria—to behold)* by following a delicate form of the empirical that grows out of an intimate experience with what we make. Centrally the task is to show how you have arrived at new and independent understandings that were birthed from a reading of this formative text.

Describe in a short reflective passage (300 words) the re-understanding that emerged from attending to this core text in an open interpretive way. Write about the process of alteration.

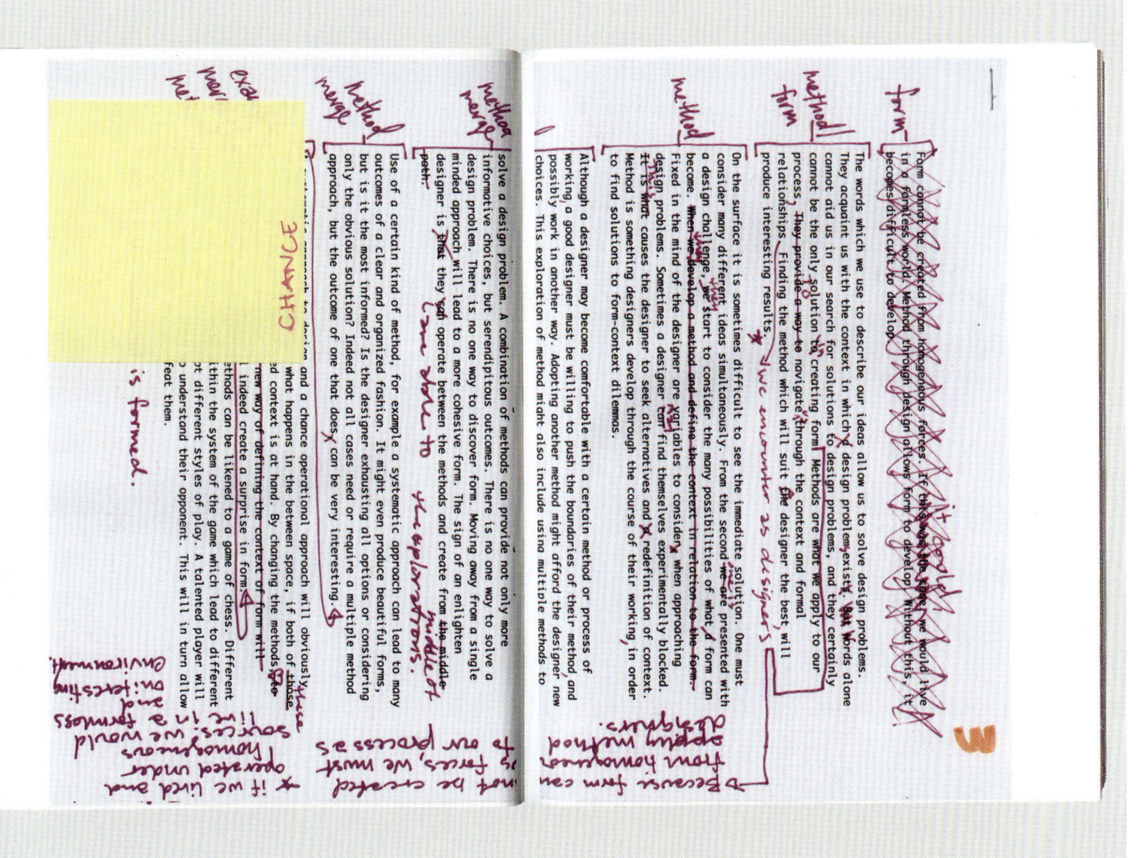

Form cannot be created from homogeneous forces. If this was the case, we would live in a formless world. Method through design allows form to develop. Without this, it becomes difficult to develop.

The words which we use to describe our ideas allow us to solve design problems. They acquaint us with the context in which a design problem exists. But words alone cannot aid us in our search for solutions to design problems, and they certainly cannot be the only solution to creating form. Methods are what we apply to our process. They provide a way to navigate through the context and formal relationships. Finding the method which will suit the designer the best will produce interesting results.

On the surface it is sometimes difficult to see the immediate solution. One must consider many different ideas simultaneously. From the second we are presented with a design challenge, we start to consider the many possibilities of what a form can become. When we develop a method and define the context in relation to the form. Fixed in the mind of the designer are variables to consider when approaching design problems. Sometimes a designer can find themselves experimentally blocked. It is what causes the designer to seek alternatives and a redefinition of context. Method is something designers develop through the course of their working in order to find solutions to form-context dilemmas.

Although a designer may become comfortable with a certain method or process of working, a good designer must be willing to push the boundaries of their method and possibly work in another way. Adopting another method might afford the designer new choices. This exploration of method might also include using multiple methods to solve a design problem. A combination of methods can provide not only more informative choices, but serendipitous outcomes. There is no one way to solve a design problem. There is no one way to discover form. Moving away from a single minded approach will lead to a more cohesive form. The sign of an enlighten designer is that they can operate between the methods and create from the middle path.

Use of a certain kind of method, for example a systematic approach can lead to many outcomes of a clear and organized fashion. It might even produce beautiful forms, but is it the most informed? Is the designer exhausting all options or considering only the obvious solution? Indeed not all cases need or require a multiple method approach, but the outcome of one that does can be very interesting.

A systematic approach to design and a chance operational approach will obviously ... what happens in the between space, if both of those ... ed context is at hand. By changing the methods, to ... new way of defining the context of form will ... l indeed create a surprise in form. ... ethods can be likened to a game of chess. Different ... ithin the system of the game which lead to different ... ot different styles of play. A talented player will ... o understand their opponent. This will in turn allow ... feat them.

repository of insight

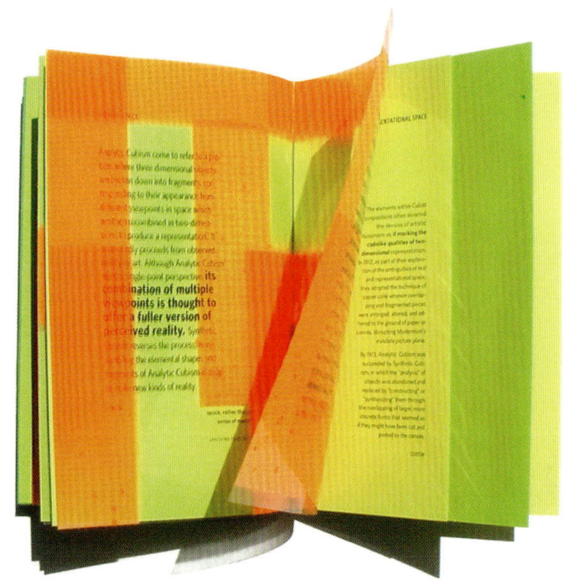

PHOTO AGNES PIERSCIENIAK

German philosopher Walter Benjamin was an inveterate collector of books. He also tirelessly collected quotations from books in little notebooks with black covers. Quotations became the very center of his written work. They were the way he entered into the vision of another's work and listened to tradition. To Benjamin, to achieve the essential in the quotation was to bring the truth to light.[136]

Project

Step One

Produce a small book of your most salient quotations. Think of these quotations as offering a repository of insight. These quotations must, in the spirit of Benjamin's practice, "be systematically and clearly arranged" to compose a series of vital strands that offer a portrait of your work. Group them by theme.

Step Two

Select one of these quotations and explain how it is relevant to your thinking. Read this passage aloud.

Step Three

At the end of this book of quotations, include an annotated bibliography. Explain how the development of your work was aided by the content of each book listed.

136 Walter Benjamin, *Illuminations*, ed. Hannah Arendt, trans. Harry Zohn (New York: Schocken Books, 1969), 58.

137 From thesis writing exercise, Ambereen Siddiqui, RISD, December 2010.

Bhabha, Homi K. *The Location of Culture*. London: Routledge, 1994.

Chapter 8, 'Dissemination,' and chapter 9, 'The Postcolonial and the Postmodern,' informed ideas about polarities in a nation's description of itself, with a lack of heterogeneous histories and minority narratives. Bhabha's ideas about the duality that exists between the migrant and the metropolitan and the recurring metaphor of the landscape as an 'inspace of national identity' have helped clarify and articulate my own ideas of diasporic experiences.[137]

ghostwriting interview[138]

Project

Team up with a partner to engage in an in-depth interview. Based on what you discover, fabricate an artist statement of 300 words in your partner's voice.

This statement should reflect both the style and content of your partner's work as it is filtered through the objectivity of your understanding. The Ghostwriting Interview allows the interviewee the freedom to explore ideas, concepts, and meaning without the immediate need to structure a coherent delivery. Similarly it allows the interviewer, or ghostwriter, the opportunity to work with language without having to be personally invested in content. The partnership will result in a rich gift of raw material for your own artist statement.

138 Inspiration for this vignette came from Sarah Walker, Associate Professor of Studio Art, in the Visual and Performing Arts department, Clark University, who led a seminar by a similar title for seniors, Spring 2002.

139 The appreciative interview builds upon the work of David L. Cooperrider and Diana Whitney, *Appreciate Inquiry* (San Francisco: Berrett Koehler, 1999).

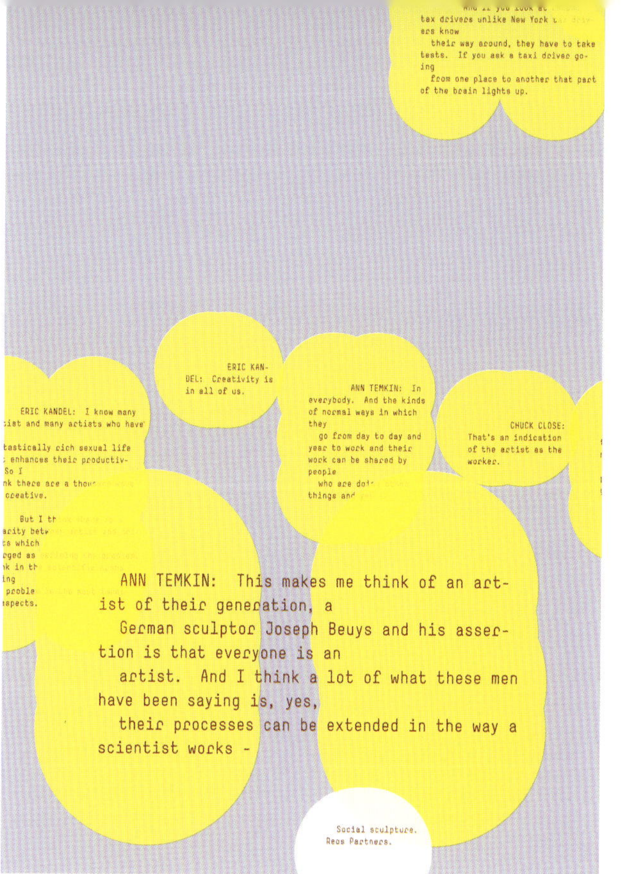

SARA RAFFO, *CONVERSATION MAP*, 2010

Interview Guide

Before you begin your interview, review these tips for conducting an appreciative interview.[139]

Engage your curiosity. Be a hungry questioner. Try to get to the substance of the images and experiences that shape your partner's creative practice. Search out opinions. Pursue truth, not just facts.

Ask your partner to provide as much detail as possible.

Allow time for give and take. Make room for silence. If someone doesn't want to, or cannot answer a question, let it go and move on to the next question.

Note key phrases and memorable quotes. Capture the eloquence of what is said and of the individual's interests. See the world through the other person's eyes.

What are you taking away from this?

The physical movement that can come with making. I wouldn't have understood this comment in quite the same way without making large collages last week.

How does work change when our whole body is involved? This brings up thoughts of gestural interfaces and Johannes Itten's Bauhaus classes.

[LAUGHTER]

This is really an a
thing. But I think in terms
ended
up doing what we're doing
there's' common misundersta
ho generations of artists
from other people's work. W
those people so much and
we'd be doomed to be followe
continued to make work th
like everyone else.

s
n

hat

CHUCK CLOSE:
resting thing about the paint-
could he
with a diagonal grid or hori-
rtical grid. They would have
the same reduced, but I decided do a horizon-vertical grid
eye would splash down the
ke a waterfall. And though the
different shape it was a
experience.

ifferent
about

ANN TEMKIN: I thin
it's very rare for a painter
or sculptor to be as
explicit about that interest in the viewer's experience. But I mean,
Richard, for you to image, it's the opposite, you didn't get step by step
gratification at all.

ERIC KANDEL:
One thinks of the
observer's participation in the art as
a modern day experience. This idea
long walk that you
taking, some of
these.

And to go from an idea in your head to what it is when these things
are complete that will make the viewer's experience be what it is, you're
envisioning it to be
can you at all describe that?

RICHARD SERRA: I went
conical shapes that were inverted
then
dealing with torque shapes. And
became a series of torqued ellipses
and
passage ways where the viewer
periencing a space he's implicated
that is somewhat stalking in the
they have no previous information that
would allow them to understand the
complexity of the curve leaning to
you. And it gave me an opening
a language.

RICHARD SERRA: I'm interested not just the
steel is a vessel that allows one to underst
to
the space in the way the room is round we kn
table. It was rectilinear table we'd know each
Those things have interested me since
on
the beach and backward the other way confou
things, being in a telephone booth as diffe
I
could never get back together in my head.
At one point I was building a work fo
and
I was splashing led and he asked me to buil
I'll shove this in the corner. And when I p
ized
that oh, the corner is holding the sheet of

And I thought I wonder. And so went
immediately it got me out of the studio. I
ten
by twenty feet long and mad the who volume
place
as interesting as the metal. And there was
The
architecture was holding the work in place.

But it's in the process of working t
The work isn't scripted or confined only to i
process of revealing itself to me is when I
hadn't foreseen in what I projected.
And one doesn't want to become a sla
and
the way to get around that is to constantly
about what it is I'm looking at and what it
often
times when pieces are coming together, you
imagined and they push you in a different d

CHUCK CLOSE: I think problem solving is not the issue. I think that it's a problem creation. What we did was try and find a way to ask questions of ourselves that no one else's answers would fit, and then the search was on.

ANN TEMKIN: And these look on a passport or –

[LAUGHTER]

ERIC KANDEL: This
t struck me. There
e a common set of
es whereby people
problems and other –

CHUCK CLOSE: Very important. I've said for a long time inspiration is for amateurs. The rest of us just show and go to work.

This description of creative work (kick, open door, choice, ride through) describes what I love most about design. How do we find ways of working that involve as many doors as possible? How do we recognize those doors when we see them?

. The
relation

ch the
fferently
ng one way

simp
l stadium,

is studio

I thought
, I real-

and
a plate

the

noth ing.

her ideas.
t in the
ible they

dents,

questions
nd and

not have

CHARLIE ROSE: So it only happens when you do what?

[LAUGHTER]

Because everything grows out of work. You do something and that kicks open a door and you say do I want to go through and you go yes, we'll ride through. Everything comes from that kind of approach. You don't want to sit around and wait for the clouds to part and be struck in the head with a bolt of lightning because it may never happen.

SARA RAFFO, *CONVERSATION MAP*, 2010

rubber band project

Art is a state of encounter.[140] NICOLAS BOURRIAUD

Project: Dialogue/Relational Bridges

This exercise necessitates the interaction and cooperation of two participants to create a work of dialogue. Using rubber bands as linking elements, the two perspectives of two artists are bridged through collaborative action.

Begin with an open discussion about the ideas that animate your individual working practices. Experiment. Use a bag of actual rubber bands to connect and communicate the fusion of your perspectives. With the rubber bands as linking elements show the possibility for intersection where your separate subjectivities merge into a "third mind" or relational space.

Document your process.

140 Nicolas Bourriaud, *Relational Aesthetics* (Dijon: Les Presses Du Reel, Franc, 1998), 18.

141 From thesis writing exercise, Marta Labad, RISD, March 2008.

PHOTO MARTA LABAD & SARA KIM, *REFRAMING THE SKY*, 2008 ›

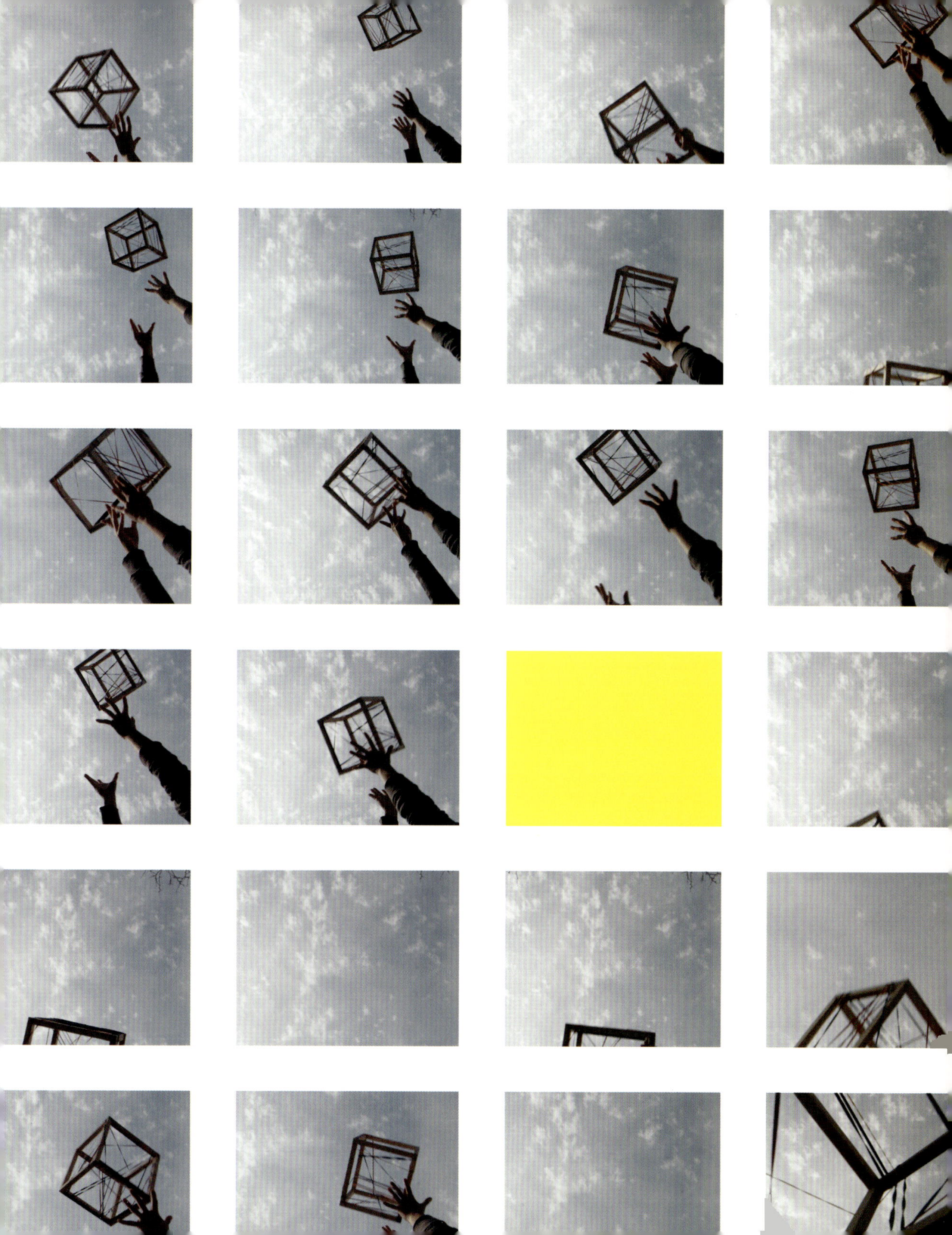

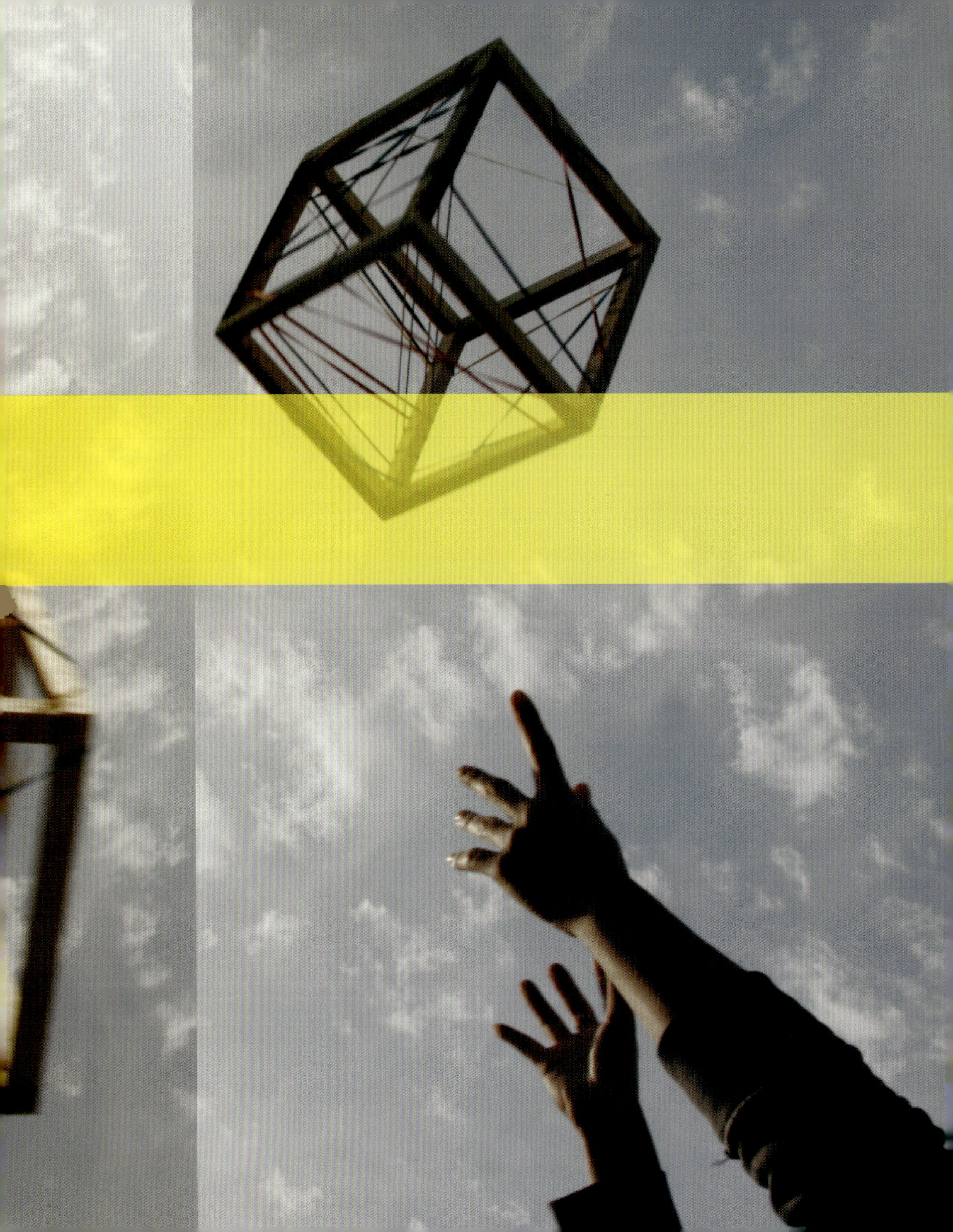

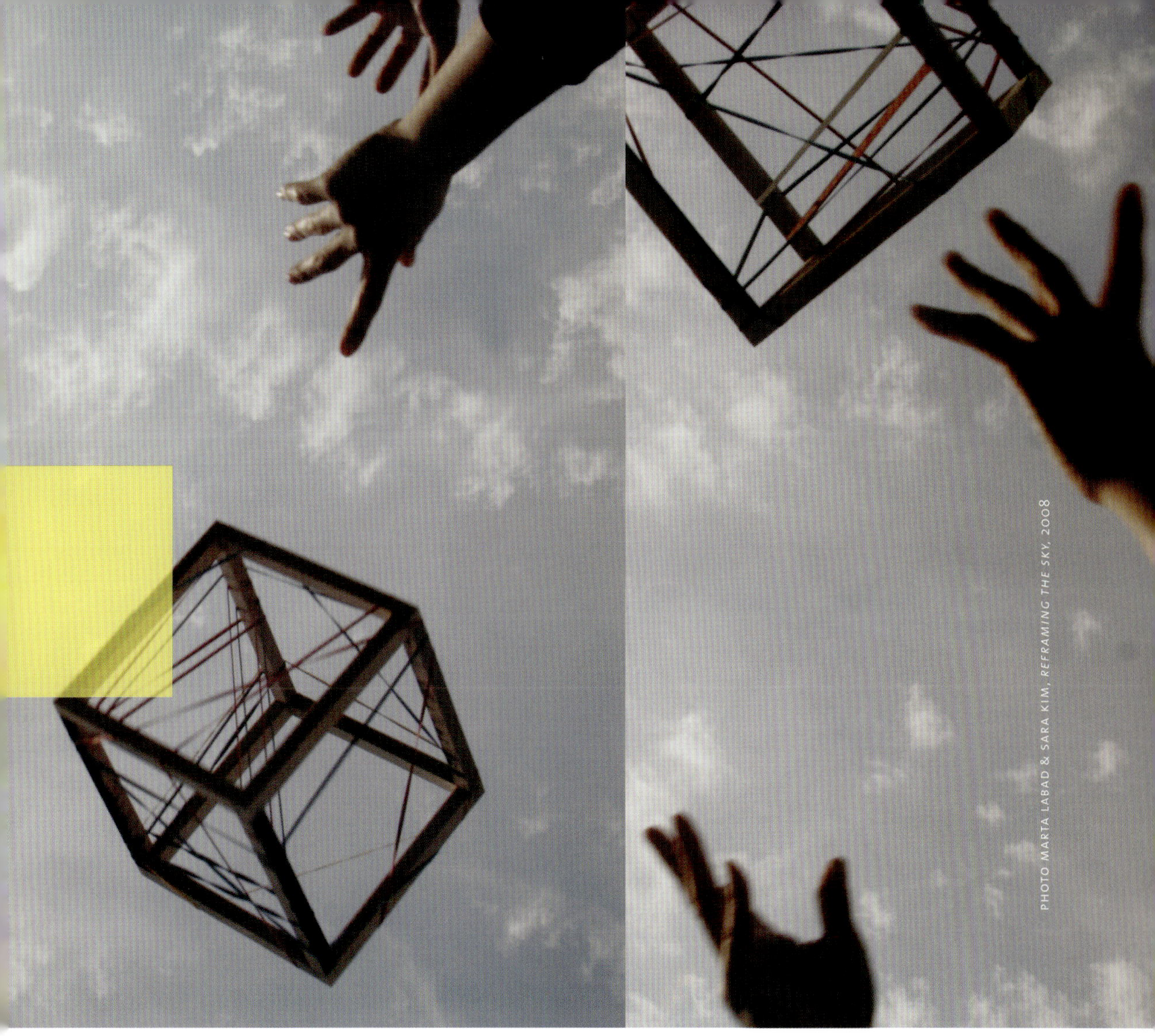

PHOTO MARTA LABAD & SARA KIM, *REFRAMING THE SKY*, 2008

ɪE RUBBER BAND PROJECT, *Reframing the Sky*

ɪis project is the result of a dialogue with my partner Sara Kim over several days as we worked to find a link between ır projects—an experience of the sky and personal circumstances of dislocation. I thought of how materials influence ɛrception, and of philosopher-feminist-psychoanalyst Luce Irigaray's words, "I see only through the touching of light." ere we found our connection point, using rubber bands to modify our perception. We constructed a cube and videotaped e flexible and unstable movement it made when thrust into the sky. The different and simultaneous movements of the quenced video stills became the "third mind," which reinforces Bakhtin's ideas of dialogue as "responsive understanding," ith not only a possible solution, but a multiplicity of possible results.[141] MARTA LABAD, PHOTOGRAPHER

metaphor as an artistic tool

The greatest thing by far is to be a master of metaphor.[142]
ARISTOTLE

You don't see something until you have the right metaphor to let you perceive it.[143] ROBERT STETSON SHAW

Finding a good metaphor is an opportunity to broaden an understanding of our work by getting past a literal reading of it. Metaphors offer image crystallizations for our often complex and somewhat indescribable feelings and musings about a particular subject. They can reshape the way we think about our work and also include others in a loop of understanding. The new context the metaphor creates gives power. We see something new through association. They illuminate each other's meaning.

The word metaphor comes from the Greek *metapherein, meta* "beyond" *pherein* "to carry." Metaphors are bridges to a larger perspective. They expand our point of view by offering another frame through which we see our work and the world. A good metaphor will permit a "perspective by incongruity," to recall the words of the philosopher Kenneth Burke.[144] In the end we compare two things which don't seem alike but are.

In her documentary, *Muse. Mute. Mutiny.* (2009), graphic designer Gunta Kaza uses the hand-woven domestic dishtowel as the metaphor that captures the essential discourse of her work. With intimate attention she studies cloth after cloth soiled with stains and deteriorated with tattered edges. The dishtowel becomes a glaring sign of a different presence—one that counters the ersatz of consumerist mall culture and allows others to share their stories. To comprehend the dishtowel within the context of everyday life is to experience the sentiment of resourcefulness, ancestral ties, and the power of work within the home. Using metaphor as an artistic tool, she deepens a perspective of her work and evolves a new method of working, allowing others to participate in her understanding.

142 Aristotle, *Poetics* in *The Basic Works of Aristotle*, ed. Richard McKeon (New York: Random House, 1941), 1459a.

143 As quoted in James Gleick, *Chaos: Making A New Science* (New York: Penguin, 1987), 262.

144 Kenneth Burke, *Perspective by Incongruity* (Bloomington, IN: Indiana University Press, 1964).

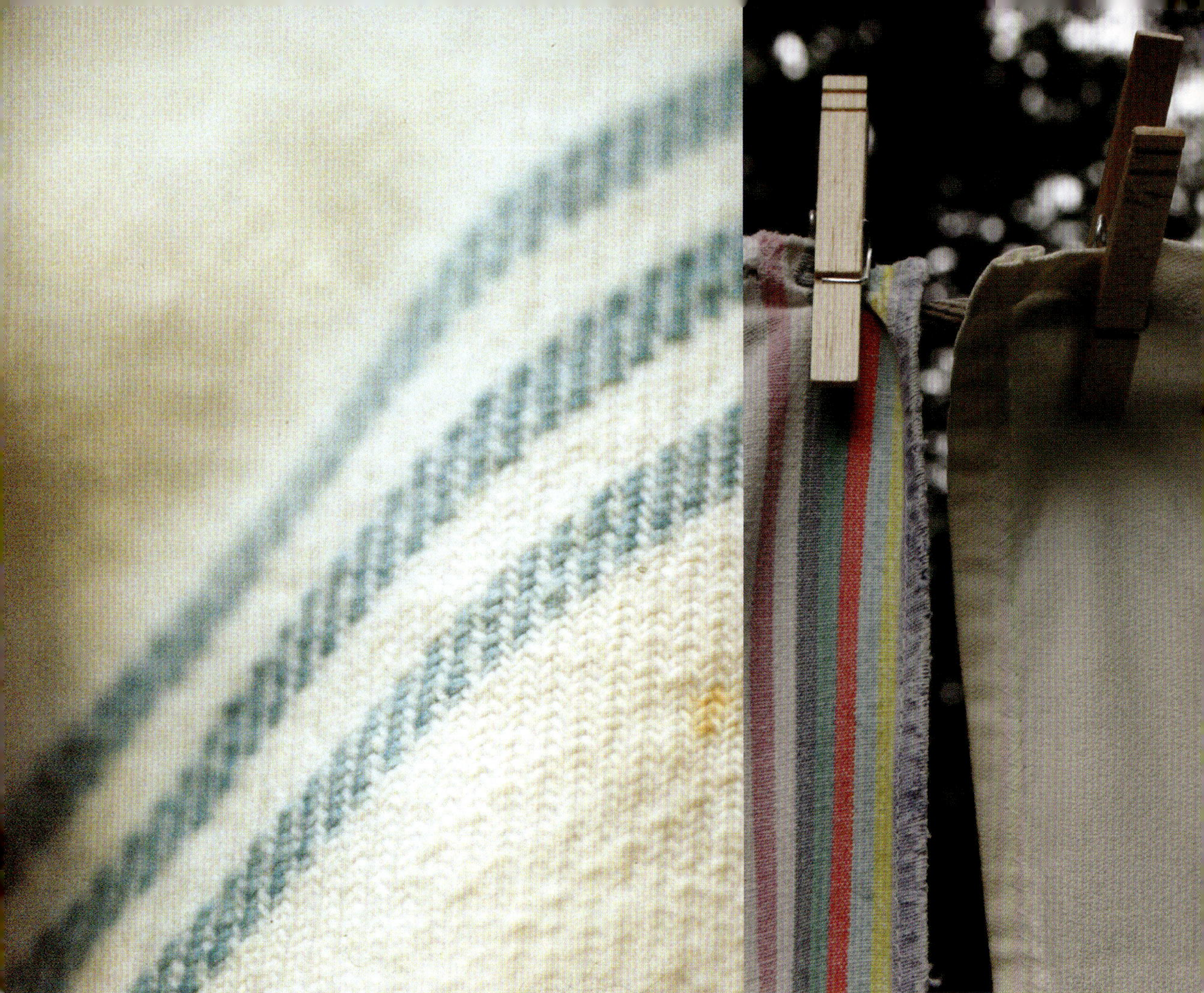

PHOTO GUNTA KAZA

Find a metaphor—a thing, image or concept—that embraces the character or essence of your work. Write it down. How has the metaphor helped you to find new relations and visual affinities?

Free write for 10 minutes.

Once you identify a productive metaphor, see how it can aid in speaking about your work.

Weave these understandings into a 500-word passage.

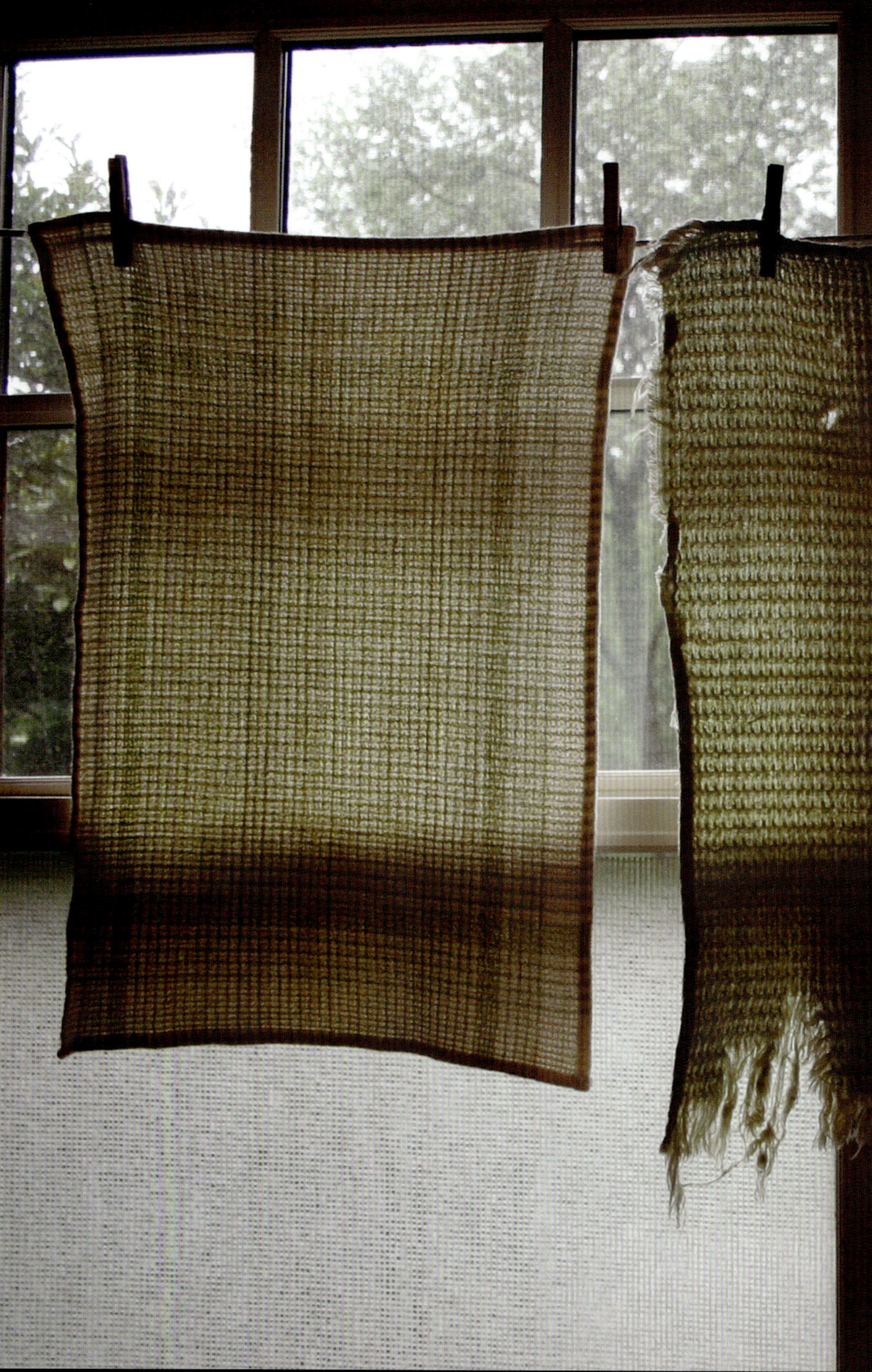

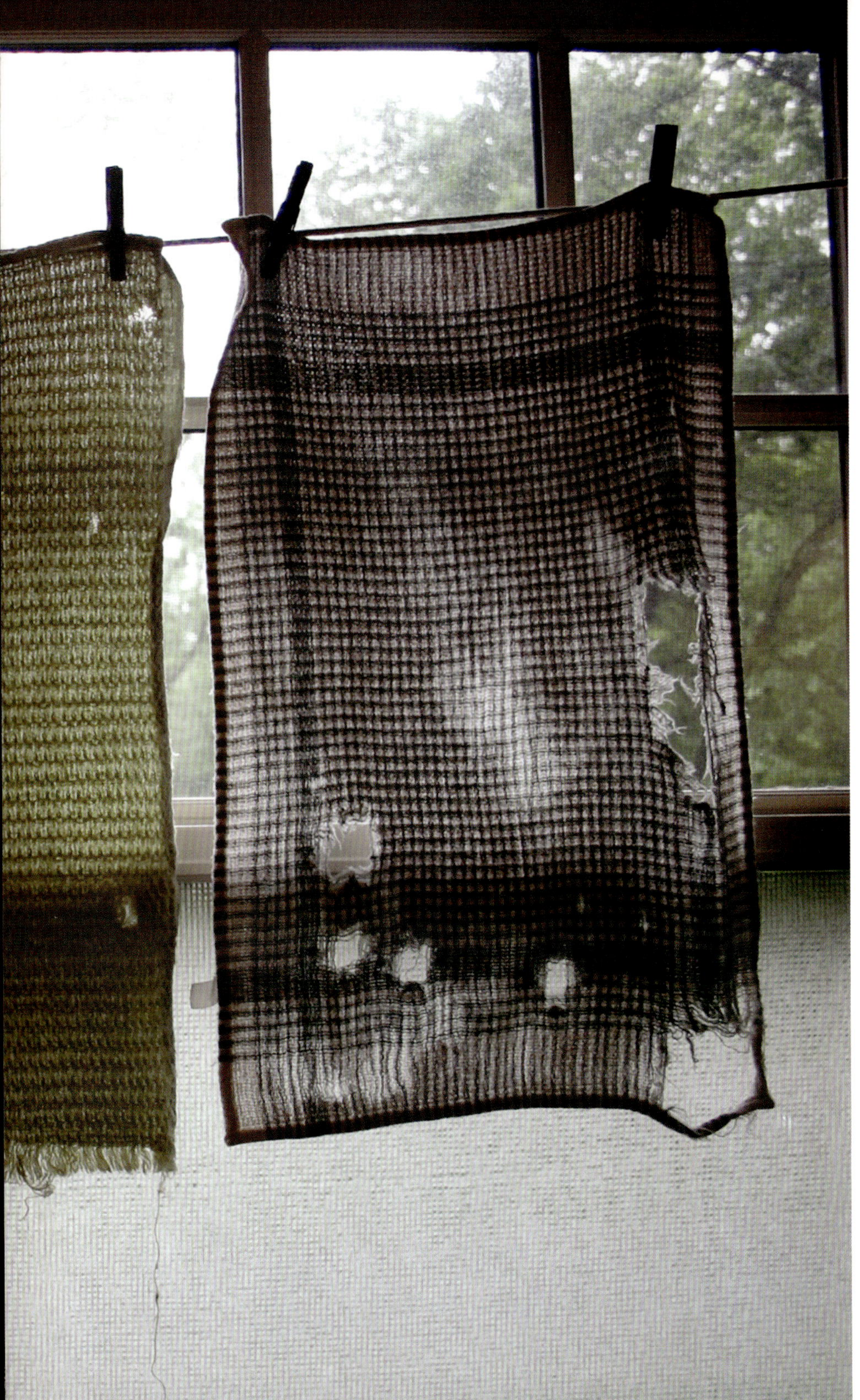

PHOTO GUNTA KAZA

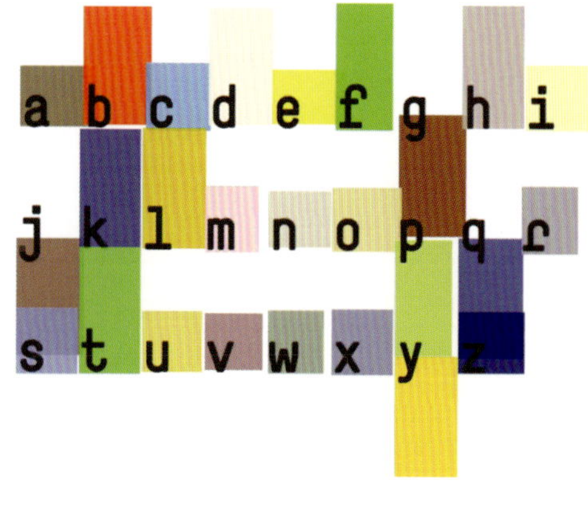

MEGAN FEEHAN

symbolic language

Ambivalence is the central theme in all my work.[145]
ANSELM KIEFER

Among the most symbolically complex contemporary art is that of the post-war German artist Anselm Kiefer. Erudite and sophisticated in his research, Kiefer draws from multiple references across religion, literature, philosophy, and politics and integrates these diverse sources into dramatic allegorical matrices. In his work for the exhibition *Heaven and Earth* at the Modern Art Museum of Fort Worth, he places us between the soiled pathos of historic reflection and spiritual transcendence, between despair and hope. Within his large-scale paintings we encounter the transformative potential of lead that is associated with air and earth, the artist's palette as symbol of the imagination, and the stairway to heaven as a bridge between heaven and earth.[146]

Symbol, from the Greek *symbolon*, means "a broken piece," one half of which signifies the existence of the other, establishing connection between what is visible and what is not visible, speakable or unspeakable.

The form of the symbol holds open a place of mystery.

145 *Anselm Kiefer: Heaven and Earth*, organized by Michael Auping (Fort Worth: Modern Art Museum of Fort Worth, 2006), 46.

146 Ibid.

147 From thesis writing exercise, Jennifer McChesney, RISD, Fall 2004.

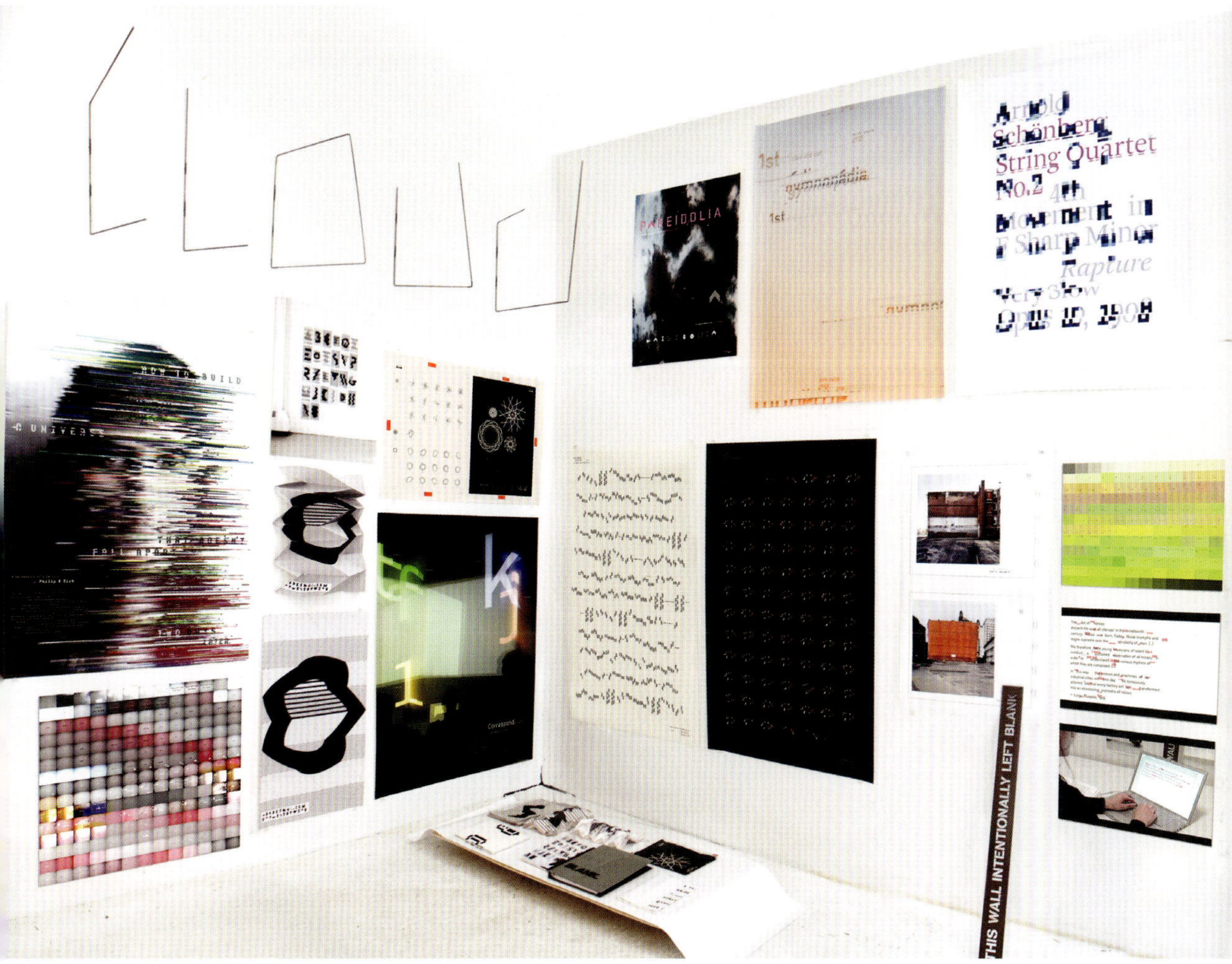

MEGAN FEEHAN, *READING TYPOGRAPHIES/PUSH & PLAY*, 2010

Identify the symbols that you use.

What is the purpose of using symbols?

Do the mythologies of other cultures play a role in the development of your symbolic language?

What themes are you articulating through the instrument of symbolic language?

Free write for 10 minutes.

five questions

Often in critiques we have neither the time nor the privilege of providing a balanced reading of what we do.

Frame five questions that you would like prospective critics to ask of your work.
Think of these questions as a means of generating the conversation you would like to have about your work. These questions should be precise probes seeking to distill the motivation of your work. They should clarify what you are doing and why you are doing it. They will delineate the breadth of your perspective and values, the spirit of inquiry at the center of your process, the epiphanies born from making, and the implications your work has for the broader community.

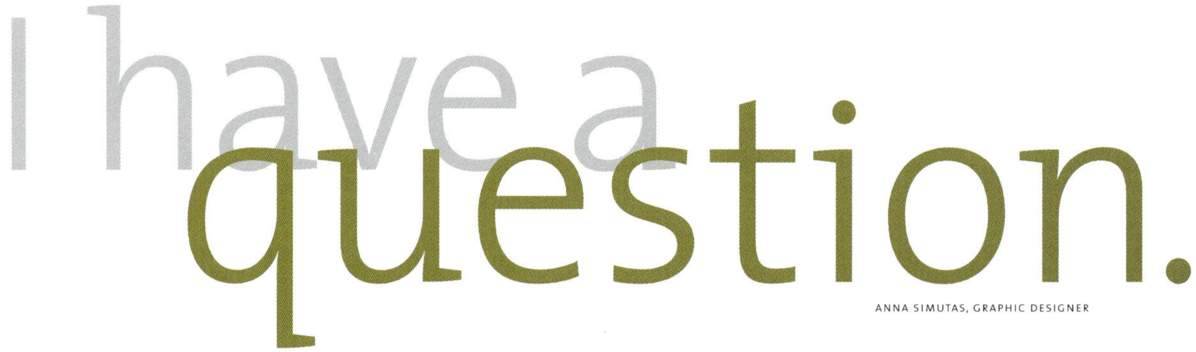

ANNA SIMUTAS, GRAPHIC DESIGNER

1 Is the use of abstraction in your work abstraction to hide or to reveal? Is the abstraction a device to provide clarity or to sketch a vision that is not visual?

2 What does the body represent in your work? Is the body present or absent? Is the body even a body at all? Is the body isolated from meaning? Can it ever not be representative of the body?

3 Is there dissonance or harmony in the rifts of meaning and metaphor in your work? Is the dissonance/harmony of meanings and metaphors constructive or deconstructive to the successful interpretation of your work?

4 Are there concrete and perceptible shifts? How important is tangibility to your work? Do the tangible and the intangible meet or collided within the genesis of your work?

5 What is the value of the work? Where does value intrinsic or otherwise play in your work? How would someone else appreciate what you create? Is this personal or perceptible?[147]

thumbnail catalogue raisonné with project descriptions

This is an opportunity to develop a comprehensive glossary of projects and to gain extreme objectivity.

[French: catalogue, catalog + raisonné, methodological, descriptive, from past participle of raisonner, to reason, analyze.]

A catalogue *raisonné* is a systematic archive of an artist's oeuvre. It celebrates a legacy of production giving clear description and analysis of each work the artist has made.

Project

Provide a good chronological sample with thumbnails of projects that is thoughtfully arranged—either ones specific to a period of intense exploration (graduate study) or a body of visual work for an exhibition or website.

Write a project description for each entry, responding to the following questions.

Describe the work. What does it consist of? How does it function? What is an audience invited to do?

What idea or theme does the work point to and build upon?

What goals did you set for the work? What inspirational source propelled the work?

How is this source reframed to achieve a new end?

What is the new idea that is offered up?

Have you omitted anything that is relevant to an appreciation of the work?

Are your thoughts clear?

Ummm, Noise

/ Interactive Custom Software, Demonstration Video

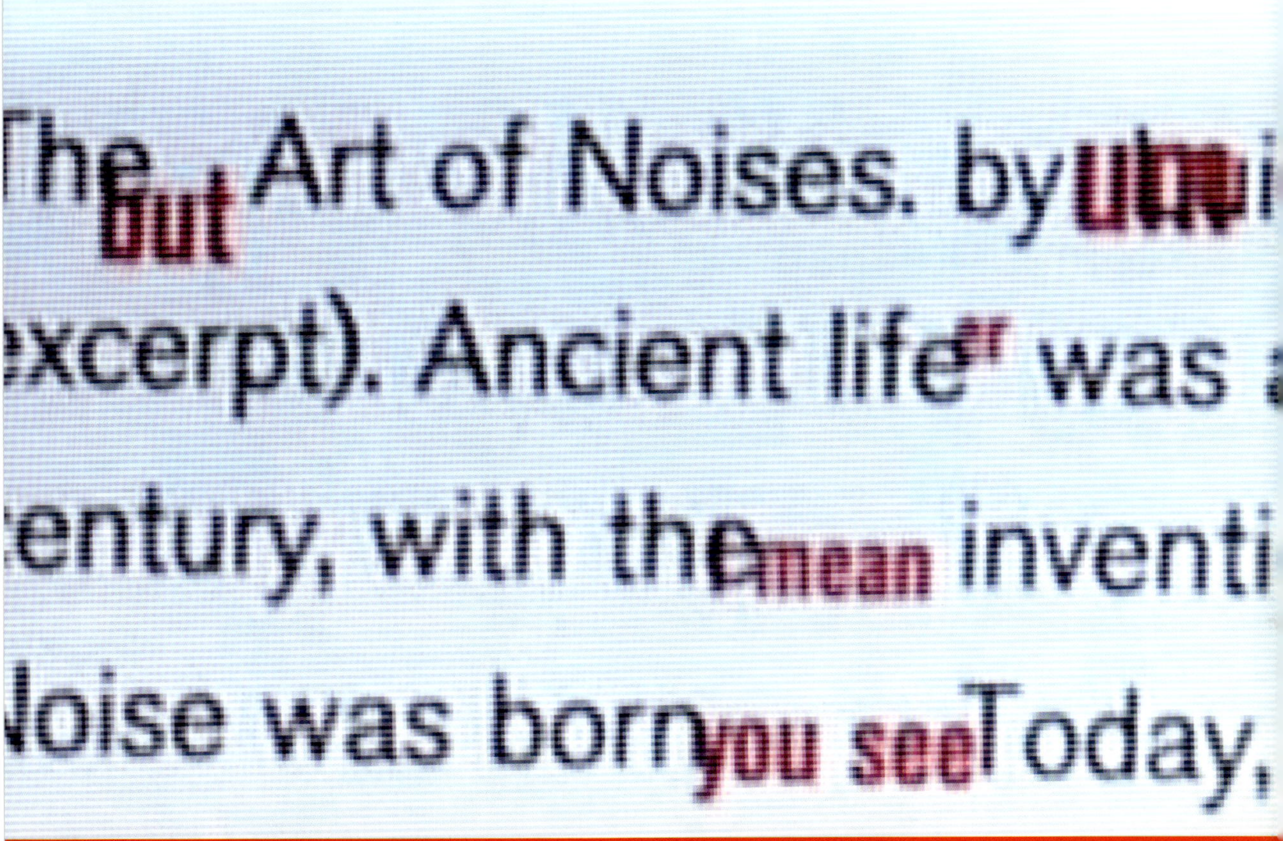

MEGAN FEEHAN, *READING TYPOGRAPHIES/PUSH & PLAY*, 2010

Ummm, Noise
Interactive Custom Software, Demonstration Video

Writing mimics speech, but only to an extent. Writing is not transcription; it requires more structure and rigor. Speech, by contrast needs not be as grammatically formed. When we speak, we pause—it's not continuous, we ramble, we stutter, we repeat, we amend. Natural conversation is fragmentary. We don't have a final product to be edited and sculpted; we speak in present time; we can take back but not erase.

What if writing actually followed how we really speak? The act of speaking is concurrent with thinking—there are gaps in speech where our brains are processing the forthcoming information. We fill these gaps with words that linguists call discourse markers or filler words. It is estimated that 20% of speech words are discourse markers—these words or phrases that are relatively syntax-independent, do not have a particular grammatical function, and are conventionally considered to have somewhat empty meaning.

It was thought that they were markers of nervousness or anxiety; some linguists dispute this and question the meaning of these words as conversation managers, holding the floor while speaking.

What if these discourse markers also invaded writing?

I wrote a program that attempts to find a form in the formlessness of filler language. As the user types, various discourse markers appear as bridges in-between words at random intervals. These words animate and become bigger the more the user types.

MEGAN FEEHAN, GRAPHIC DESIGNER

SUSTAINABLE RELATIONSHIPS

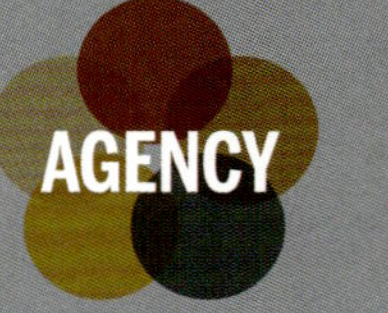

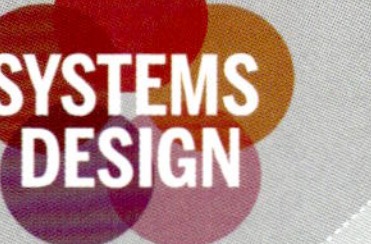

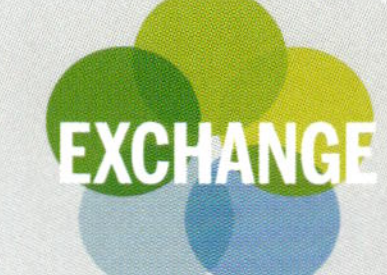

	AGENCY	EMPOWERMENT	ACCOUNTABILITY	SYSTEMS DESIGN	EXCHANGE
DEFINITION	conviction, civic responsibility, community, free will, desire to contribute, meaningful practice, change	education, authenticity, holism, presence, trust, guidance, joy, respect, understanding, empathy, kindness, manage expectations, passion, desire to contribute,	evaluation, good intentions ≠ good design, transparency, efficacy, address hypocrisy, follow through, honesty, manage expectations, trust, authority, confidence, loyalty, metrics, evaluation,	structure, flexibility, ecosystems, nature's design, address myopia, context, symptomatic design, perspective,	teaching, policy, writing, visualization, design, modeling, articulation,
INSPIRATIONS	climate change, environment, travels, life experience, advocacy, buddhism, presence,	learning organization, buddhism, taoism, alternate learning / teaching methods, dialogue, david bohm, peter, senge, transformation design,	US national design policy, LEED, Mulago, C2C, terracycle, ivan illich, nathan shedroff, dori tunstall, ef schumacher, victor papanek,	biomimicry, wendell berry, sustainable agriculture, michael pollan, peter senge, donella meadows,	tufte, ideo, think public, cup, john thackara, emily pilloton, david stairs,
PROJECTS	Design Agency 101	education, trust, guidance	transparency, address hypocrisy	structure, flexibility	teaching, articulation, design
	RD poster series	trust	efficacy	structure, flexibility,	design
	standards evaluation	authenticity, guidance	evaluation, transparency, efficacy	address myopia	policy, visualization, modelling
	writings	authenticity, holism, trust	transparency, address hypocrisy	ecosystems	articulation
	respond design	guidance, holism, education	transparency, efficacy	structure, flexibility	articulation, design
	decoy design	education, guidance, holism	efficacy, address hypocrisy	structure, address myopia	visualization, writing, articulation

EMILY SARA WILSON, *FIVE-WORD COMPOSITE MAP*, 2010

KEYWORDS ARE AS FOLLOWS

ALCHEMY

potential energy
salvage
arrange
collage
bricolage
construct
transform

Definition:

Alchemy is a form of **chemistry and philosophy** practiced from the Middle Ages through the Renaissance. It was primarily concerned with discovering methods for transmuting baser metals into gold, and with finding a universal solvent and an elixir of life.

Alchemy refers to any **magical power,** or process of **transmuting** a common substance, usually of little value, into a substance of **great value.**

Are the present-day parables clear enough here? I suspect that they are not.

Influences

Joseph Beuys
Yves Klein
Edward Kelly (Alchemical Writings from 1893)
Robert Gober
Felix Gonzales Torres
Nick Cave
Shinique Smith

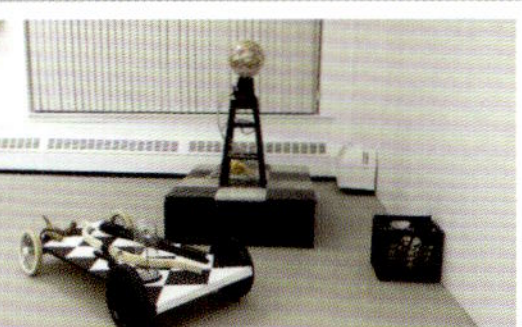

Theater of The Incompetent Alchemist, 2009

WIT

humor
serious playfulness
art historical reference

Definition:

Wit is the keen perception and clever expression of those connections between ideas that awaken amusement and pleasure.

It implies **powers of intelligent observation, ingenious contrivance**, mental acuity, composure, and resourcefulness.

Is the wit coming through? Should I be more blunt with my little jokes?

Influences

Dieter Roth
Dada (hello, Rrose Selavy)
Kalup Linzy
Phoebe Washburn
Vik Muniz
Olaf Breuning
Christian Marclay

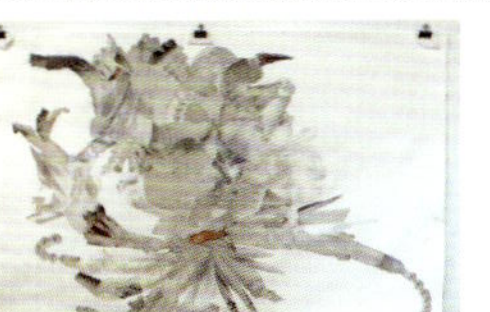

Kurt Schwitters in Venice, 2008

VULNERABILITY

self-consciousness
pain
dumb-luck
improvisation
desire

Definition:

To be vulnerable is to be susceptible to being wounded or hurt, as by a weapon: and intimates a vulnerable part of the body. Vulnerability leaves one open to moral attack, criticism, and temptation. **Vulnerability, inadvertently, can be quite brave.**

I know I'm at my best when I'm simple and dumb, but it's terrifying.

Influences

Martin Kippenberger
Richard Brautigan
Bas Jan Ader
Yoko Ono
Letters to A Young Artist, Darte, 2006

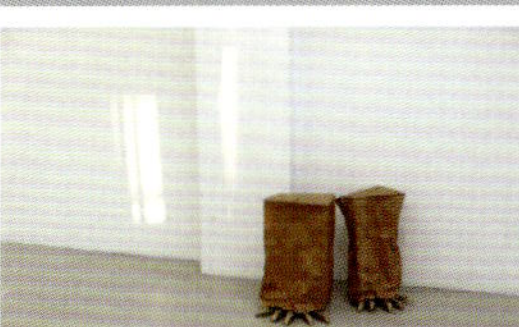

Simone, Nina, 2009

MAGIC

intangibility
rhythm
incarnations
investigations
metaphysics
suspension of disbelief
play

Definition:

Magic is the art of creating illusions as entertainment by the use of sleight of hand, deceptive devices, or conjuring.

It is also the art of producing a desired effect through the use of incantation or various other techniques that presumably assure **human control of supernatural agencies or the forces of nature.**

When I refer to magic, it's personal. Also, magic and alchemy are intrinsically connected through their transformative powers.

Influences

Ulla Von Brandenberg
Kenneth Anger
Hans-Peter Feldman
Gabriel Orozco
Delia Gonzalez
Eva Rothschild

In The Basement, 2008

ATMOSPHERE

nostalgia
tableaux
stagecraft
lighting
space
vibration
spotlighting

Definitions:

1. The gaseous envelope surrounding the earth; the air.
2. **This medium at a given place.**
3. Astronomy. the gaseous envelope surrounding a heavenly body.
4. In Chemistry. any gaseous envelope or medium.
5. **A surrounding or pervading mood, environment, or influence.**
6. The dominant mood or emotional tone of a work of art.
7. A distinctive quality, as of a place; character.

This word seemed superficial at first, but at closer inspection was quite revealing.

Influences

Pascale Marthine Tayou
Marcel Broodthaers
Ree Morton
Pippilotti Rist at the Castello di Rivoli
Bruce Nauman at Dia Beacon
Olafur Eliasson at the Castello di Rivoli
Mike Nelson

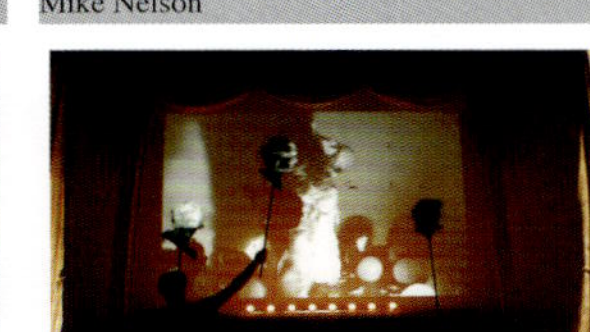

Storyville Stage, 2010

Maybe I have written to see;
to have what I never would have had;
so that having would be a privilege not of the hand that takes and encloses,
of the gullet, of the gut; but of the hand that points out,
of fingers that see, that design, from the tips of the fingers that transcribe
by the sweet dictates of vision.[149]

HÉLÈNE CIXOUS

149 Hélène Cixous, *Coming to Writing and Other Essays*, trans. Sarah Cornell and others (Cambridge, MA: Harvard University Press, 1999), 4.

MARIANA ACOSTA CONTRERAS, *COLOR IN FUSION*, 2009

COMMUNICATING

map as voice

REBECCA KLEIN GANZ, *BALANCING IN THE BETWEEN*, 2003

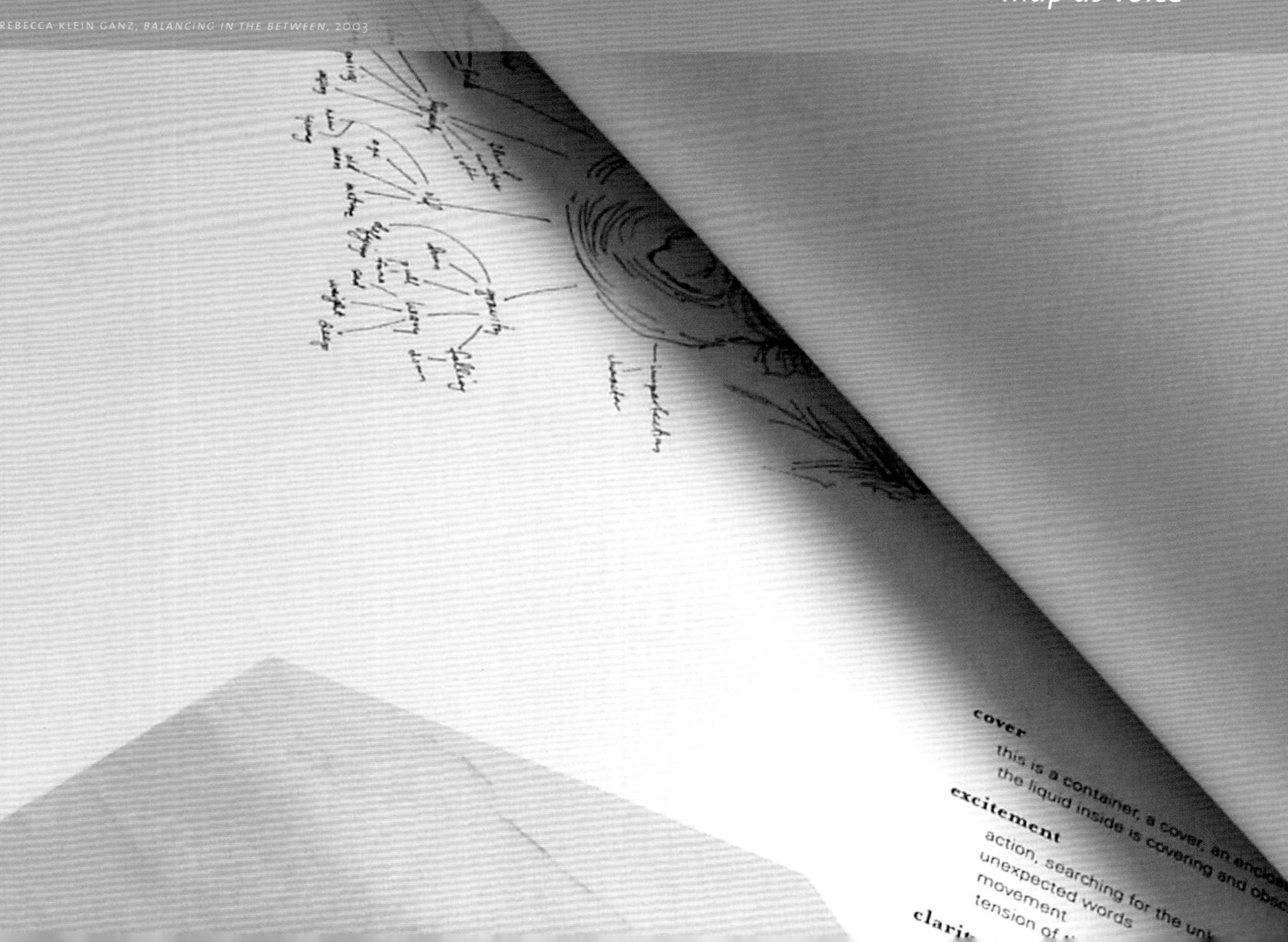

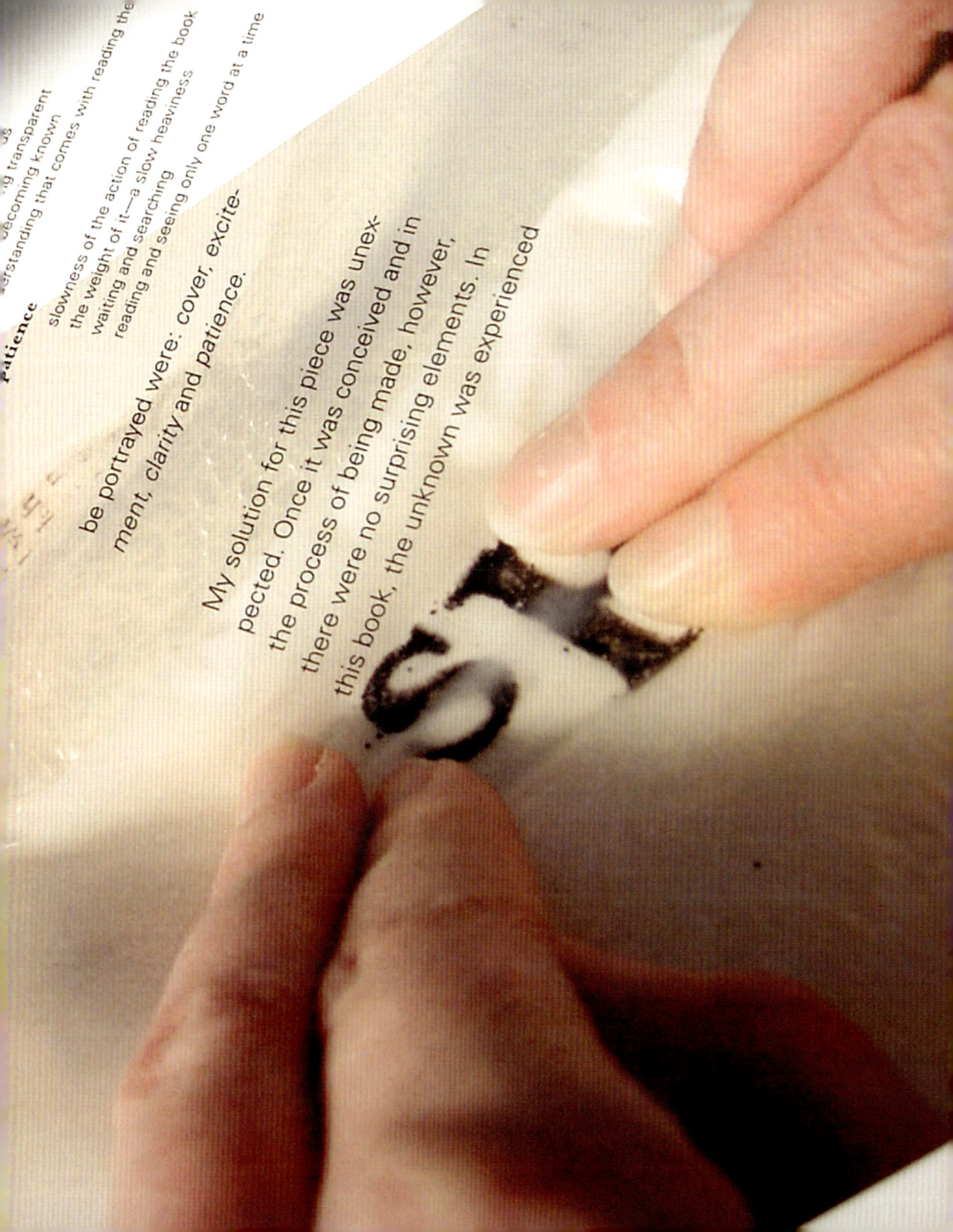

g transparent
becoming known
erstanding that comes with reading the

Patience
slowness of the action of reading the book
the weight of it—a slow heaviness
waiting and searching
reading and seeing only one word at a time

be portrayed were: cover, excitement, clarity and patience.

My solution for this piece was unexpected. Once it was conceived and in the process of being made, however, there were no surprising elements. In this book, the unknown was experienced

COMMUNICATING
map as voice

Our explorations have yielded, up to this point, much raw material. Through disciplined exploring we connected with the vast underbelly of creativity. Having dropped the plumb line into the murky, wonderfully rich subsoil of our work, we then illuminated the interconnectedness of seemingly random intuitions through considered research. Moving from subconscious to conscious thought now takes us to a fuller expression of our vision through the art of public communication, the third and final component of mapping.

Communicating with an audience is the culminating step in the process. It involves shifting from reading our work to writing and speaking about it. We now become authors, which implies responsibility and action. In giving voice to our work, we embrace and sift all previous raw material, moving it to a higher level of synthesis while offering it to others for their consideration. This section is about making rational sense of our inspirations, perceptions, experiences, influences, and precedents. The charge to speak coherently about our work requires that we be grounded in our instincts, yet clearly and persuasively present our own unique ways of seeing. In the words of poet Marvin Bell, good communication "requires of us the courage of clarity—linear, syntactical, and referential—which in no way compromises the great wildness of experience and imagination.[150]

At its core, this section on Communicating is about finding the voice of our work. We live in a world where much—too much—is interpreted for us. Many of the hoops we are asked to jump through are a way of sustaining the biases and interpretations of others. We want to gain access to our own speech and to exchange with others the lived experience of our work convincingly.

What we get from this process.

Working within certain conventions—a wall text for an exhibition, a letter to the editor, an artist statement, an abstract, a layout for a limited edition publication—we shape with word and image our knowing, in order to establish a connection with our audience.

150 Marvin Bell, *A Marvin Bell Reader: Selected Poetry and Prose* (Hanover, NH: Middlebury College Press, 1994), 220.

IN THIS SECTION

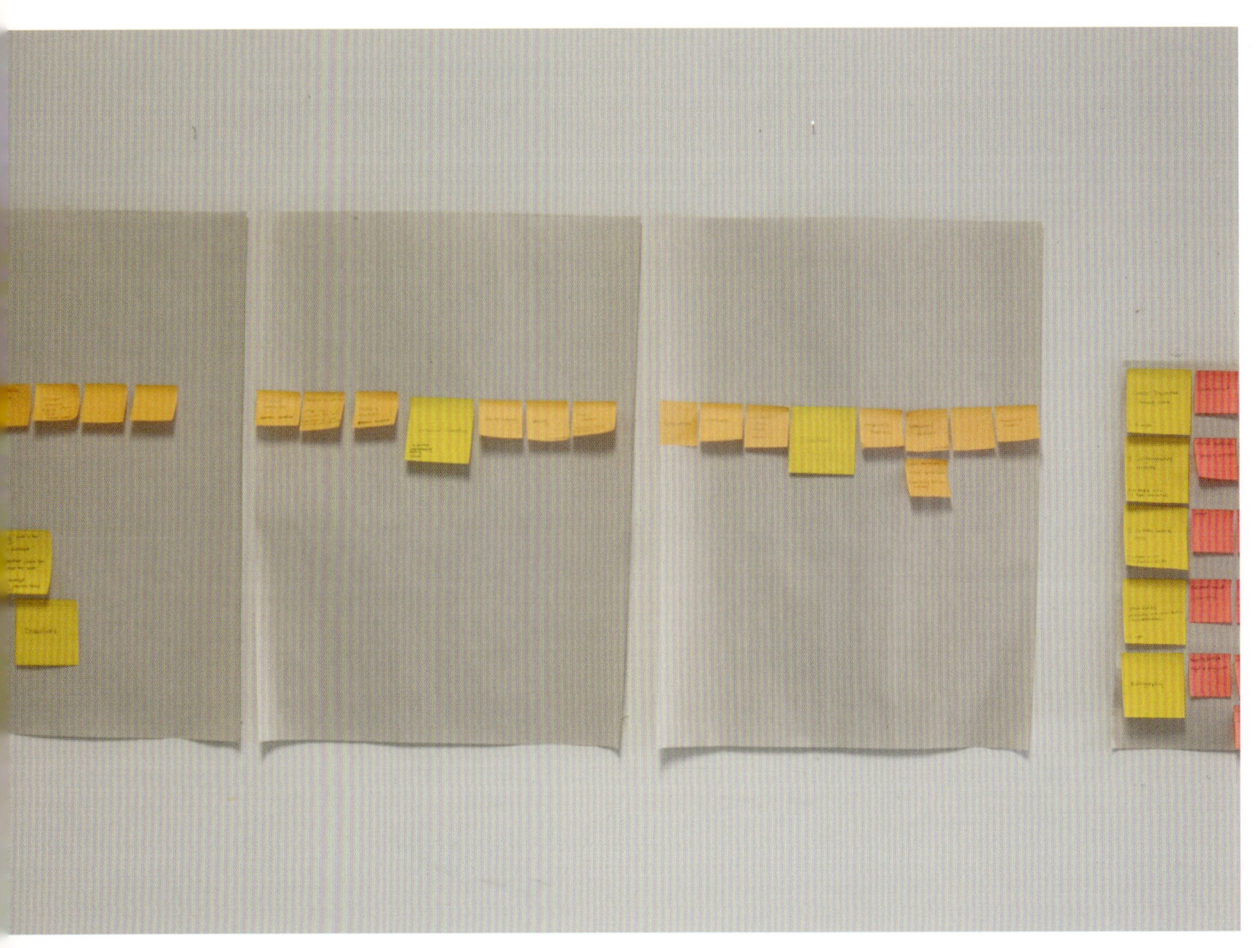

AMBEREEN SIDDIQUI, *MAPPING EXERCISE*, 2010

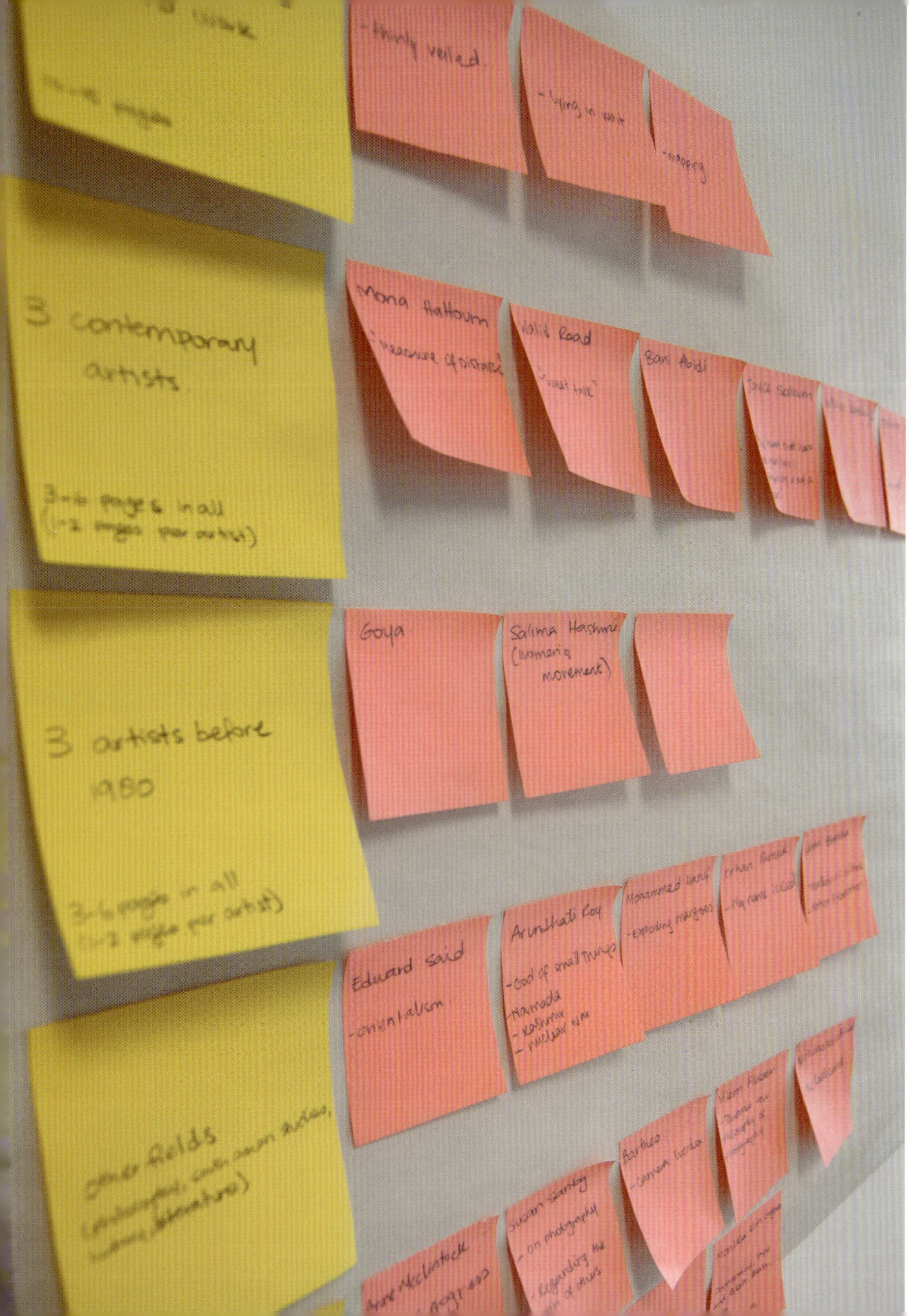

AMBEREEN SIDDIQUI, *MAPPING EXERCISE*, 2010

titles

titles vivify all to me...[151] EVA HESSE

Titles can be an important part of a work, affecting its meaning and responses to it. They can bring into focus, making more specific what the work is supposed to be about.

How do you assign titles to your work?

Jot down three possible titles for one of your works. Explain simply and directly why you chose each of these three titles and how they affect the work's meaning in different ways.

Measuring Niagara with a Teaspoon, 1997

TITLE OF A WORK BY ENGLISH SCULPTOR AND INSTALLATION ARTIST CORNELIA PARKER

151 Eva Hesse. In *Eva Hesse: A Retrospective*, eds. Lesley K. Baier, Maurice Berger, and Helen A. Cooper (New Haven, CT: Yale University Press, 1992), 17.

titles are hints

titles have suggestive power

titles are provocative

titles are bait

titles can corral

titles hold secrets

titles are punch lines

titles stimulate the imagination

titles offer a handhold on a work

titles are part of the fiction of a work

titles put an object into a new context

titles complete the sensibility of a work

titles anchor meaning

titles can be entire works

inventive grouping

Every object well contemplated creates a new organ of sight.[152]
JOHANN WOLFGANG VON GOETHE

Project

Write an extended label (350 words) for a hypothetical installation that pairs one of your works with that of another artist or designer found in a museum of your choice.

Inspired by Pierre Schneider's *Louvre Dialogues* (1971), Michael Kimmelman, chief art critic for the *New York Times*, published *Portraits: Talking with Artists* (1998), a collection of interviews he conducted with eighteen contemporary artists in celebrated museums around the world.[153] Kimmelman's interviews offer rich insights into what these artists chose to look at, as well as the relevance of past art to their current studio practice.

Begin by developing a visual and verbal sketch of the work of another artist in a museum. Palestinian artist Mona Hatoum says, "We relate to the world through our senses. ... Meanings, connotations and associations come after the initial physical experience as your imagination, intellect, psyche are fired off by what you've seen."[154] Write down a question that arises as you look at the work. Note the formal and poetic parallels that you are aware of between your work and this object.

The Extended Label

Imagine that a curator from the museum has asked you to create an installation that places one of your works alongside the selected museum object. In order for this display to have relevance for museum visitors, you must write a 350-word detailed label that brings to life, with clarity, the reasons for this inventive grouping. Explain why you picked this work and why it has significance and meaning for you. Allow viewers to see with fresh eyes—your eyes—the specifics of the inspirational connection.

Employ appropriate conventions for labeling. Include information about the work of the selected artist and your own work.

152 Johann Wolfgang von Goethe, *Theory of Colors* (London: John Murray, 1840).

153 Michael Kimmelman, *Portraits: Talking with Artists at the Met, The Modern, The Louvre and Elsewhere* (New York: Random House, 1988).

154 Michael Archer, Guy Brett, and Catherine de Zegher, *Mona Hatoum* (London: Phaidon Press Limited, 1997), 8.

155 From thesis writing exercise, Anjali Srinivasan, RISD, January 2007.

Jim Hodges
Somewhere between Here and There, 2001

Mirror on canvas, 6' x 48"

Anjali Srinivasan
Here and There all at once, 2007

Mirrored blown glass on silicone, air pump, capacitance sensor. Basic stamp program interface, 6' x 24"

Somewhere between Here and There is a "mirror painting" by Jim Hodges. The large mosaic is made of small rectilinear mirror shards, laboriously cobbled together. Reflection of light transforms your, the viewer's, image on canvas. In return, the canvas becomes an object that is transformed constantly. As you see yourself pixilated and dissolving in the work, the distance between you and the painting becomes a medium of both loss and transcendence.

Anjali Srinivasan's *Here and There all at once* is composed of myriad mirror fragments, each convex and irregularly shaped. Reflection of light in this work converts the singular images of your presence into innumerable mite-sized images—one on each shard to be exact. When the hypnotic pattern generated by your images causes a closer examination of the full-length mirror-sized work, *Here and There all at once* inhales and exhales your silhouette. By breathing back at you, your reflection transforms into a responsive alter ego.

Both artists explore reflection as creation using similar media and form. The works, however, function differently. Using the metaphor of skin, *Here and There all at once* asks the viewer to consider that to reflect (upon) something is to respond, to act. Using the metaphor of shimmering light-on-water, *Somewhere between Here and There* presents reflection as a new relationship between you and the immediate environment. Hodges' work relies on dissolution of image for loss and transcendence while Srinivasan's work uses reincarnation to do the same. Unlike *Somewhere between Here and There*, where "distance" is a key medium, *Here and There all at once* asks you to bridge the physical distance.

This pairing of seemingly similar works makes apparent the subtle shifts that interest each artist within a common theme and enable us to see the world lending generously to poetic re-creation.[155]

ANJALI SRINIVASAN, GLASS ARTIST

to the editor (or author)

Write a letter of response to an article featured in a contemporary journal relevant to your field.

Select a contemporary periodical relevant to your field, for example, *Art in America, Artforum, cabinet, Ceramics Monthly, e-flux journal, eye, Frame, FX, grafik, Landscape Journal, Leonardo, Metropolis, Ornament, Surface.*

Choose an article from a recent issue that connects to your visual search. Carefully read the article and make notes.

Now compose a short (500 words) letter to the editor that tells him or her what you think of the ideas in the article. By shaping your point of view for publication, you are putting your thoughts into action in the community. Begin your response by writing a brief recapitulation of what you have read.

 From thesis writing exercise, Jessica Roundy, RISD, Fall 2010. Jessica submitted her response to *Metropolis* where it was accepted for publication.

"By using a systems approach that links the building process, site, materials, aesthetics, and function together, the LBC is a holistic take on sustainability."

A Shining Example

FROM JESSICA ROUNDY;

I applaud *Metropolis* for its coverage of the Living Building Challenge ("Radical Green," by Suzanne LaBarre, October 2009, p. 98). LaBarre successfully introduces the LBC by way of the Omega Center for Sustainable Living at the Omega Institute for Holistic Studies. Her description of the building as it relates to the mission of the nonprofit illustrates the greater principles behind the Cascadia Region Green Building Council's prerequisites for truly sustainable and regenerative design. The Omega Institute's mission of awakening the best in the human spirit emphasizes health, a connection to place, and an appreciation of aesthetics. These principles set the LBC apart from LEED certification. By using a systems approach that links all aspects of the building process, site, materials, aesthetics, and function together, the LBC is a more holistic take on sustainability. The new LBC (version 2.0) expands this thinking into other forms of design, beyond built structures, to include site and community design.

The graphic representation of the LBC (p. 102) clearly demonstrates the Cascadia Region Green Building Council's underlying principles. Rather than breaking the 16 design rules into six categories, as LEED does, the version of the Challenge published in *Metropolis* weighs all rules equally. I encourage the magazine to delve further into this commentary as the LBC 2.0 is implemented and both the Omega Center for Sustainable Living and Washington University's Tyson Living Learning Center are evaluated for certification. The design community can learn a great deal from the Cascadia Region Green Building Council's ambitions and the case studies that have risen to meet their challenge.[156]

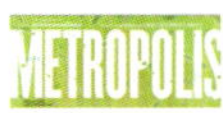

blog post as extended artist statement

Contribute a 1000-word essay to a blog that explains what your work is about.

This assignment is intended to conjure a relevant context within which to present your voice. Writing directly to a community of critical thinkers (your professional peers), you will communicate the framework of your creative and intellectual processes in a manner that is a clear, concrete, engaged, and thorough. For this commentary, you must know your arguments and back your claims.

Assume a straightforward presentation.

Begin by outlining your concept—the umbrella idea or issue.

Explain your key motivation for undertaking this course of exploration.

Perhaps reveal the questions that you ask yourself as you make.

What tools and means have you used to approach your subject? Explain your research methods; for example, if your work is more content or scholarly driven, have you relied on fieldwork, interviews, book reading, archival sources?

Show it. Using three projects as examples, show the development of your concept. Include images of actual work and captions.

Make explicit how other historical and contemporary artworks relate to your work.

Finally, within your definition of your discipline, explain what your work delivers to the field. What are the pragmatic and social implications of the work?

Since this is a content-driven blog, under *Bibliographic References & Notes,* offer relevant documentation. Under *Subject*, include research subjects and/or key terms.

Publish

the displayed + preserved work

Leaving a practical record with a museum or gallery about how your work is made and assembled as well as intentions for display and conservation will aid others in handling your work, installing it, and storing it.

Make a drawing with proper architectural details that describes the accurate and safe installation of your work.

Write a description that outlines the preservation and storage of your work.

PHOTO WARREN SEELIG

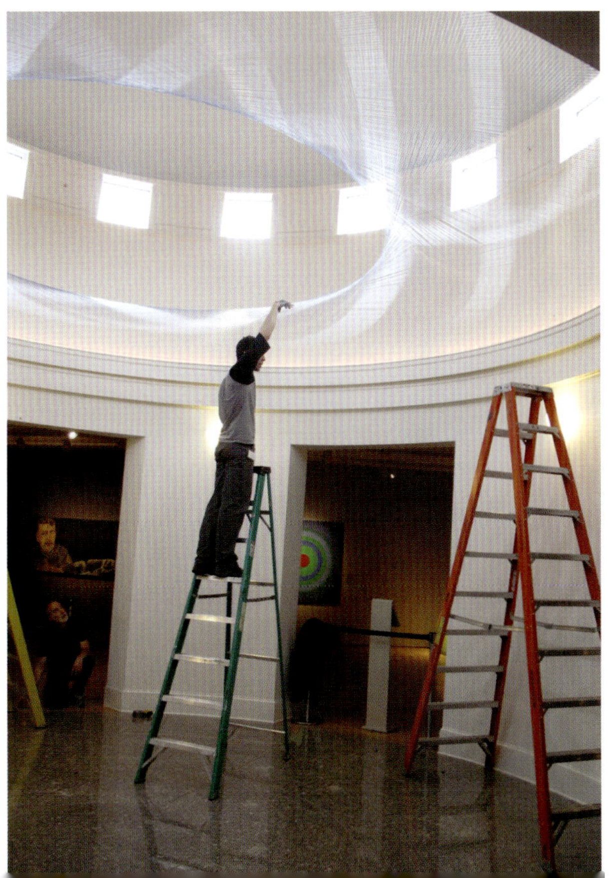

Exhibition: Four in Maine: Site Specific / Summer 2010
Location: Rotunda/ Farnsworth Art Museum, Rockland, Maine
Dimensions: 28' diameter x 1/4" thick
Material: 60 pound aqua nylon monofilament
Lighting: variable through clerestory overhead over 24 hours
The work remains in place waiting for time lapse photo documentary over 24 hour period of full moon.

your philosophy + teaching strategy

Project

Write a statement (four paragraphs) that announces the theme of your work and weaves together your personal artistic philosophy, your personal artwork, and your teaching philosophy, including a class you would teach if given the opportunity.

As an artist, teacher, and thinker offer a clear view into your work and philosophy. Be succinct. Personalize it. What matters to *you*? What drives *you* as an artist?

Once you have written your philosophy, read it to a friend. Ask him or her if your thoughts are developed clearly. Does one thought follow logically after the other? Do you sound convincing, inspiring?

157 From writing exercise, Brannin Buehner, Wheaton College, Spring 2006.

The Speed of Life

I am from rural Maine, a place of tranquility, isolated from metropolitan sprawl. I appreciate silence and a more meditative way of life that is tuned to the rhythms of nature. As a woodworker, I appreciate the time it takes for trees to grow. As a blacksmith each swing of the hammer is like a tick of a clock, timing a long, slow process. As a photographer I am compelled to document our society's overwrought speed of life.

In a film assembled from still images, I map the movement of this frenetic pace. The split second succession of images creates a rhythm that reflects the blind, insatiable consumption of American culture. As a counterpoint to this assault of hectic graphics, I construct a meditative bench, memorializing a dead cedar. The twisted roots of steel I blacksmith are burned black legs that support a blood red tree. The bench is a quiet place of contemplation that contrasts the mechanized churning of modern society captured in the film.

My workshop for children raises an awareness of optics, the behavior of light, and of images produced from time-lapse photography. Long exposure collaborative light drawings and pinhole photographs teach students to become more conscious of movement and energy, as well as stillness and slow time. This parallels explorations in my own studio work.

My film and bench are a reaction against the reckless over-development of our landscape. We obliviously squander our natural resources. The frantic tempo of our everyday lives dulls our imagination. My workshop inspires students to slow down, think, and imaginatively respond artistically and actively.[157]

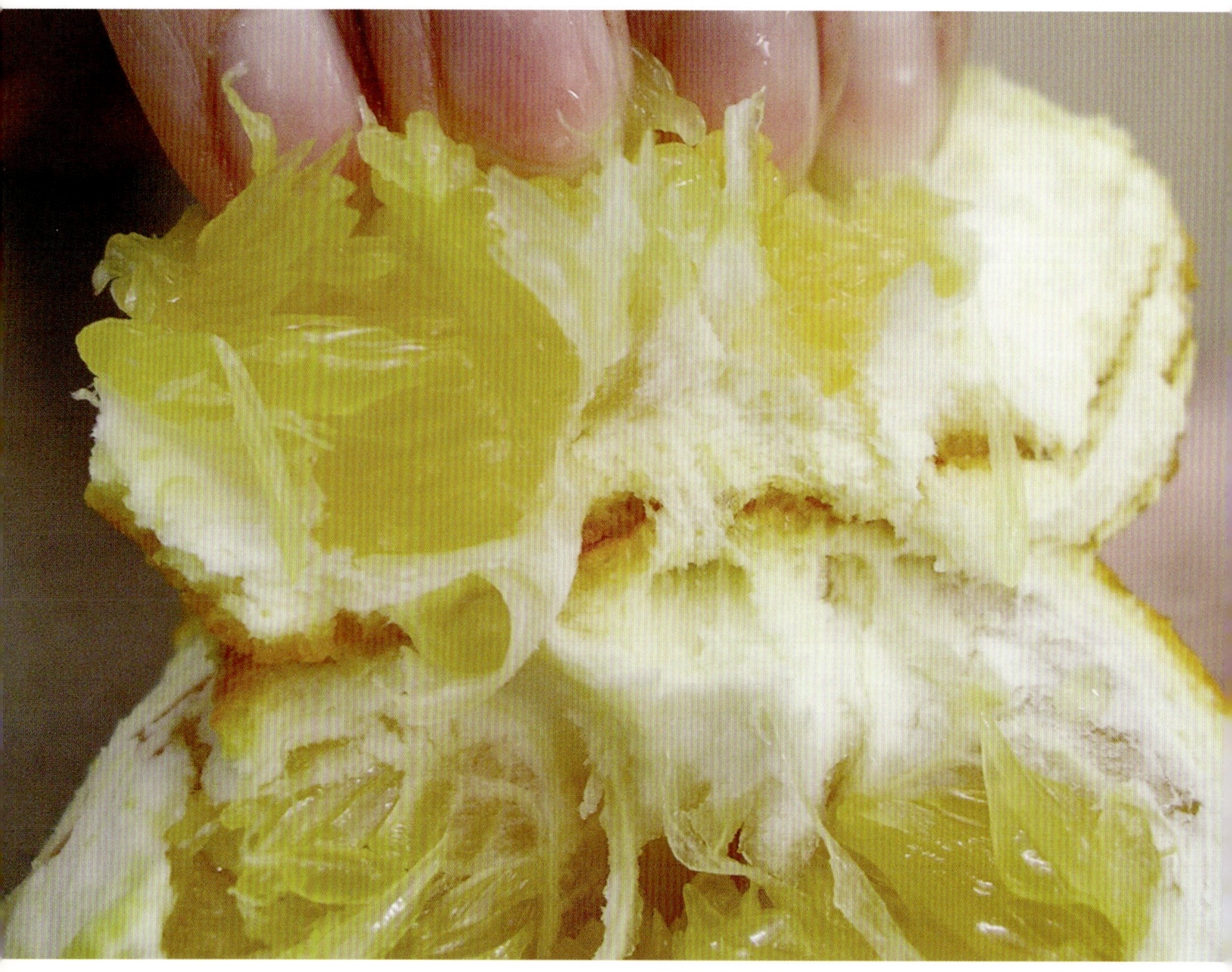

PHOTO STEPHANIE GREY

living on a diet of the work

Write a memo to a young artist that offers your point of view on art or design. Think of this as passed down knowledge or insight.

 From thesis writing exercise, Astrid Al Mkhaafy, RISD, Fall 2004.

You Are What You Make

Life is too short to become totally routinized. There are magical moments ready to be experienced at every turn. Stop projecting always into the future. Sometimes it's important to slow down, and really focus on where you are at, and sometimes it's even more important to do this with other people. To collaborate is breaking routine. Come together for a brief moment of intense playfulness.

We are driven people—by profession. We live from deadline to deadline, we organize vast collections of data, and we orchestrate projects and people. We synthesize cultures into compact messages. We work, most often alone in our heads or on a computer. One of our great challenges is in engaging with others. Even more so in unpredictable settings. It is too easy when we are limited with time—and challenged with multiple projects and unpredictable hurdles—to let what can be routinized become static. This becomes a fossilized life.

Remember never to let your gusto and eccentricity become undernourished. Remember to gravitate towards kindred spirits. Remember to laugh and let down your façade. Remember to let labels act as layers—not to trap yourself or others in rigid definitions. Remember to be fluid. To be a shape shifter, to pop up where least expected, to surprise yourself and others by your ever changefulness.

Travel. Far and wide and alone. Put yourself in situations that are foreign to you. Feel what it is to be alone, new, fresh, and awake. The more often you can test your boundaries, the more likely you are to redraw your map of self identity. Grow. Delight in newness. And share your journeys with those who care.

If you feel others are limiting your creativity, don't invite them to play again. Or invite them over and over and hope they mellow out. Do not change for them. Do not limit yourself. This is your life.

It's short. Make what you are and live what you make.[158]

manifesto, or words to live for

Write a manifesto.

As a gesture of self-definition and self-advocacy, and as a means of working out the tenets of a practice, positioning the work, energizing it, and establishing a point of view, write a short manifesto.

As we engage the high-spirited form of the manifesto, we participate in a long tradition of artistic declaration, among them Edvard Munch's *The St. Cloud Manifesto* (1889), Umberto Boccioni's *Manifesto of the Futuristic Painters* (1910), Naum Gabo and Antoine Pevsner's *Realist Manifesto* (1930), Lucio Fontana, *Manifesto of Spatialist Art* (1951), Yves Klein's, *The Chelsea Manifesto* (1961). Many artists—especially the modernists—worked out their ideological stance using the form of the manifesto. The manifesto is generally a document of dramatic assertion. It is often opposed to something. It is loud—a shout. Know that the strident manifesto (I assert), may begin as a personal creative credo (I believe), and eventually turn into a public charter or mission statement (I wish to institute this agenda).[159]

While the manifesto thrived amid "isms," which have largely disappeared in postmodern times, the practice of writing a manifesto is an opportunity to develop a statement of extravagant self-assurance that invites others into your way of thinking. It may be the first step in working out an artistic philosophy.

What gets you out of bed in the morning? What drives you to make the work that you make? What is your artistic urgency? Convince your audience of the tenets of your practice with optimism.

159 See Mary Ann Caws, ed., *Manifesto: A Century of Isms* (Lincoln: University of Nebraska Press, 2002), xx-xxxix.

160 Conditional Design, last accessed December 16, 2010, http://www.conditionaldesign.org/pages/about-us/

Conditional Design is a method/mentality/approach.

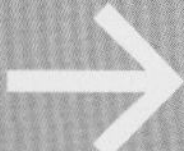

A manifesto for artists and designers by Luna Maurer, Edo Paulus, Jonathan Puckey, and Roel Wouters.

Through the influence of the media and technology on our world, our lives are increasingly characterized by speed and constant change. We live in a dynamic, data-driven society that is continually sparking new forms of human interaction and social contexts. Instead of romanticizing the past, we want to adapt our way of working to coincide with these developments, and we want our work to reflect the here and now. We want to embrace the complexity of this landscape, deliver insight into it and show both its beauty and its shortcomings.

Our work focuses on processes rather than products: things that adapt to their environment, emphasize change and show difference. Instead of operating under the terms of Graphic Design, Interaction Design, Media Art or Sound Design, we want to introduce Conditional Design as a term that refers to our approach rather than our chosen media. We conduct our activities using the methods of philosophers, engineers, inventors, and mystics.[160]

>>

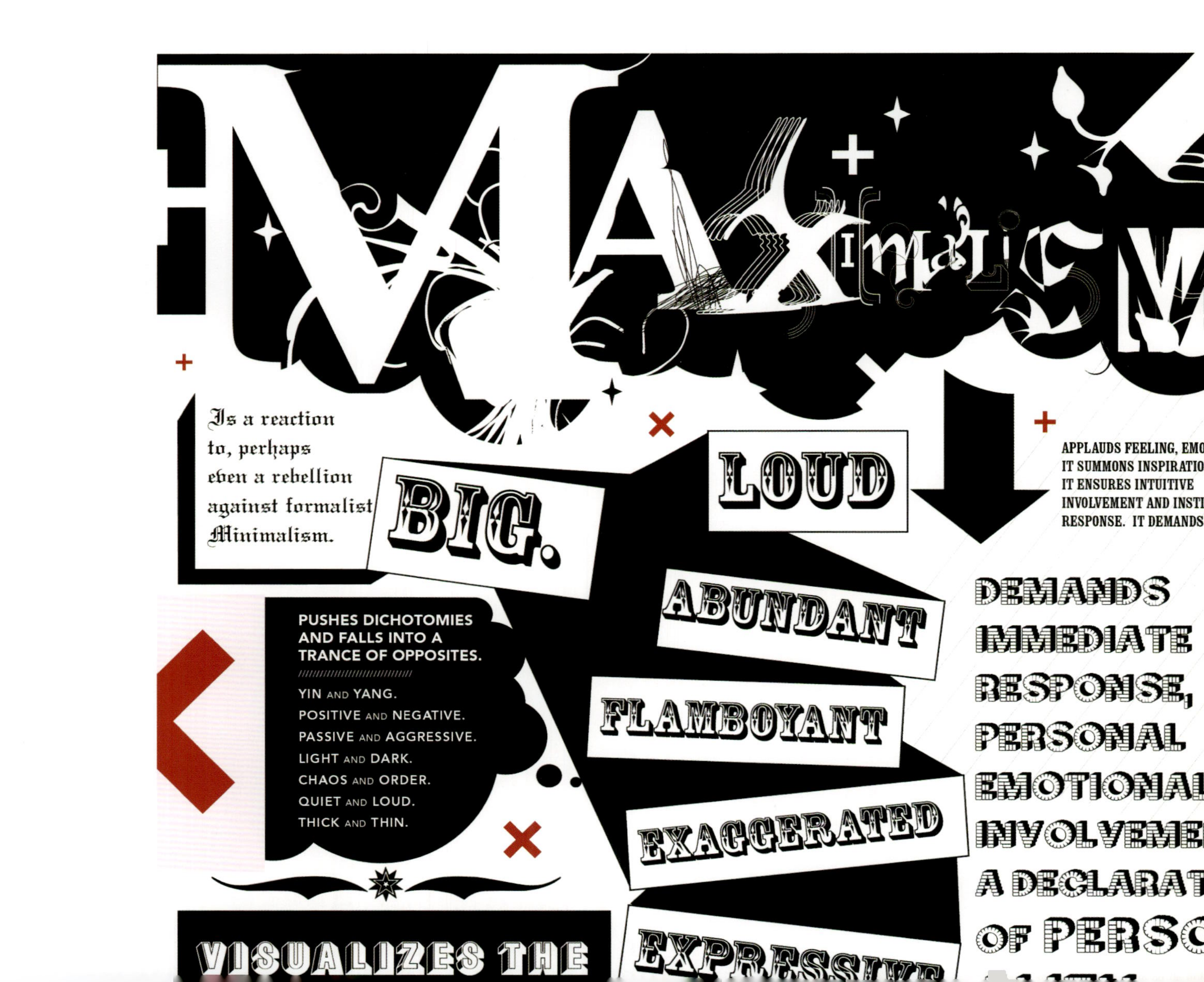

MAXIMALISM
Is a reaction to, perhaps even a rebellion against formalist Minimalism.
BIG.
LOUD
ABUNDANT
FLAMBOYANT
EXAGGERATED
EXPRESSIVE
APPLAUDS FEELING, EMOTIO
IT SUMMONS INSPIRATION.
IT ENSURES INTUITIVE
INVOLVEMENT AND INSTINCT
RESPONSE. IT DEMANDS HON
DEMANDS
IMMEDIATE
RESPONSE,
PERSONAL
EMOTIONAL
INVOLVEMEN
A DECLARATI
OF PERSO
PUSHES DICHOTOMIES AND FALLS INTO A TRANCE OF OPPOSITES.
YIN AND YANG.
POSITIVE AND NEGATIVE.
PASSIVE AND AGGRESSIVE.
LIGHT AND DARK.
CHAOS AND ORDER.
QUIET AND LOUD.
THICK AND THIN.
VISUALIZES THE

OF OUR CULTURE IT
TRAPS THE
NOISE OF OUR
CULTURE
IN A BOTTLE
AND TAKES A CLOSE
LOOK AT IT.

BARRIERS OF AGE,
CLASS, GENDER, AND
DEMOGRAPHICS BY
AIMING TO STIMULATE
THE SOUL.

inflates. But it does so by playing
fine line between refinement and
It plays with pattern, scale, multit
and magnitude to evoke trance.

IS INSPIRED BY AND
CELEBRATES AMERICA'S
CULTURAL INTOXIFICATION
WITH EXCESS. IT FEEDS
ON THE SENSIBILITY OF
OVERLOAD AND INFLATION

DEMANDS A SENSE
OF RECKLESSNESS,
SPONTANEITY, AND
A WILLINGNESS TO
BREAK THE RULES.

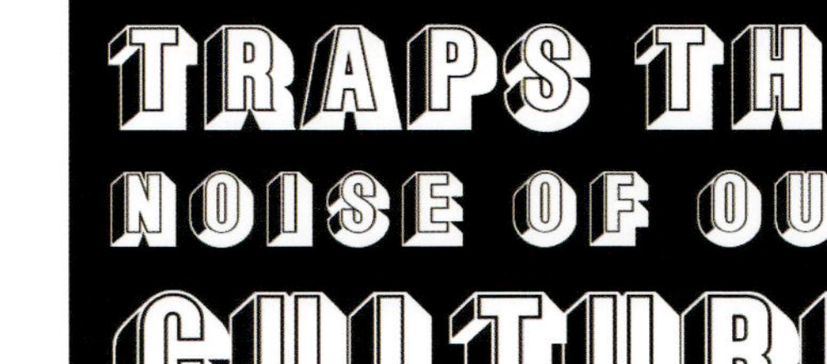

Pushes color to create TEXTURE and ACTION. Lots of action, through vibrating COLOR and overloads of bold PIGMENT.

MINES THE BASIC PREMISES OF DESIRE
AND ATTEMPTS TO DISCOVER WHY WE
EXAGGERATE OURSELVES AND
SURROUNDINGS TO EXUDE IMPACT.

CLARA SIMS, *E UNIBUS PLURUM*, 2007

for immediate release

Project: A Sales Pitch for Your Work.

As a way to keep the public in your head, write a short press release about an upcoming exhibition of your latest work.

What would you choose to say if you were to announce your work to the public?

Link the reader to the who, the what, the where, the why, the when.

Remember: While there is room for a small degree of self-promotion or embellishment, there is no room for empty adjectives. Each word must count.

161 Jessica Tomlinson, Director of Public Relations, Maine College of Art, 2009.

MAINE COLLEGE OF ART
522 CONGRESS STREET
PORTLAND, MAINE 04101

MECA Freshmen Address Maine Hunger Crisis

More than 100 first year students at Maine College of Art have participated in a unique freshman experience that has resulted in an exhibition called Food, Hunger, Justice. As part of a new curriculum called FY-In that has a service learning component, students have spent their first semester researching the food crisis in Maine. In response, they have volunteered on local farms, created artwork and will use the proceeds from art sales to provide food for low-income senior citizens in Portland.

Students partnered with Cultivating Community to visit their urban and suburban farms: Turkey Hill Farm, Boyd Street Urban Farm and Oxford Street garden. During these visits, students harvested food, put gardens to bed, moved rocks and assisted with farm chores.

Based on their academic study and on-site experiences, students created artwork that reflected their learnings. These original works includes prints, painting, drawings, photographs, t-shirts, mixed media and videos. Their goal is to use artwork to raise awareness about the pending food crisis in Maine. The work will be on view from November 19 to December 6 throughout Portland at Maine College of Art at 522 Congress Street, Aurora Provisions at 64 Pine Street, Rabelais Books at 86 Middle Street and Local 188 at 685 Congress Street. Proceeds from the sale of student work benefit the Elder Share fund of Cultivating Community, which delivers a weekly bag of produce to seniors living in one of three low-income housing in Portland.[161]

abstract as convergent process

Writing an abstract is a convergent process. It will summarize and cohere your new body of writing about your work. We generally submit abstracts for conference proceedings where we must outline the nature of a paper we will present. If you are writing a graduate thesis, you will be asked to briefly summarize the nature of your work and provide an overview of the contents of your inquiry.

An abstract is an original piece of writing—a succinct and powerful stand-alone passage. It demonstrates a clear grasp of the contents of your writing in abbreviated form and if about published writing, aids researchers searching on databases. An abstract is 250 to 300 words in length. It should express your fundamental ideas, research, and methodology. A list of keywords is useful. Remember that your focus must be sharp to bring an integration of your ideas forward as public declaration.

Write a 250–300 word abstract.

Why would another researcher or artist be interested in your work?

What are the most important aspects of your work?

What are the subjects you have explored?

What are the main points in your writing?

Summarize these points in one sentence, if possible.

What is your title?

Revise often to correct weaknesses in organization; improve transitions from point to point; drop unnecessary information; add important but previously omitted information; and eliminate wordiness.

ARABISH

With the influx of foreign cultures and economic globalization, the United Arab Emirates (UAE) is undergoing a major identity transformation. While many feel the threat of this transformation on the Emirati identity, some use it as an inevitable process to be embraced.

I believe that the UAE is not losing its identity, it is creating a vivid new one. This new identity is Arabish. Arabish, initially known as a hybrid form of text messaging—where Latin characters are used to replace Arabic pronunciation—is now more than just that. It is a way of speaking and a way of life, especially for Emirati youth.

As a designer, I address this emerging Arabish culture from a personal and global perspective. Graphic design is a powerful method of research and communication. I use it as a means to comment on hybrid cultural elements—dress, language, and urban landscape. It is my vehicle, helping me and others better understand the UAE identity and its emerging Arabish culture.[162]

162 From thesis writing exercise, Salem Al-Qassimi, RISD, Spring 2011.

graphic inspiration

If you have aspirations to publish, it is important that you find the appropriate structure to relate word to image, balancing textual material with a visual experience.

To design is much more than simply to assemble, to order, or even to edit: it is to add value and meaning, to illuminate, to simplify, to clarify, to modify, to dignify, to dramatize, to persuade, and perhaps even to amuse. To design is to transform prose into poetry. Design broadens perception, magnifies experience, and enhances vision. Design is the product of feeling and awareness, of ideas that originate in the mind of the designer, and culminate, one hopes, in the mind of the spectator.[163] PAUL RAND

Every semester I take my students to the Rhode Island School of Design Library to view artists' books selected from the Artists' Book Collection, which numbers over 1,200 volumes. I want them to see how artists conceive, design, and produce books that are complete artworks in themselves, so they can effectively visualize and present their own work as a printed document. I want them to see what can be done. We also view exhibition catalogues of artists' works and monographs that offer an overview of a corpus of work. I call this session the "sensations of reading," to borrow a title from an exhibition of artists' books I saw many years ago.[164] I like this title because it considers the practice of reading as intimate and pleasurable, one that brings the reader into a way of viewing the world that is full and sensorial. When we create a printed document, whether it is a promotional portfolio of our work, a residency proposal, a graduate thesis, or a limited edition book, we want to invite others to our forms of perception. We want our ideas to be felt and imaginable. As the philosopher Gaston Bachelard says, we want to "make the reader a poet on the level of the image."[165]

163 Paul Rand, *Design, Form, and Chaos* (New Haven, CT: Yale University Press, 1993), 3.

164 Tim Guest, *Sensations of Reading* (London: London Regional Art Gallery, 1984), 4.

165 Gaston Bachelard, *The Poetics of Space*, trans. Maria Jolas (Boston: Beacon Press, 1994), xxv.

166 From thesis writing exercise, Chelsea Green, RISD, Fall 2007.

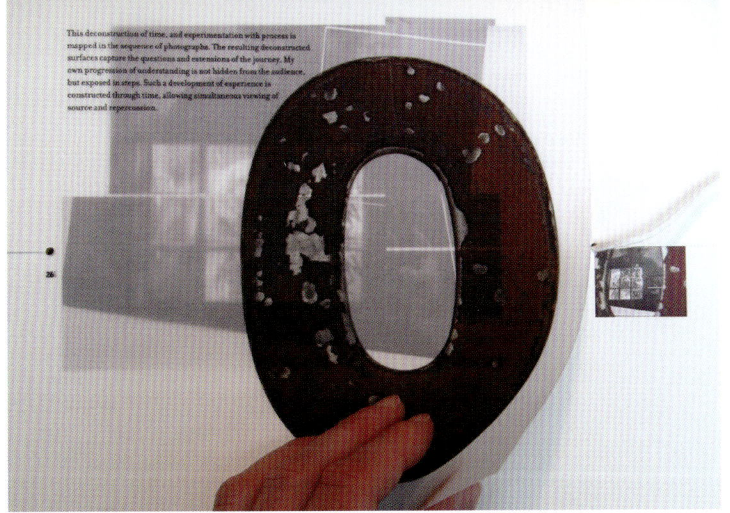

KELLY SALCHOW MACARTHUR, *FROM EXPERIENCE TO CONSTRUCTION: FOCUSING, EXPANDING AND ROTATING THE LENS OF AWARENESS*, 2003

Creating a printed document that conveys images and ideas in book form is a means of showing and telling. For this, we can invent the reading experience and define the proper show versus tell balance. We are allowed to come up with new formats, new ways to connect the reader to the visual and conceptual ground of our work. By carefully considering the design layout we can ensure the integrity of our message. How our images integrate with our written text is important. Careful consideration of the structure and material components can further the concept and create interest.

All of these elements tell a story, carrying and connecting our voice to our readers. The scale and character of type and how typography can be used to render voice is just as much visual as verbal. Different qualities of paper and uses of materials, page size, as well as the rhythm of layout and text and image, if treated together, reinforce one another. The beauty of varied texts, sequencing, pacing, pauses in the text, the role of blank space, layering, and transparency modifies dialogue across pages. Bindings ensure ease of readability and the survivability of a book over time.

Step One
Find a model that you will serve as graphic inspiration for the layout of your publication.

Step Two
Refine a layout from the *Pairing Words and Images* project, (p. 178), using this model to dictate graphic direction.

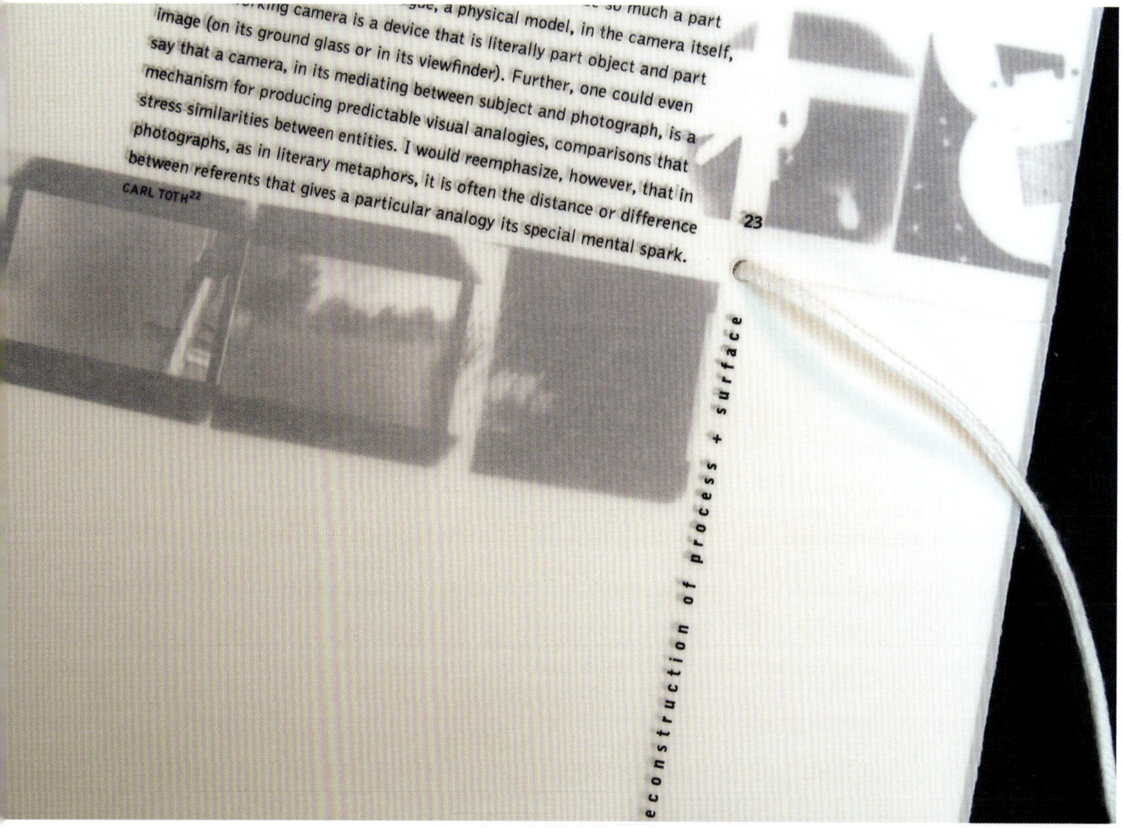

KELLY SALCHOW MACARTHUR, *FROM EXPERIENCE TO CONSTRUCTION: FOCUSING, EXPANDING AND ROTATING THE LENS OF AWARENESS*, 2003

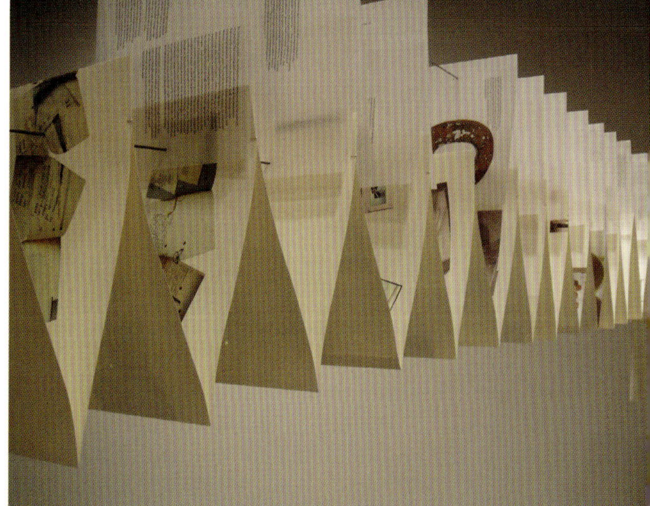

One reference I will be using as graphic inspiration is the book *Hella Jongerius* by Phaidon. The book, *Campanas*, by Estudio Campana and published by Editora Bookmark has also inspired me. I am going to try to keep it simple with lots of white space to create moments of pause. I would really like the final books to be a map of process to practice. I am hoping for it to be a living container for the content of each workshop as well as to invite or inspire further participation.[166]

say it! launch it!

> I admire open and closed forms, the pungency of colloquial idiom and the play of literary puns and allusions; evocative metaphor and dream abstraction; the disparate voices of the lyric cry, satiric jibe, conversational inflection, prophetic incantation. The house of poetry has many mansions.[167]
>
> ALICIA SUSKIN OSTRIKER

Creating a Fresh and Comprehensive Publication

Our final effort brings together and presents the results of the mapping process. We now become authors, which implies responsibility, voice, and action. Here we seek to embrace all previous raw material, moving it to a higher level of synthesis while offering it to others for consideration.

We want to ensure that our publication has aesthetic intelligibility, clarity, definition, and authority. It must be informative and experiential. It will be a fertile bed from which to pull out phrases for grant proposals, residency applications, or professional articles as well as define a path for growth, spurring future making. It serves as a manual, a book of ideas, a "gift that keeps on giving," as one student proudly remarked.

167 Alicia Suskin Ostriker, *Stealing the Language: The Emergence of Women's Poetry in America* (Ypsilanti, MI: Beacon Press, 1987), 18.

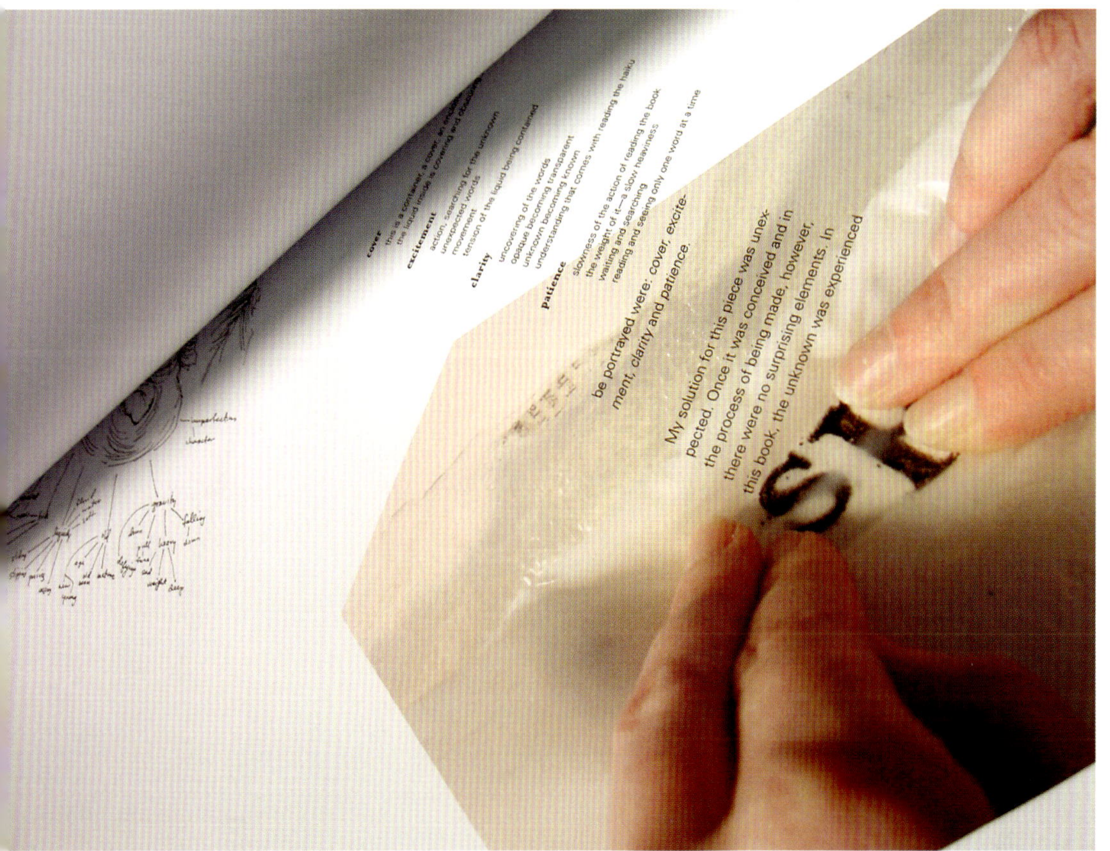

REBECCA KLEIN GANZ, *BALANCING IN THE BETWEEN*, 2003

Essentially we must tailor the design of our document to the tone and content of our material and conceptual inquiry. We present this communication as a map of complex interactions, which are personal, material, and conceptual. Process drawings, diagrams, photographs, insights, journal notations, interviews, questions, and other graphic descriptions may be presented within the explanatory text to give variety to the texture of the whole. Every element tells part of the story.

Return to your *Sharing the Blank Page* exercise for clues. Include quotations from your *Repository of Insight*. Pin down your terminology with a glossary of terms from your *Composite Map*. Include a haiku or a manifesto. Refer to notes from your *Research Spree* and study of precedents. Include critical responses developed in your *Inventive Grouping* or *Letter to the Editor (or Author)*. Bring as many examples forward as a means to "tell in full" a story of your own work and ideas. This is more than a private archive. Help the reader to truly understand your process. Coalesce the document so that projects speak to a coherent view.

>>

The Limited Edition Publication or Thesis Document

Step One: Exposition of Creative Process
As you create this final document, you might ask yourself:

Where did I start?

What does my process look like?

How can I allow others into my process?

What has my inquiry permitted me to say?

Who is my audience?

What are the factors that are important for someone to know?

What is integral to my message?

How can I make visible to others the connections that I have made?

How can I help a reader to look critically at my work?

Is there a way of evoking rather than showing?

If there were a sound track to my book, what would it be?

Remember: this is a "living document" that while comprehensive, is not fixed. The artist world is not a vacuum. It is iterative. It is intensely alive. You should never tire of shifting things around, reshaping the document. Every new idea may lead to an alteration of your map.

Books
Making and Breaking the Grid, A Graphic Design Layout Workshop, Timothy Samara

Thinking with Type, A Critical Guide for Designers, Writers, Editors, & Students, Ellen Lupton

Software Resources
Adobe InDesign
(best for page layouts)

Lynda.com
(online tutorials)

Self-Publishing
Lulu.com

Blurb.com

EditionOneBooks.com

Step Two: Graphic Layout
A considered use of text and image on the page holds the potential to add value and meaning to your publication or thesis document. Below are suggestions to help guide you. On the following pages you will find visual examples.

Negative space, or "white space" allows for a more comfortable reading experience and increases legibility. White space can also be used to tell the story of your work, creating moments of pause and particular points of focus.

A considered juxtaposition of words and images can draw out relationships and emphasize meaning.

Typographic hierarchy can help readers understand the structure of your content and guide a reader through your document. Hierarchy of information can be displayed in a number of ways through scale, weight, color, and alignment.

An underlying grid organizes elements on the page and provides an overall cohesiveness to your document.

Whether playful, quiet, or commanding, typography is used to express meaning and bring clarity to your artistic voice. Thoughtful consideration is given to choice of typeface, placement, scale, and texture.

The overall form of your document can also make a statement about its contents. If your book is being created through an online publisher you may follow a standard format that is provided to you and focus on graphic elements. If you have the opportunity to create your book by hand, you may consider the shape, materials, and structure of the book itself as a way for the reader to experience the content. Do pages fold out to make a particular statement? Which paper is most appropriate for your message? Is your book heavy, light, square, round, small and intimate, or oversized?

Step Three: Make a Dummy Book
Before you print your document, make a full-scale prototype. This will help bring clarity to the details before you create the final piece.

>>

WHITE SPACE

IMAGE JUXTAPOSITION

THESIS abstract

Design decisions, conditioned by culture and preconceptions, are often too trained and formula-driven, leading to convention and predictability. This thesis takes the position that, in our search for fulfilling design, a balancing act between control and disruption must be engaged. By loosening the limitations of control and embracing disruption, we invite the unpredictable and unexpected into our work. This thesis process navigates the space *between* intention and non-intention, *between* inside and outside, and *between* the known and the unknown as a break from conditioned response. The "between" is explored as a means to establish a connective harmony from an emerging, creative center.

01

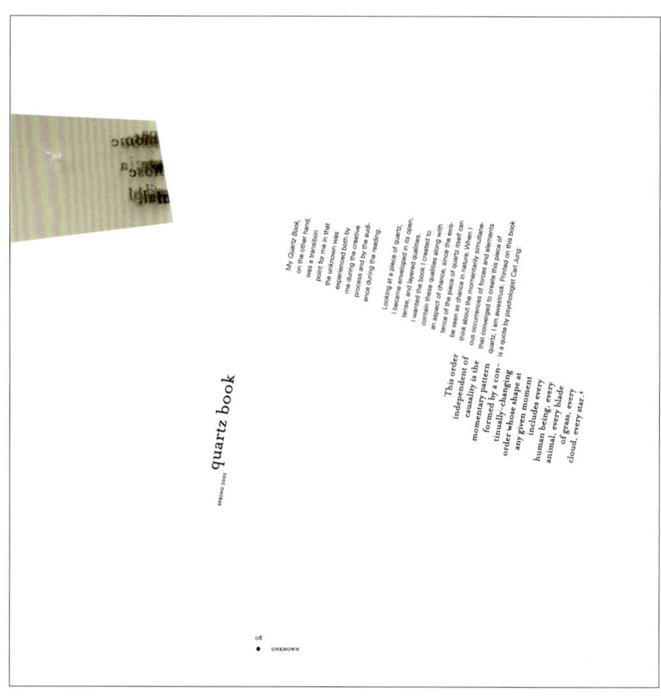

COMMUNICATING

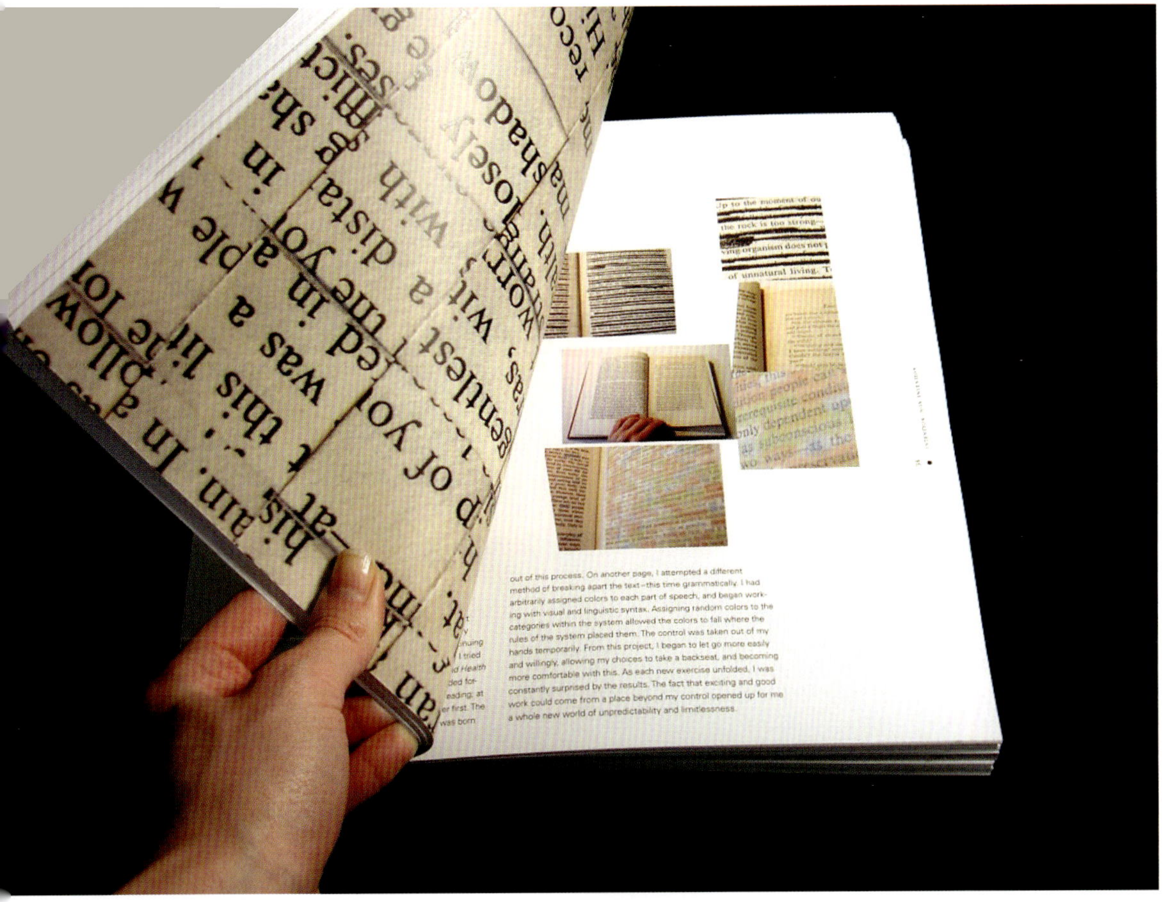

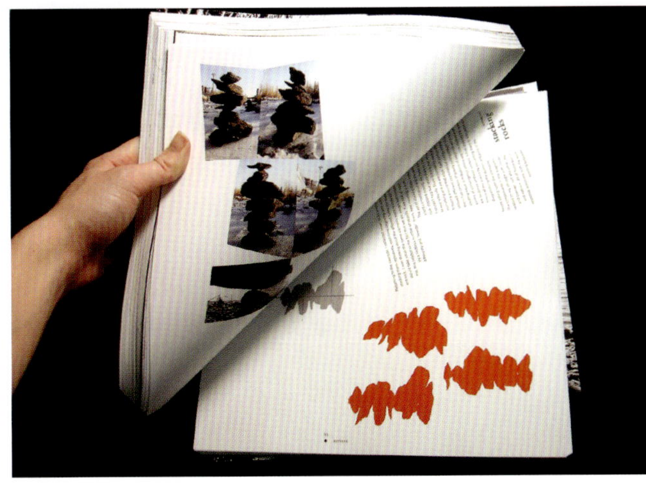

REBECCA KLEIN GANZ, *BALANCING IN THE BETWEEN*, 2003

TYPOGRAPHIC HIERARCHY

UNDERLYING GRID

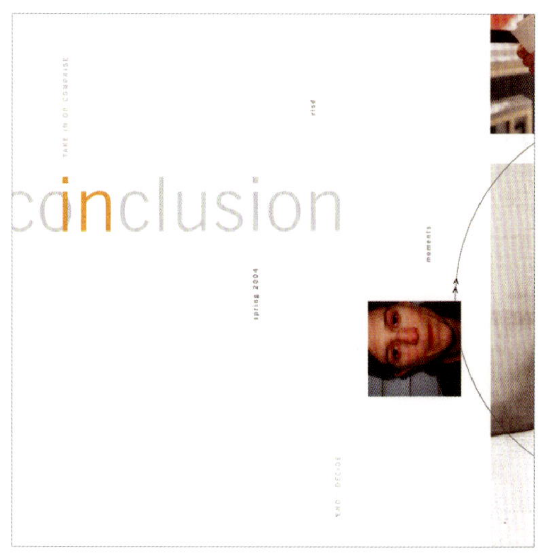

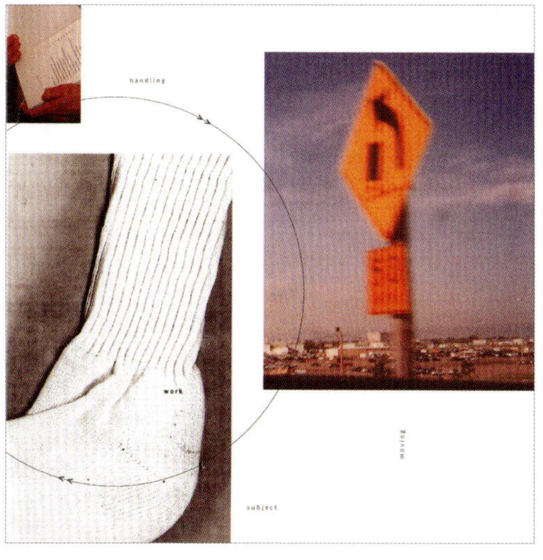

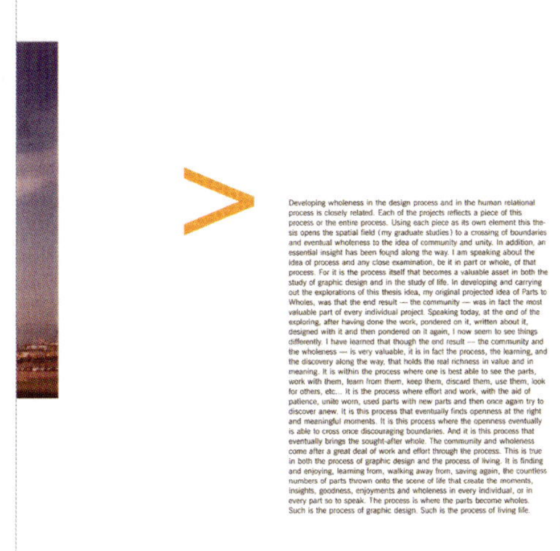

Developing wholeness in the design process and in the human relational process is closely related. Each of the projects reflects a piece of this process or the entire process. Using each piece as its own element this thesis opens the spatial field (my graduate studies) to a crossing of boundaries and eventual wholeness to the idea of community and unity. In addition, an essential insight has been found along the way. I am speaking about the idea of process and any close examination, be it in part or whole, of that process. For it is the process itself that becomes a valuable asset in both the study of graphic design and in the study of life. In developing and carrying out the explorations of this thesis idea, my original projected idea of Parts to Wholes, was that the end result — the community — was in fact the most valuable part of every individual project. Speaking today, at the end of the exploring, after having done the work, pondered on it, written about it, designed with it and then pondered on it again, I now seem to see things differently. I have learned that though the end result — the community and the wholeness — is very valuable, it is in fact the process, the learning, and the discovery along the way, that holds the real richness in value and in meaning. It is within the process where one is best able to see the parts, work with them, learn from them, keep them, discard them, use them, look for others, etc... It is the process where effort and work, with the aid of patience, unite worn, used parts with new parts and then once again try to discover anew. It is this process that eventually finds openness at the right and meaningful moments. It is this process where the openness eventually is able to cross once discouraging boundaries. And it is this process that eventually brings the sought-after whole. The community and wholeness come after a great deal of work and effort through the process. This is true in both the process of graphic design and the process of living. It is finding and enjoying, learning from, walking away from, saving again, the countless numbers of parts thrown onto the scene of life that create the moments, insights, goodness, enjoyments and wholeness in every individual, or in every part so to speak. The process is where the parts become wholes. Such is the process of graphic design. Such is the process of living life.

with + WATER

PROJECT TITLE Water with Hope
INSTRUCTOR Tom Ockerse
CLASS Graduate studio I
SEMESTER Fall 2002

HOPE

hope

This project was actually completed my first two months of graduate school. I have reserved it for the end because I found it very interesting to see that the process explored here was so closely related to what my end thesis project became. I had no idea it would be like this.

In short, we were asked to visually show what water was from the perspective of hope. I used elements of socks, laundry detergent, the color blue for water and the idea of hope. The medium was print. The interaction and crossing of these images or parts came into a new community because of the element of hope. This single part that could not be seen is the very element that allowed the parts to open themselves in relation to one another and to build connections and relationships that ended in strong visual examples of pieces working together and uniting in meaning. SEE EXAMPLES.

fall 2002

>>

TYPE AS VOICE

CONSIDERATION OF FORMAT AND MATERIALS

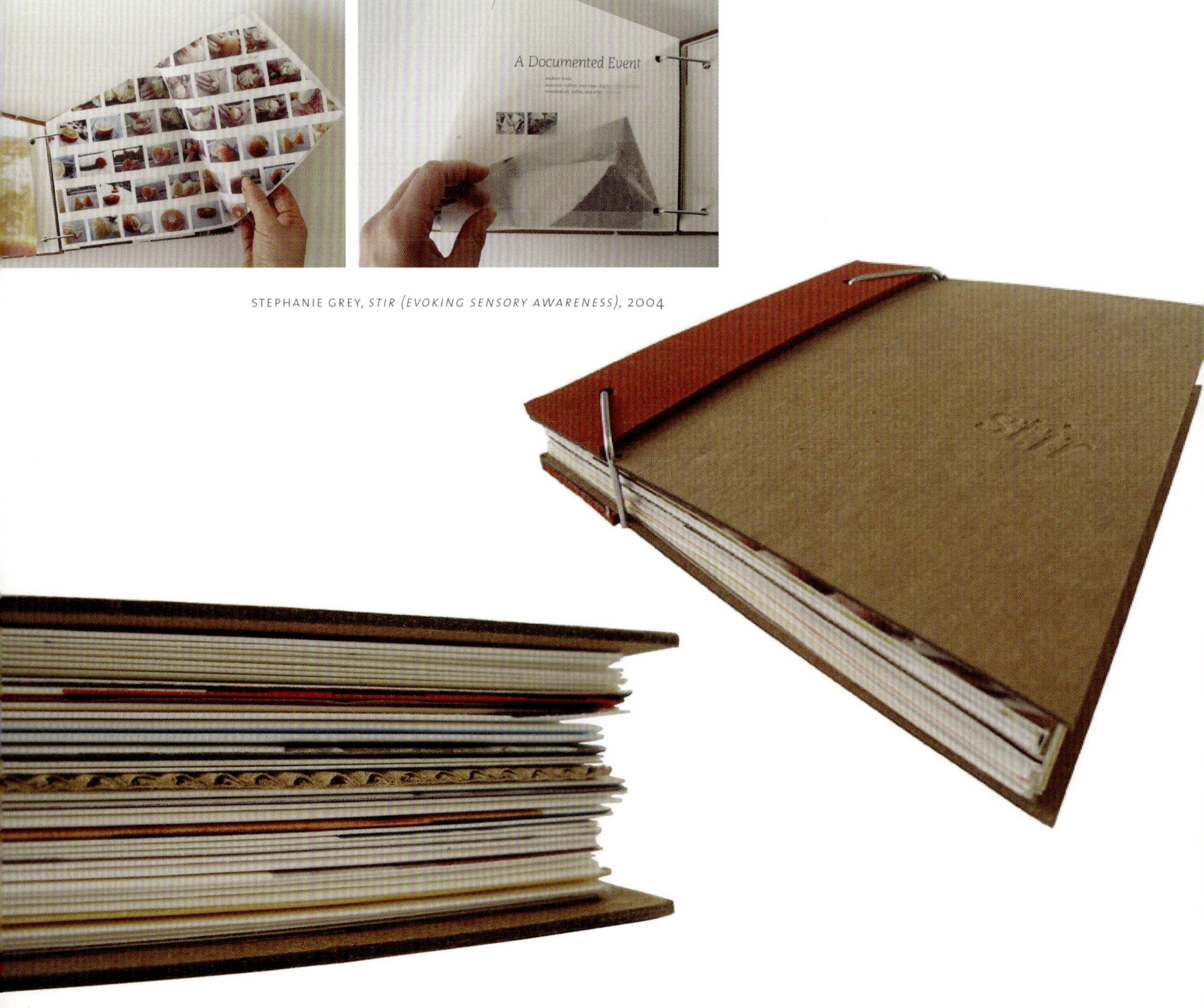

STEPHANIE GREY, *STIR (EVOKING SENSORY AWARENESS)*, 2004

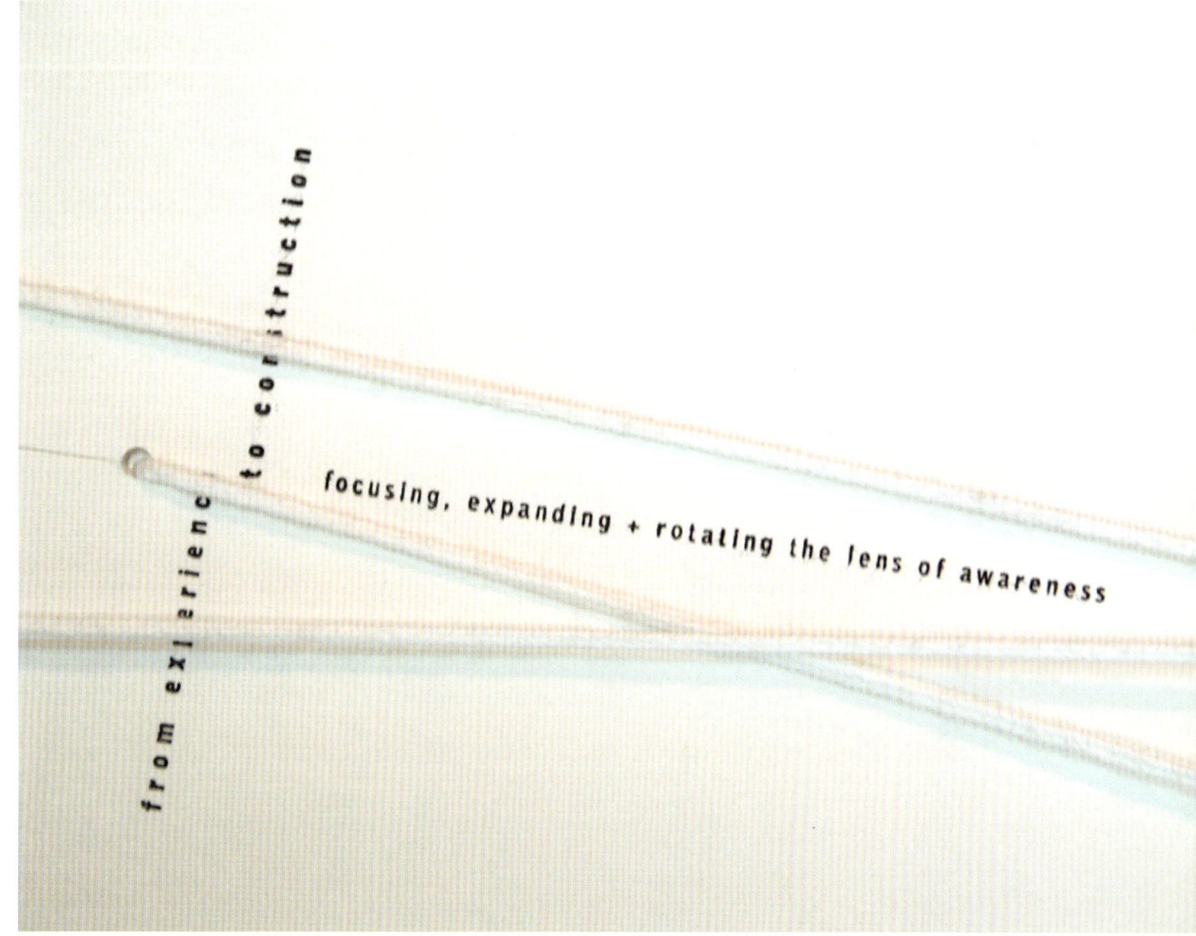

KELLY SALCHOW MACARTHUR, *FROM EXPERIENCE TO CONSTRUCTION: FOCUSING, EXPANDING AND ROTATING THE LENS OF AWARENESS*, 2003

leaving some things unsaid

If writing is thinking and discovery and selection and order and meaning, it is also awe and reverence and mystery and magic.[168]
TONI MORRISON

The process of explaining images and artistic process does not mean that we must fully redeem the ambiguity of the visual. Meaning and mystery are inseparable. There may be aspects of the work that will remain unavailable or are outside the scope of language. While direct communication and clarity are our goals, it is possible that within the layout of our text and images we can preserve rhythms of silence and complexity. Not all things need to be said to their completion. Not all answers are complete. Leave space for the reader's imagination to fill in the text.

Future Directions

What are some questions you still hope to ask through your work?

List areas and ideas still open for exploration.

168 Toni Morrison, "The Site of Memory," in *Out There: Marginalization and Contemporary Culture*, eds. Ferguson, Gever, Minh-ha, and West (Cambridge, MA: MIT Press, 1990), 302.

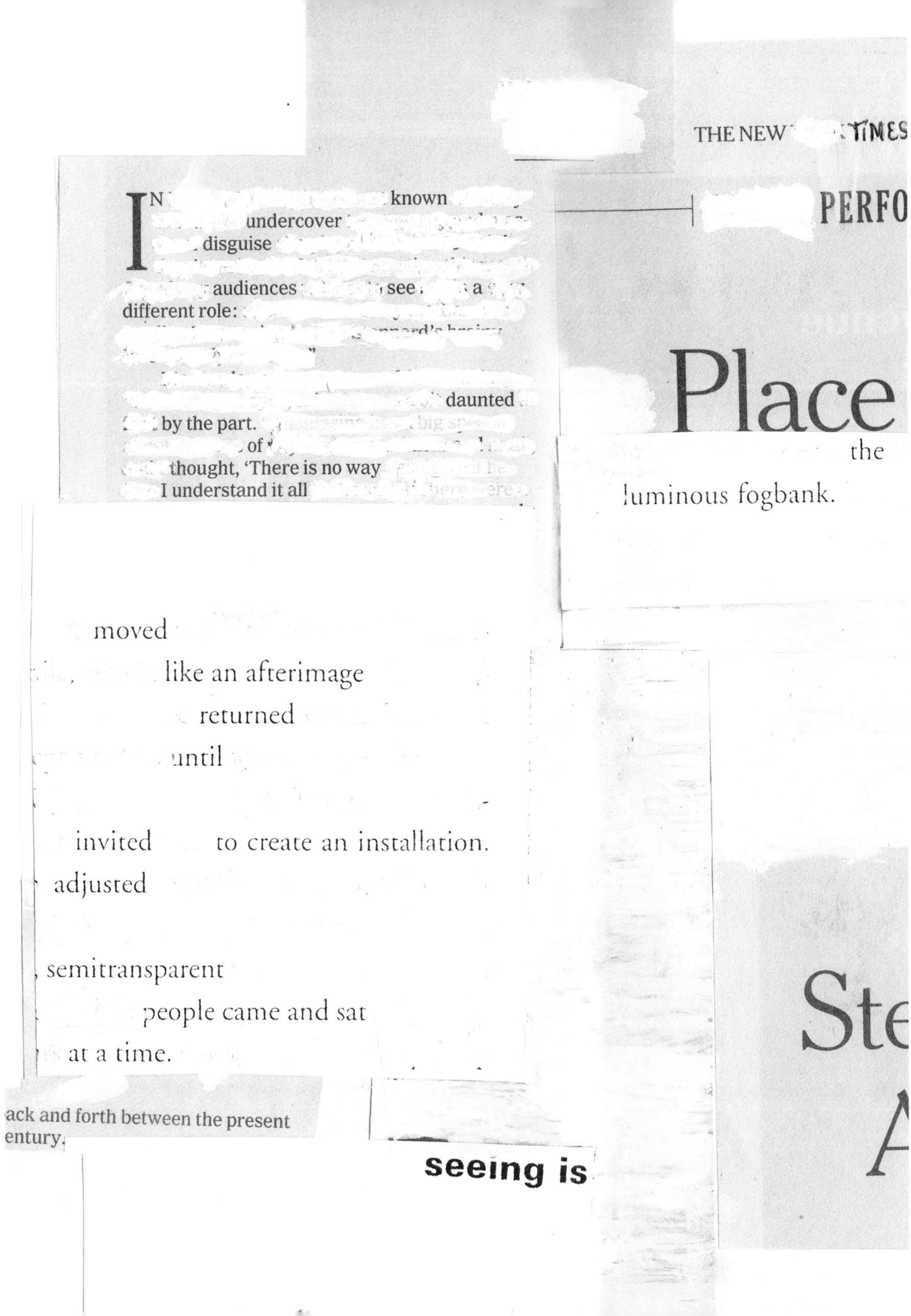

THE NEW TIMES

PERFO

IN known
undercover
disguise

audiences see a
different role:

daunted
by the part.
of
thought, 'There is no way
I understand it all

Place

the
luminous fogbank.

moved
like an afterimage
returned
until

invited to create an installation.
adjusted

semitransparent
people came and sat
at a time.

ack and forth between the present
entury.

seeing is

Ste
A

I always keep very active notebooks.

Not notebooks like sketchbooks, which I have never kept,

but notebooks like a journal or a kind of travelogue, mapping a personal course

through various readings, quotations, associations, observations, experiments,

and ideas for pieces, all jumbled into one.[169]

BILL VIOLA

169 Bill Viola, *Reasons for Knocking at an Empty House: Writings 1973–1994*, ed. Robert Violette (Cambridge, MA: MIT Press, 1998), 267.

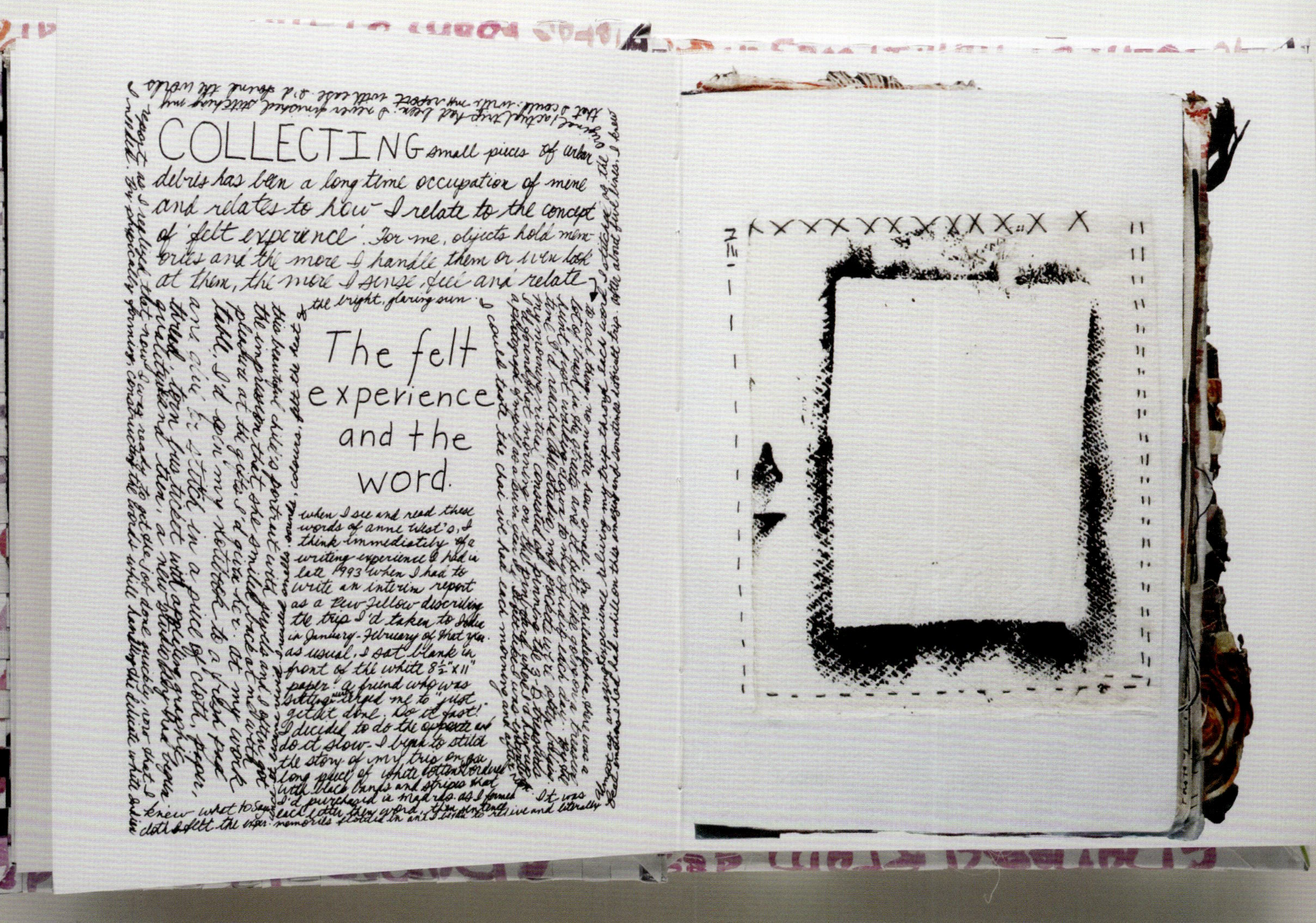

SANDRA BROWNLEE, *THE FELT EXPERIENCE AND THE WORD*, DEPARTURES AND RETURNS, 2009   PHOTO JACK RAMSDALE

Start a Mapping Notebook

Frequently my students tell me that their ideas are recorded in a hundred different places and that one of their major obstacles to writing is breaking free from a disorganized mind. Establishing a mapping notebook is one way to organize bits and pieces of information and free creative energy and insight.

The mapping notebook is a "material space" for writing, logging insights, entering quotations, cataloguing visual material, and for recording bibliographic references. The notebook is also a "vision space" for meaningfully tracking and linking sensation, perception, emotion, idea, attitude, and intuitive spark. The notebook may be a paper notebook and/or a digital document, even a blog. Either way, make it an easily accessible, dynamic system.

I use two formats. I have a three-ring binder—a mapping binder—with lined paper where I sketch my thoughts first. Here I thought-doodle. I explore ideas with immediate gratification. I fixate on one idea and then move to another.

In my paper notebook, I also generate a list of bullet points or stream of consciousness lists to chart thought paths. Later I shape these impressions into syntax on the computer. For example, when my ideas take root and I need to generate a developed piece of writing, I open a new text document on my laptop, identified by subject or theme. After each passage finds its own legs, I print out a copy. I revise these writings again and again. Each copy is placed in the mapping binder or folder.

I find that once I have identified prominent themes in my work, then I can return to folders every two weeks or so, to winnow and conceptualize what is there.

Keep Showing Up

Ah, yes, we must show up! Writing demands effort. Establish a time each day just for writing. Discipline is often resisted as oppressive but the paradox is that a clearly defined timeframe enhances insight and freedom of expression. A specific timeframe anchors and focuses attention. Be sure to bring your mapping notebook and a favorite writing tool. Write on your bed. Write in your studio. Set a timer. Use the questions in this book to inspire more writing. Set the mind free. Listen to the imagination. Allow the words to surface as they may on the page.

Trust Your Radar

According to the pre-Socratic philosopher Heraclitus, "All things are in process and nothing stands still."[170] Recent research on consciousness suggests that it is not a single state but instead an active process whose focus, like the focus of vision, is restless, continually searching for orientation in the dynamic flux of information that is life.[171]

During aesthetic work, the mind is an active radar. Pay attention to what engages you. Notice nuance. Relish the insights, the vivid images, and the discoveries as they appear. Cement fragile thoughts in motion. Connect a dot. If you discover something in a book, on the web, or from a lively radio discussion, log it in your mapping notebook with your comments. Never throw away these jottings. Every attempt to write creates a pathway into your work or may be the stepping stone to your next undertaking. Brilliant things start to happen.

Keep Your Ideas Wet[172]

Counteract writer's block by establishing a secondary venue to record thought patterns. Spread out your ideas on a table. Fix them on a corkboard or on your studio wall with Post-it™ notes. One of my writer friends mounts a clothesline in her apartment and pins her thoughts on the line.

Ask for a Candid Response

Ask another person if your thoughts are developed clearly. Does one thought follow logically after the other? The practice of reflecting back will help you to find gaps in your thinking and writing.

Tell It Out Loud

Improvise a story of your work on an audio recorder or video—anything to activate your unscripted voice. Many times explanations and insights are clearest when they flow from the natural cadences of the spoken word. Turn the recording into a transcript.

Jettison the External Critic

12th-century mystic and writer Hildegard von Bingen says, "We cannot live in a world that is not our own, in a world that is interpreted for us by others. An interpreted world is not a home. Part of the terror is to take back our own listening. To use our own voice. To see our own light."[173] Question the authority and the sanity of the other. Banish the censor from your mind. You don't have to use institutional language to give credibility to how you think. You are the unifying theme.

Target a Reader

To make your writing clear, concrete, engaged, and passionate, know your audience. Conjure up an imaginary reader and write directly to that person. Help your reader to see what you see.

Not Just a Polished Apple

Perfectionism tyrannizes the imagination; imperfection is an invitation. Think of your work as imperfect, agile, and in motion. Keep the evolving momentum of discovery by fearlessly asking questions. Why? Why? Why? Maintain the tension of the question by zooming in, by rotating the lens. Revisit ideas for their inherent possibilities. Research. Henry David Thoreau advises, know your own bone. "Pursue, keep up with, circle round and round. ... Know your own bone; gnaw at it, bury it, unearth it, and gnaw it still.[174]

Present the Voice of Others Clearly

Distinguish the voices of others —artists, critics, and observers. Permit the reader to hear these commentaries as distinct from your own.

Winnow and Distill

Use a highlighter to draw attention to core ideas and relevant phrases. Filter, discard, append, and clarify. Rewrite. Separate the wheat from the chaff. Keep only the essential words. Crystallize thought. Name the essence. Seek synthesis. Good writing is precise. It follows clear thinking and enables you to take ownership of your artistic intentions.

Build Connective Tissue

A coherent, cohesive story of your work has diverse elements. Be aware of the transitions from paragraph to paragraph in your writing. Aid the reader in making connections.

Refine Writings

Return to passages that hold promise and focus your attention on the content and form of these passages. After you edit these texts, you are ready to post them on a blog or web site, or incorporate them into your publication.

Give it Your Best Shot, Your Most Accurate Voice

170 Richard Gelhard, *Remembering Heraclitus* (Great Barrington, MA: Lindisfarne Books, 2000), 158. Fragment 22.

171 Wallace Chafe, *Discourse, Consciousness and Time*, as quoted in Carol Laing, *Katherine Knight. Five Strands, In Order to Stop Time* (Lethbridge, Alberta: Southern Alberta Art Gallery, 1996), 4.

172 Francisco J. Varela, "The Reenchantment of the Concrete," in *Incorporations*, eds. Jonathan Crary and Sanford Kwinter (New York: ZONE, 1992), 324. I am borrowing from Varela's reference to "wet" as connected to living experience, not abstract process.

173 As quoted in, Hildegard von Bingen, www.nac-cna/pdf/eth/0706/theatre_0706.pdf. Accessed June 21, 2011.

174 Henry David Thoreau, "Letters to a Spiritual Seeker," ed. Bradley P. Dean (New York: W.W. Norton & Company, 2004), 38.

the spirit of mapping through writing

KATARINA WESLIEN *Titling your book **Mapping the Intelligence of Artistic Work** requires a little explanation. How do the acts of making, mapping, and writing come together?*

ANNE WEST I call this work "mapping" because the metaphor best serves the intention of this practice, which is to make more apparent the hidden texture of artistic seeing and knowing. Mapping through writing is the catalyst for plumbing the hidden correspondences in our image language. It is the means we use to probe the dynamic space of the imaginative mind and to plot the intricacies of this composite world. The metaphor of the map links writing to the creative imagination and brings to consciousness a more authentic understanding of an artist's work.

KW *How did the connection between the two arise in your mind?*

AW Over a decade ago, an artist friend introduced me to Charles Hampden-Turner's *Maps of the Mind.* The spirit of mapping in his book set me on a path of thinking and teaching. Hampden-Turner's maps are windows into the complex minds of leading thinkers in philosophy, psychology, and sociology. His maps portray diagrammatically, with visuo-spatial imagery, the thought worlds of great thinkers. We see the intelligence of each mind's unique approach to configuring reality. In fact, his maps read as landscapes of essential ideas which, when rendered as image, frame mental paradigms. With his emphasis on "connectedness, coherence, relationship, organicism, and wholeness," we are able to see a convergence of their thought patterns and worldview.[175] In one instance we see a map of Martin Luther King's mind: the ecology of his values and how he broke from dualism.[176] Immediately I felt his work was a powerful interpretive tool for seeing, thinking, and writing about visual work. Over time, I have witnessed the power of using mapping as a vehicle for revealing and celebrating the visual mind.

KW *You teach a course by a similar title at the Rhode Island School of Design. Is this book an outgrowth of that course?*

AW Since 1996 I have taught an image-based form of critical writing to graduate students who are preparing their written theses. Employing the technique of "mapping through writing," students discover the underlying intelligence of their work and through this discovery their voices as artists and designers. Mapping enables them to forge vital links to the meaningful messages of their work, making them more effective and confident communicators. Inspired by these classes, I decided to capture the essence of these group processes into book form for an expanded audience. This process was built in successive stages within group settings. Utilizing carefully planned exercises (vignettes), the students examine the connections, both concrete and abstract, that inform their creative processes. The idea was to get to the pith of the experience via connections, gaps, bridges, and to express it in words.

KW *Can we backtrack a little? If you were initially intrigued by Hampden-Turner's ways of mapping the mind, how has this translated into mapping the artistic mind? How is the mind of the artist different?*

AW Mapping the artistic mind involves a kind of spatial poetics where image-based thinking in brought into dialogue with the written word. Imagination—the way we make sense of reality—is not a clear-cut rationalist process. It is an immersive, non-linear process directed by images. In the hands of artists and designers, mapping through writing is a way to inquire, document, and constellate meaning within an open, interpretive space. In this flexible space multiple centers of awareness exist simultaneously and in dynamic relationship—real experiences, fundamental transformations that occur through media, charged aesthetic considerations, intuitive insights, and much more.

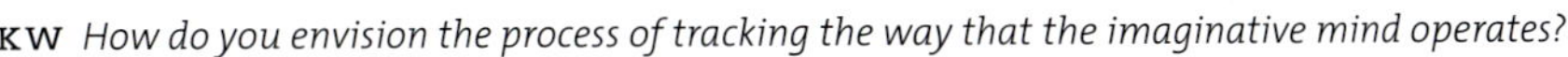

KW *How do you envision the process of tracking the way that the imaginative mind operates?*

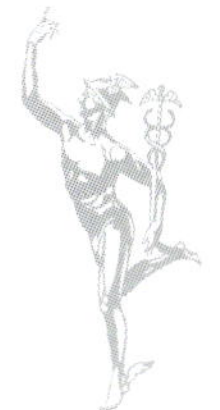

AW For me, the idea of the god Hermes presents a way to envision this process. Hermes, the messenger god of Greek mythology, is the interpreter. According to Homeric legend it was Hermes who invented writing. He has wings on his heels that make him adept in forging links across different zones of experience. He is cunning in his *modus operandi*. How artists trace out what they know requires a similar cunning approach. The artist-writer obeys a different kind of logic as s/he, like Hermes, wanders along non-linear paths. It's a form of chaos theory at work. Painter Christine Hwang expresses this process so clearly when she writes,

"Mapping through writing is landing in one spot, exploring the area around it, discovering the boundaries, and then moving on."[177]

KW *Chaos theory at work. Can you expand on the idea of chaos theory at work?*

AW Nothing that is alive lives by being enclosed and separated from the environment. If a system remains enclosed, it is subject to entropy. Structures will dissipate within this entropy. They need an initial variant—a strange attractor—from outside the system to give them life.[178] The initial variant and its behavior cannot be predicted. Weather is a good example. Our imagination is also a dynamic system. Images nudge our consciousness and behave as unpredictable variants—strange attractors that come from outside the system and affect the system, giving it life. The initial unpredictable behavior in turn results in creating a vital new pattern of thought. Artistic awareness is built upon the power to respond to these strange attractors which come in the form of idea, intuition, sense impression, recognition, memory. I believe they connect to the body's deep level of knowing—Eros. They alter the field of attention and break the chain of familiar response. For me mapping is the best way to work with images and dynamic systems. It allows us to see the way we combine, recombine, organize, and reorganize meaning.

KW *This is the main point of mapping.*

AW Yes. The non-linear dynamics of the imagination cannot be interpreted from a single fixed angle or with an anticipation of a set behavior. Mapping asks us to follow the paths that the "strange attractors" activate and to bring these insights to consciousness. When artistic consciousness is viewed through mapping, artmaking no longer functions as a subset of life but rather as a human process operating within a dynamic field of potential and as a system of relationships. Maps give us eyes to this larger analogue. We zoom in on the intimate. And then through the wide aperture of the mapping lens, we link with the generative matrix. It's all one vision.

KW *You seem genuinely intrigued by the multiple ways the artist's mind is animated, what you call vision. How do you think vision works?*

AW As you well know, artists do not *see* from a single vantage point but holistically from many angles. Vision, which includes a space for the body, not just the eyes, comes from multiple centers of awareness: visual, visceral, emotional, experiential, abstract, and inquisitory.

KW *Can you speak to how we build a clear map based on our field of vision?*

AW The imaginative mind is disciplined and inextricably connected through persistent vision and developed visual language. From this persistent vision, a cohesive body of work emerges. Jean-Paul Sartre, in *On Imagination*, speaks of images as "conscious events."[179] When images are strung together, forming a group of interrelated elements, they acquire cohesion—a field of vision.

KW *What do you think informs this persistent vision?*

AW Images are ideas and thus a way of seeing and knowing. It is imagery that carries the life spirit and energy of the work. These "mental events" form a vision of reality. For example, author James Hillman opens our understanding to the link between ideas and insight. He writes,

> "The word idea itself points to its intimacy with the visual metaphor of knowing, for it is related both to the Latin *videre* ("to see") and the German *wissen* ("to know"). Ideas are ways of seeing and knowing, or knowing by ways of insighting. Ideas allow us to envision, and by means of vision we can know."[180]

KW *So, we create a map of these mental events and build from there. Perhaps it is simply paying attention, noticing what we do? I am thinking about how important the first-person point of view is, and that our experience of life is being mapped in each moment when we truly slow our pace down and pay attention.*

AW Yes. By naming the images that fire the imaginative mind, we understand the structures through which we perceive. Italo Calvino discusses at length how images are potentialities and how we get caught in their web. He writes,

> "As soon as the image has become sufficiently clear in my mind, I set about developing it into a story; or better yet, it is the images themselves that develop their own implicit potentialities, the story they carry with them. Around each image others come into being, forming a field of analogies, symmetries, confrontations."[181]

I like this idea that images develop their own implicit potentialities.

KW *Yes, I agree. Then the challenge becomes how do we work with these implicit potentialities? What do we do and make with these images in the process of writing?*

AW Through a "poetic logic," meshing image and language.

CONVERSATION

KW *What do you mean by the term "poetic logic"?*

AW I first encountered this term in the writings of Marcel Danesi about the Neapolitan philosopher Giambattista Vico.[182] In the 18th century, Vico was writing about artistic knowing as "poetic logic." He was perhaps the first to speak for a knowledge that stemmed not from reason but from imagination. According to Vico, imagination and metaphor are the essence of the mind.

The Greek word *poeisis* means, "to make, create, invent." The word poet means "maker with words."[183] *Logos* is the Greek word for "speech, articulate discourse, rational word, and idea." According to Vico, iconic, perceptual thought inaugurates the first act of knowing and images are our first-order thought forms. These images become the foundation stones where we first "make," "create" sense. The images wallow deep in the imagination and form an interference pattern in the mind that incites creativity. Through a metaphoric capacity in the mind, these impressions are translated into conceptual thought. So, in a Vichian sense, when one translates into language the roots of one's visual knowing, a poetic logic gives validity to the experience.

KW *In other words, one starts with perceptions and sensations to get to the underlying images and then comes language.*

AW Yes. Visual work teaches us to reside differently at the threshold of language. Initially the work is unaffected by words (unless language is the basis of the work). If images are the means of thinking, then one must consider the weight of sensation and perception as the means to connect with language.

KW *In the encounter between art and writing, how does this poetic logic work?*

POIESIS	LOGOS
making	writing
sensation	language
intuition	rationality
sensing	knowing

AW To write on behalf of visual work, we function in the space between *poiesis* (the making) and *logos* (the speaking). *Poiesis* and *logos* are inseparable; one cannot be without the other. They work like opposing magnets and through a union arrive at communication. *Poiesis* needs the glimpse of inspiration revealed through the imagination to inaugurate a form. *Poiesis* represents the expressive potential and syntax of the visual field. *Logos* requires imaginative capacity to generate linguistic form. The verbal is accessed through the visual. The map is a complementary cross-fertilization emanating from the overlapping of *poiesis* and *logos* (image and language).[184]

KW *How is the spirit of mapping relevant to this encounter?*

AW Mapping allows us to locate the place of identity in the work and to know both in form and in language our most accurate truth, authentic voice. It tracks the persistence of the imagination and generates a narrative structure that communicates the intelligence of the visual work. The non-linear dynamics of artistic vision cannot be interpreted from a single fixed angle. Writing encourages shifts of stance in accessing the matrix of the work. Mapping is the lens, the generous optic revealing the intimate facets as well as the larger field of artistic vision. One of my students, sculptor Laura Kaufman, who has worked with this process, remarks,

> "Mapping grants me reprieve from eliminating what may have been true before, but is not what is before me now. In other words, there is no need to amputate ideas—they are all mine—some farther from the center but the center will shift and the once far away idea glows in the spotlight of focus. Mapping allows me a state of mind/being that shifts and includes, not one that prunes errant branches before they bloom. It allows my small, fearful mind to accommodate the big world."[185]

This awareness and ability to adapt is essential to generating a meaningful map.

KW *I have heard you refer to this writing practice as a practice in holism. What do you mean by this expression?*

AW To write about imaginative understanding, we must enter the "picture" as an experiment in holism. To appreciate and understand the work is to experience it whole. It is viewed like a hologram, where a number of complex relationships are packed into a concise image or form. When writing, we unpack the hologram to see what has fired the imagination. Mapping through writing is a way to see the work holistically. Seeking wholeness allows us to find validity in the ambiguity of an open, non-linear process. It fosters a graceful balance between knowing and non-knowing and sidesteps the perfection that can easily become a tyranny on the imagination. Writing into this wholeness is a gesturing toward something that is in a constant state of evolution.

KW *What does it mean to be a fierce or comprehensive mapmaker?*

AW When I was writing this book, I was also learning to sail. I learned, while out at sea, what it means to be a keen mappist of a world in a constant state of flux. Like the creative process, sailing requires minute-to-minute perceptual attentiveness to information coming simultaneously from multiple sources. Extending this metaphor to the practice of writing in the mapping mode, artists work like sailors charting their course. At various points along the way, they become privy to what informs consciousness. As they move to another place of thought, they reframe their position and perform the same exercise again. With each shifting angle, perspective becomes more intelligible. Each nuance of awareness develops a more generous optic with which to see the larger picture. Vision comes into sharp relief, moving one from tunnel vision to the largesse of a more prismatic way of seeing and knowing. The writings of architect Christopher Alexander helped me to understand this process of attending to the multiple centers that carry the vitality of work. According to Alexander, the centers are the building blocks that give a work a sense of the whole. Using the metaphor of the early Turkish carpet, he shows that the degree of wholeness that a carpet has is directly correlated to its number of centers. The more centers the more powerful and deep its degree of wholeness. Likewise the deeper the ideas that inform our visual work the more powerful its degree of wholeness.[186]

KW *As you speak about the drive of mapping and map-making, I wonder if there is a danger of thinking too rigidly about this mapping process, that is, of attributing closure to a process that is in fact an open one?*

AW I recall one student asking,

> "Can I really know these impulses and describe them or are my notions just signposts, agreements with a spirit I can only obey but not fully describe, map, or understand?"[187]

The richness of visual language is speculative and indeterminate. The moment we compartmentalize, find a formula, pigeonhole, establish a niche, the act of interpretation becomes finite. If we set out to explain it, we may draw the life out of it. Artistic knowing does not exist in the domain of direct correlation between fact and meaning. Art permits us to be carried away from this type of determination. Art serves notice that the world of meaning is an open one that is constantly being created and recreated.

Mapping artistic work is about becoming more perceptually aware, about making connections for the sake of consciousness. By becoming more aware of the processes, the sources, the actions, and materials, we stimulate artistic consciousness. As Gilles Deleuze and Felix Guattari said,

> "Art is never an end in itself; it is only an instrument for tracing the lines of lives."[188]

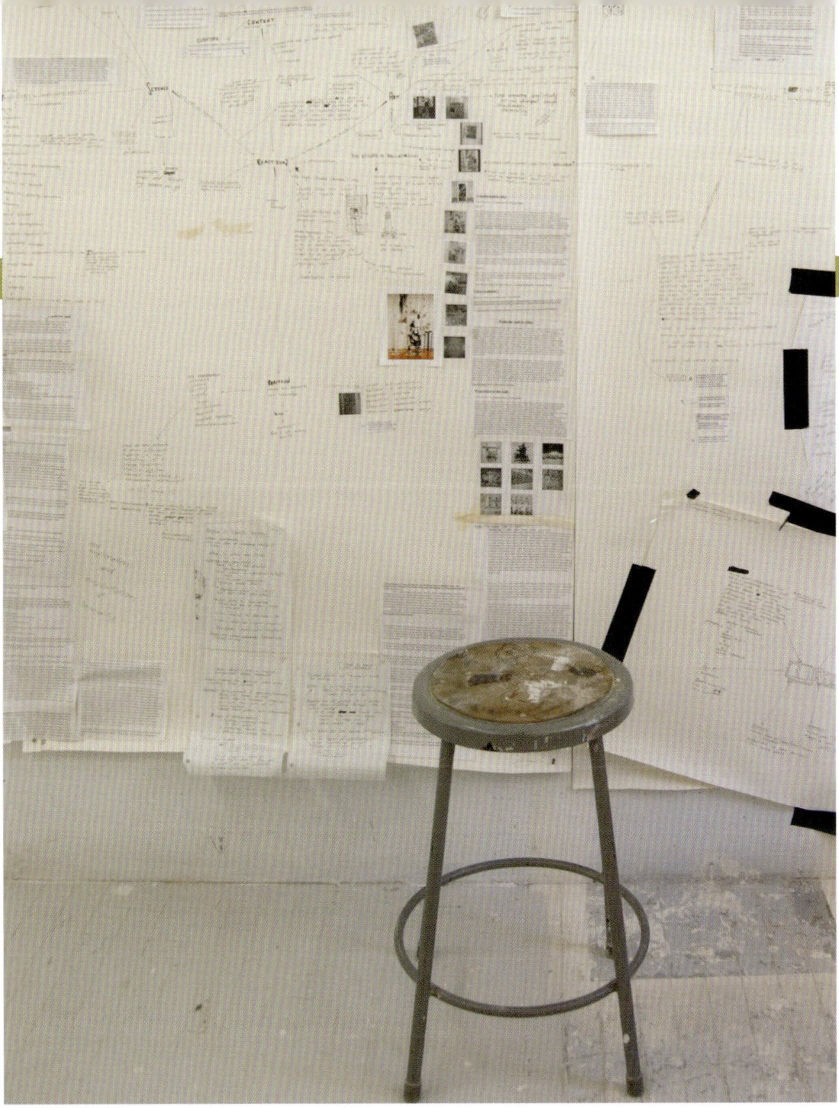

LEE JOHNSON, *MAPPING EXERCISE*, 2010 PHOTO ADAM LUCAS

175 Charles Hampden-Turner, *Maps of the Mind* (New York: Macmillan Publishing Company, 1982), 8.

176 Ibid., 204–07.

177 In conversation with painter Christine Hwang, RISD, January 2007.

178 This passage builds upon an interpretation of chaos theory offered by Reb Zalman Schachter-Shalomi in his *Wisdom of the Elders* recording (Fetzer Institute, 2004).

179 Jean-Paul Sartre, *Imagination: A Psychological Critique*, trans. Forrest Williams (Ann Arbor: The University of Michigan Press, 1972). Sartre offers a critical investigation of the history of the imagination, in which the character of images and the nature of the imagination are revealed as a type of consciousness.

180 James Hillman. *A Blue Fire: Selected Writings*, ed. Thomas Moore (New York: Harper & Row Publishers, 1989), 53.

181 Calvino, "Visibility" in *Six Memos*, 88–89.

182 Marcel Danesi, *Vico, Metaphor, and the Origin of Language* (Bloomington & Indianapolis: Indiana University Press, 1993). "The first language of humanity was an iconic one that crystallized in the deep level of the mind when the imagination transformed the images produced by the brain into iconic signs." (Danesi, 117)

183 *The American Heritage Dictionary of the English Language*, 4TH ed., s.v. "poiesis."

184 The writings of Denis Wood also informed my thinking about the exchange between image and language. See Wood, 95–142.

185 In conversation with sculptor Laura Kaufman, at the *Art & Writing Institute*, Aldrich Museum of Contemporary Art, Connecticut, 2007.

186 Christopher Alexander, *A Foreshadowing of 21st Century Art: The Color and Geometry of Very Early Turkish Carpets* (New York: Oxford University Press, 1993), 31–51.

187 In conversation with photographer Noah David Smith, RISD, January 2004.

188 Gilles Deleuze and Felix Guattari, in Deleuze's *Essays Critical and Clinical* (Minneapolis, MN: University of Minnesota Press, 1997), 1.

Abakanowicz, Magdalena. *Magdalena Abakanowicz.* Museum of Contemporary Art, Chicago. New York: Abbeville Press, 1983.

Abram, David. *The Spell of the Sensuous: Perception and Language in a More-Than-Human World.* New York: Vintage Books, 1996.

Abrams, Janet, and Peter Hall, eds. *Else/Where: Mapping New Cartographies of Networks and Territories.* Minneapolis: University of Minnesota Design Institute, 2006.

Adolphs, Volker. "The Body and the World." In *Mona Hatoum*, edited by Christoph Heinrich, 43. Ostfildern, Germany: Hatje Cantz Publishers, 2004.

Alexander, Christopher. *A Pattern Language.* New York: Oxford University Press, 1977.

---. *A Foreshadowing of 21st Century Art: The Color and Geometry of Very Early Turkish Carpets.* New York: Oxford University Press, 1993.

---. *The Timeless Way of Building.* New York: Oxford University Press, 1979.

American Heritage Dictionary of The English Language, The. 4th edition. Boston: Houghton Mifflin Company, 2000.

Anderson, Laurie. Interview. "The End of the Moon." *Pomegranate Arts.* Transcript accessed from http://artscenter.uhh.hawaii.edu/?Archives:2006_Season:Laurie_Anderson. August 1994.

Anderson, Laurie. "Same Time Tomorrow." *The Ugly One With the Jewels.* Warner Bros. Records, 1995.

Ankori, Gannit. *Palestinian Art.* London: Reaktion Books Ltd., 2006.

Archer, Michael, Guy Brett and Catherine de Zegher. *Mona Hatoum.* London: Phaidon Press Limited, 1997.

Ault, Julie, ed. *Felix Gonzalez-Torres.* Gottingen: Steidl Publishers, 2006.

Auping, Michael, ed. *Heaven and Earth.* Fort Worth: Modern Art Museum of Fort Worth, 2006. An exhibition catalogue.

Bachelard, Gaston. *The Right to Dream.* Translated by J.A. Underwood. Dallas: The Dallas Institute Publications, 1988.

---. *The Poetics of Reverie: Childhood, Language, and the Cosmos.* Translated by Daniel Russell. Boston: Beacon Press, 1960.

---. *The Poetics of Space.* Translated by Maria Jolas. Boston: Beacon Press, 1994.

Baldessari, John, "My Files of Movie Stills." In *Blasted Allegories: An Anthology of Writings by Contemporary Artists,* edited by Brian Wallis. 100–103. Cambridge, MA: The MIT Press, 1989.

Barthes, Roland. *Camera Lucida: Reflections on Photography.* Translated by Richard Howard. New York: Hill and Wang, 1981.

Basho, Matsuo. *Narrow Road to the Interior: And Other Writing.* Translated by Sam Hamill. Boston: Shambhala Publications, 1998.

Beckley, Bill, and David Shapiro, eds. *Uncontrollable Beauty: Toward a New Aesthetics.* New York: Allworth Press, 1998.

Bell, Marvin. *A Marvin Bell Reader: Selected Poetry and Prose.* Hanover: Middlebury College Press, 1994.

Benjamin, Walter. *Illuminations.* Edited by Hannah Arendt. Translated by Harry Zohn. New York: Schocken Books, 1969.

---. *Reflections.* Edited by Peter Demetz. New York: Schocken Books, 1969.

---. "A Berlin Chronicle", in *One Way Street and Other Writings,* NLB, London, 1979.

---. "The Collector." In *The Arcades Project.* Translated by Howard Eiland and Kevin McLaughlin, 204. Cambridge, MA: The Belknap Press of Harvard University, 1999.

Berger, John, and John Christie. *I Send You This Cadmium Red...A correspondence between John Berger and John Christie.* Barcelona: Actar, 1999.

Berry, Wendell. *Standing by Words.* San Francisco: North Point Press, 1983.

Boldt, Lawrence G. *Zen and the Art of Making a Living: A Practical Guide to Creative Career Design.* New York: Penguin, 1993.

Boltanski, Christian. *"Christian Boltanski: Lessons of Darkness."* The New Museum of Contemporary Art, December 9–February, 1988.

Bourriaud, Nicolas. *Relational Aesthetics.* Dijon: Les Presses Du Reel, Franc, 1998.

Brakhage, Stan. *Metaphors on Vision.* New York: Anthology Film Archives, 1976.

Brownlee, Sandra. *Departures and Returns.* Nova Scotia Center for Craft and Design, 2009. An exhibition catalogue.

Bruce, Chris, Buzz Spector, and Rebecca Solnit. *Ann Hamilton: Sao Paulo and Seattle.* Henry Art Gallery, 1992. An exhibition catalogue.

Brusatin, Manilio. *A History of Colors.* Boston: Shambhala, 1991.

Burke, Kenneth. *Perspective by Incongruity.* Bloomington, IN: Indiana University Press, 1964.

Cage, John. *Silence.* Middletown, CT: Wesleyan University Press, 1973.

Calvino, Italo. *Six Memos for the Next Millennium.* Cambridge, MA: Harvard University Press, 1988.

---. *Invisible Cities.* New York: Mariner Books, 1978.

Canetti, Elias. *The Conscience of Words.* Translated by Joachim Neugroschel. London: Picador, 1979.

Cardinal, Roger. "The Case of Kurt Schwitters." In *The Cultures of Collecting,* edited by John Elsner and Roger Cardinal, 75. Cambridge, MA: Harvard University Press, 1994.

Careri, Francesco. *Walkscapes: Walking as an Aesthetic Practice.* Barcelona, Spain: Editorial Gustavo Gili, 2002.

Cather, Willa. *My Antonia.* Boston: Houghton Mifflin Company, 1918; 1995.

Caws, Mary Ann, ed. *Manifesto: A Century of Isms.* Lincoln: University of Nebraska Press, 2002.

Cennini, Cennino d'Andrea. *The Craftsman's Handbook.* New York: Dover, 1954.

Chafe, Wallace. "Discourse, Consciousness and Time." In *Katherine Knight. Five Strands, In Order to Stop Time...*, edited by Carol Laing, 4. Lethbridge, Alberta: Southern Alberta Art Gallery, 1996.

Chatwin, Bruce. *Anatomy of Restlessness: Selected Writings 1969–1989.* Edited by Jan Borm and Matthew Graves. New York: Penguin Books, 1987.

Cixous, Hélène, and Catherine Clement. "The Newly Born Woman." In *Theory and History of Literature, Vol. 24,* translated by Betty Wind, ix. Minneapolis: University of Minnesota Press, 1986.

---. *Coming to Writing and Other Essays.* Translated by S. Cornell, D. Jenson, A. Little and S. Seller. Cambridge: Harvard University Press, 1991.

Cooperrider, David L., and Diana Whitney. *Appreciate Inquiry.* San Francisco: Berrett Koehler, 1999.

Cragg, Tony. *In Camera.* S'Hertongenbosch, Netherlands: European Ceramics Work Centre, 1993.

Curiger, Bice. *Rebecca Horn.* Zurich: Kunsthaus, 1983. An exhibition catalogue.

Danesi, Marcel. *Vico, Metaphor, and the Origin of Language.* Bloomington & Indianapolis: Indiana University Press, 1993.

Deleuze, Gilles. *Essays Critical and Clinical.* Minneapolis, MN: University of Minnesota Press, 1997.

Deleuze, Gilles, and Claire Parnet. *Dialogues II.* New York: Continuum, 2006.

Dillard, Annie. "Write Till You Drop." In *New York Times Book Review,* May 28, 1989.

---. *The Writing Life.* New York: Harper & Row, Publishers, 1989.

Drucker, Johanna. "The Artist's Book as Idea and Form." In *A Book of the Book: Some Works & Projections About the Book and Writing,* edited by Jerome Rothenberg and Steven Clay, 376–388. New York: Granary Books, 2000.

Dudley, Michael. *A Man in a Hotel Room.* Toronto, 1986.

Dumas, Marlene. *Marlene Dumas: Give the People What they Want.* Philadelphia: Goldie Paley Gallery, Moore College of Art and Design, November 5–December 17, 1993.

Durban, Pam. *The Laughing Place.* New York: Charles Scribner's Sons, 1993.

Eccher, Danilo, ed. *Anselm Kiefer: Stelle cadenti.* Bologna: Galleria D'Arte Moderna Di Bologna, 1999. An exhibition catalogue.

Eliot, George. *Middlemarch.* New York: Harper and Brothers, 1873.

Ellery, Johns, Adrian Shaughnessy, Martin Parr, Erik Spiekermann, Lawrence Weiner and Alan Fletcher. *136 Points of Reference.* London: Ellery/Browns, 2005.

Ermen, Reinhard. "Work comes out of work." *Kunstforum International* no. 192. July/August 2008.

Feehan, Megan. "Reading Typographies/Push & Play." MFA thesis in Graphic Design Rhode Island School of Design, 2010.

Fichte, J.G. *Addresses to the German Nation.* Edited by George Armstrong Kelly. Translated by R.F. Jones and G.H. Turnbull. New York: Harper and Row Publishers, 1968.

Fine, Ruth E. "Books as Bones." In *The Book Room: Georgia O'Keeffe's Library in Abiquiu,* 11–16. New York: The Georgia O'Keeffe Foundation, 1997.

Finlay, Victoria. *Color: A Natural History of the Palette.* New York: Random House, 2002.

Forster, E.M. *Aspects of the Novel.* Edited by Oliver Stallybrass. Harmondsworth, England: Penguin, 1976.

Foucault, Michel. "Of Other Spaces." In *The Visual Culture Reader*, edited by Nicholas Mirzoeff, 237. New York: Routledge, 1998.

Freeman, Judi. *The Dada & Surrealist Word-Image.* Los Angeles: Los Angeles County Museum of Art and Cambridge: MIT Press, 1989.

Fuller, R. Buckminster, with Jerome Agel and Quentin Fiore. *I Seem to be a Verb.* New York: Bantam Books, 1970.

Garcia-Marquez, Gabriel. *One Hundred Years of Solitude.* New York: Cambridge University Press, 1990.

Gelardin, Arianne, Patricia C. Phillips, and Mat Stevens, eds. *Speculations: A Collective Exchange on the Creative Process.* Providence: Rhode Island School of Design, Division of Graduate Studies, 2010.

Gelhard, Richard. *Remembering Heraclitus.* Great Barrington, MA: Lindisfarne Books, 2000

Gerz, Jochen. "People Speak." Vancouver, Canada: Vancouver Art Gallery, September 18–November 28, 1994.

Gladwell, Malcolm. *The Tipping Point: How Little Things Can Make a Big Difference.* New York: Little, Brown and Company, 2000.

Gleick, James. *Chaos: Making A New Science* New York: Penguin, 1987.

Glimcher, Arnold B. *Louise Nevelson.* New York: E.P. Dutton & Company, Inc., 1976.

Goldberg, Natalie. *Writing Down the Bones.* Boston: Shambhala Publications, 1986.

Goldsworthy, Andy. *Hand to Earth: Sculpture 1976–1990.* Edited by Terry Friedman and Andy Goldsworthy. New York: Harry N. Abrams, 1993.

Grauerholz, Angela. *Aporia.* Oakville, Ontario: Oakville Galleries, 1995.

Guest, Tim, ed. *Sensations of Reading.* London: London Regional Art Gallery, 1984. An exhibition catalogue.

Hampden-Turner, Charles. *Maps of the Mind: Charts and Concepts of the Mind and its Labyrinths.* New York: MacMillan Publishing Company, 1982.

Handke, Peter. *Across.* Translated by Ralph Manheim. New York: Macmillan, 1987.

Hara, Kenya. *Designing Design.* Baden, Switzerland: Lars Müller Publishers, 2007.

Harmon, Katerine. *You Are Here: Personal Geographies and Other Maps of the Imagination.* New York: Princeton Architectural Press, 2004.

Hass, Robert, ed. *The Essential Haiku: Versions of Basho, Buso & Essa.* Hopewell, New Jersey: The Ecco Press, 1994.

Hesse, Eva. In *Eva Hesse: A Retrospective,* edited by Lesley K. Baier, Maurice Berger, and Helen A. Cooper. New Haven, CT: Yale University Press, 1992. An exhibition catalogue.

---. *Voicing Today's Visions: Writings by Contemporary Artists.* Edited by Mara R. Witzling. New York: Universe Publishing, 1994.

Higginson, William J., and Penny Harter. *The Haiku Handbook.* New York: Kodansha International, Inc., 1985.

Hillman, James. *A Blue Fire: Selected Writings.* Edited by Thomas Moore. New York: Harper & Row Publishers, 1989.

Hillman, James. "The Practice of Beauty." In *Uncontrollable Beauty: Toward a New Aesthetics,* edited by Bill Beckley and David Shapiro. New York: Allworth, 1998.

Holt, Nancy, ed. *The Writings of Robert Smithson.* New York: New York University Press, 1979.

Hughes, Langston. *The Big Sea.* New York: Alfred Knopf, 1940.

Irwin, Robert, "Being Available in Response." In *Seeing is Forgetting the Name of the Thing One Sees* by Lawrence Weschler. Berkeley: University of California Press, 1982. 163–167.

Jackson, John Brinckerhoff. *A Sense of Place, a Sense of Time.* New Haven, CT: Yale University, 1999.

James, William. *The Principles of Psychology.* New York: Henry Holt and Company, 1890.

Jensen, Hans. *Sign, Symbol and Script: An Account of Man's Effort to Write.* Translated by George Unwin. New York: G.P. Putnam's Sons, 1969.

Kandinsky, Wassily. *Concerning the Spiritual in Art.* Translated by M.T.H. Sadler. New York: Dover Publications, 1977.

Kaza, Gunta, producer. *Mute. Muse. Mutiny.* 9 min. 2000. Boston: Massachusetts College of Art, DVD.

Kimmelman, Michael. *Portraits: Talking with Artists at the Met, The Modern, The Louvre and Elsewhere.* New York: Random House, 1988.

Kotik, Charlotta, "The Locus of Memory: An Introduction to the Work of Louise Bourgeois." In Louise Bourgeois, *Louise Bourgeois: The Locus of Memory, Works 1982–1993.* New York: Brooklyn Museum, 1994.

Kundera, Milan. *The Unbearable Lightness of Being.* New York: HarperCollins, 1984. An exhibition catalogue.

Kunitz, Stanley, and Genine Lentine. *The Wild Braid: A Poet Reflects on a Century in the Garden.* New York: W.W. Norton & Company, 2005.

Kuspit, Donald. "Beuys or Warhol?" www.griffinila.com/Portals/0/Beuys%20or%20Warhol.pdf. Accessed November 28, 2010.

Laing, Carol, ed. *Katherine Knight: Five Strands in Order to Stop Time.* Lethbridge, Alberta: Southern Alberta Art Gallery, 1996. An exhibition catalogue.

Levi-Strauss, Claude. *The Raw and the Cooked.* Translated by John and Doreen Weightman. New York: Harper & Row Publishers, 1969.

Lippard, Lucy R. *The Lure of the Local: Sense of Place in a Multicentered Society.* New York: W.W. Norton & Company, 1977.

Lopez, Barry. *About This Life.* New York: Vintage Books, 1998.

---. *Light Action in the Caribbean.* New York: Alfred A Knopf, 2000.

Lorca, Federico Garcia. "The Irresistible Beauty of All Things." *Harper's Magazine,* September 2004.

Lupton, Ellen. *Thinking with Type, A Critical Guide for Designers, Writers, Editors, & Students.* Princeton Architectural Press, 2010.

Lynch, Kevin. *The Image of the City.* Cambridge, MA: The MIT Press, 1980.

Martin, Agnes. "Beauty is the Mystery of Life" and "Journal Excerpts." In *Agnes Martin,* edited by Barbara Haskell. New York: Whitney Museum of American Art, 1993.

Mays, John Bentley. "Comment." In *Globe and Mail.* Toronto, 1992.

McKeon, Richard, ed. *The Basic Works of Aristotle.* New York: Random House, 1941.

McLuhan, Herbert Marshall. *Essential McLuhan.* Edited by Eric McLuhan and Frank Zingrone. London: Routledge, 1995.

Missias, A.C., "Contemporary Haiku: Origins and Directions." Web de Sol. http://webdesol.com/Perihelion/acmarticle.htm. Accessed December 16, 2006.

Morrison, Toni. "The Site of Memory." In *Out There: Marginalization and Contemporary Cultures,* edited by Russell Ferguson, Martha Gever, Trinh T. Minh-ha, and Cornell West, 299–305. New York: The New Museum of Contemporary Art, 1990.

Mumford, Lewis. *Technics and Civilization.* New York: Harcourt, Brace & Company, 1934.

Nabokov, Vladimir. *Speak, Memory.* New York: Vintage International, 1989.

Neruda, Pablo. *Ode to Common Things.* Boston: Little, Brown and Company, 1999.

Ostriker, Alicia Suskin. *Stealing the Language: The Emergence of Women's Poverty in America.* Ypsilanti, MI: Beacon Press, 1987.

Rand, Paul. *Design, Form, and Chaos.* New Haven: Yale University Press, 1993.

Rich, Adrienne. *Arts of the Possible.* New York: W.W. Norton & Company, 2002.

---. *What Is Found There: Notebooks on Poetry and Politics.* New York: W.W. Norton & Company, 1993.

Rinder, Lawrence, and George Lakoff, "Consciousness Art: Attending to the Quality of Experience." In *Search Light: Consciousness at the Millennium,* edited by Lawrence Rinder, 25–62. New York: Thames and Hudson Publishers, 1999.

Ross, David A., Peter Sellars, and Bill Viola. *Bill Viola.* New York: Whitney Museum of American Art in association with Flammarion, Paris-New York, 1997. An exhibition catalogue.

Safransky, Sy. *Four in the Morning.* Chapel Hill: The Sun Publishing Company, 1993.

Samara, Timothy. *Making and Breaking the Grid, A Graphic Design Layout Workshop.* Rockport Publishers, 2005.

Sartre, Jean-Paul. *Imagination.* Translated by Forest Williams. Ann Arbor, MI: The University of Michigan Press, 1972.

Shapiro, David, "Mondrian's Secret." In *Uncontrollable Beauty: Toward a New Aesthetics,* edited by Bill Beckley and David Shapiro, 307–323. New York: Allworth Press, 1998.

Shulman, Alix Kates. *Drinking the Rain.* New York: Penguin Books, 1995.

Smith, Keith. "The Book as Physical Object." In *A Book of the Book: Some Works & Projections About the Book and Writing,* edited by Jerome Rothenberg and Steven Clay, 54–70. New York: Granary Books, 2000.

Smithson, Robert. *The Writings of Robert Smithson.* Edited by Nancy Holt. New York: New York University Press, 1979.

Spirn, Anne Whiston. *The Language of Landscape.* New Haven, CT: Yale University Press, 1998.

Srinivasan, Anjali. "Particle Activism." MFA thesis in Glass, Rhode Island School of Design, 2007.

Stafford, William. *The Way It Is.* Saint Paul, MN: Graywolf Press, 1998.

Steiner, George. *Real Presences.* Chicago: The University of Chicago Press, 1989.

Stewart, Susan. *Poetry and the Fate of the Senses.* Chicago: The University of Chicago Press, 2002.

Stiles, Kristine, and Peter Selz, eds. *Theories and Documents of Contemporary Art: A Sourcebook of Artist's Writings.* Berkeley: University of California Press, 1996.

Tanizaki, Jun'ichiro. *In Praise of Shadows.* Translated by Thomas J. Harper and Edward G. Seidensticker. Sedgwick, ME: Leete's Island Books, 1977.

Theroux, Andrew. *The Primary Colors: Three Essays.* New York: Henry Holt and Company, 1994.

---. *The Secondary Colors.* New York: Henry Holt and Company, 1996.

Thompson, Philip, John Williams, and Gerald Woods, eds. *Art Without Boundaries.* New York: Praeger Publishers, 1974.

Thoreau, Henry David. "Letters to a Spiritual Seeker", edited by Bradley P. Dean. New York: W.W. Norton & Company, 2004.

Tisdall, Caroline. *Joseph Beuys.* New York: The Solomon R. Guggenheim Museum, 1979.

Tuan, Yi-Fu, *Passing Strange and Wonderful: Aesthetics, Nature and Culture.* Washington D.C.: Island Press, 1993.

Tufnell, Miranda, and Chris Crickmay. *Body Space Image.* London: Virago Press, 1990.

Turchi, Peter. *Maps of the Imagination: The Writer as Cartographer.* San Antonio: Trinity University Press, 2004.

Turner, Robert. "Born Remembering." *Studio Potter,* June, 1982.

Twombly, Robert, ed. *Louis Kahn: Essential Texts.* New York: W.W. Norton, 2003.

Varela, Francisco J. "The Reenchantment of the Concrete." In *Incorporations,* edited by Jonathan Crary and Sanford Kwinter, 328. New York: Zone Books, 1992.

Vernon, John. "Language and Speech" and "Language and Writing." In *Poetry and the Body,* 22–40. Chicago: University of Illinois Press, 1986.

Viola, Bill. *Reasons for Knocking at an Empty House. Writings 1973–1994.* Edited by Robert Violette. Cambridge, MA: MIT Press, 1998.

Von Bingen, Hildegard. www.nac-cna/pdf/eth/0706/theatre_0706.pdf. Accessed June 21, 2011.

Von Goethe, Johann Wolfgang. *Theory of Colors.* London: John Murray, 1840.

Weschler, Lawrence. *Seeing is Forgetting the Name of the Thing One Sees.* Berkeley: University of California Press, 1982.

White, E.B. *Writings From The New Yorker 1927–1979.* Edited by Rebecca M. Dale. New York: HarperCollins, 1990.

Wolff, Virginia. *Moments of Being.* London: Triad Grafton Books, 1976.

Woodman, Betty. *5 x 7: Seven Ceramic Artists Each Acknowledge Five Sources of Inspiration.* New York: Division of Ceramic Art, School of New York State College of Ceramics at Alfred University, 1993. An exhibition catalogue.

Wood, Denis. *The Power of Maps.* New York: The Guilford Press, 1992.

Woods, Alan. *Being Naked Playing Dead: The Art of Peter Greenaway.* Manchester: Manchester University Press, 1996.

ABOUT THE AUTHOR

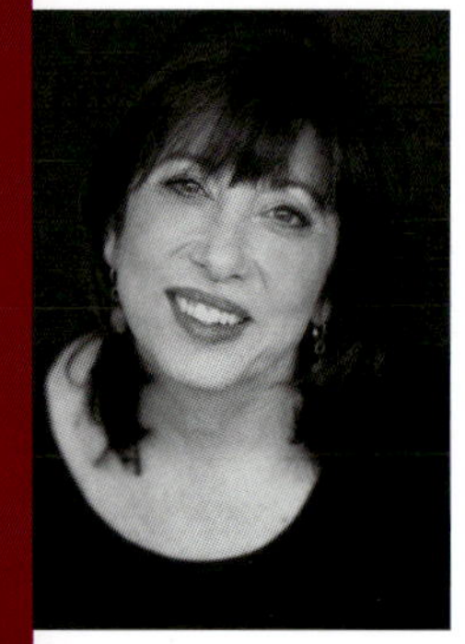

PHOTO GVK IMAGES

Anne West is an educator, writer, and independent curator with a lifelong interest in creativity. Her research focuses on phenomenology and interpretive human studies, including poetics and mapping. With a Ph.D. in Arts and Media Studies from the University of Toronto, she is Senior Critic, Division of Graduate Studies, at Rhode Island School of Design. West is a Fellow of Syracuse University.

Her interpretive projects have been featured on C.B.C. Radio, in catalogue essays for museums and galleries in Canada and the United States, in art journals, as well as through initiatives with numerous art schools, The Aldrich Contemporary Art Museum, The Big Picture Company, and Fetzer Institute.

www.annewest.net

This book, which offers an in-depth method for writing about visual work, has been at the forefront of my intellectual curiosity for many years. It is a synthesis of my research in phenomenology and interpretive human studies, including poetics and mapping. I could not have accomplished this work without the help of many individuals.

I wish to express my debt to two professors—Vivian Darroch-Lozowski and Ronald Silvers—who were central in shaping the direction of this work while I was a doctoral student at the University of Toronto, Canada.

I am grateful for the privilege to work at Rhode Island School of Design. I began teaching in 1996 with an invitation from Christina Bertoni, Dean of Graduate Studies, to offer a workshop on thesis writing. In a number of contexts and courses, and over many years of teaching, this work has matured and informed this book's content and form. Two Professional Development Fund awards (2004, 2010) from Rhode Island School of Design also provided support for the development and realization of the design of this book.

I am indebted to Jim Barry, my initial editor, who read the manuscript in its entirety. The essential care he gave to its content offered me great encouragement and confidence.

I am deeply grateful to my editor/publisher Katarina Weslien, Moth Press, Maine College of Art, who believed in the book strongly and offered ready support. She has been the most remarkable ally in bringing this book to completion.

I extend my thanks to Jennifer Liese for her editorial savvy, as well as to my copy editors, Dominique Bartels, Liz Elia, Marayia Lotts, and Karel Olsson, who insisted on clarity and accurateness.

Thank you to Steven McDonald, General Counsel at RISD for his astute guidance, Ellen Petraits for helping me track down innumerable sources, and to Hasan Askari, Tom Ockerse, Frances Musco Shipps, and Laurie Whitehill-Chong for their continuing conversation as colleagues and friends.

I would like to thank Seth Stem for encouraging me to write this book. David Barg, Laura Kaufman, Ed Merck, and Jessie Shefrin read the manuscript at pivotal moments and offered dialogue essential to the growth of the book. My utmost gratitude to each of them.

Generous family and friends have offered base support and renewal of spirit. I thank them for their strong and quiet influence: Sandra Brownlee, Sarah Buie, David Chandler, Cindy Davis, Doreen Eiteneir, Diane Elofson, Linda LeBelle Flood, Liliana Ferraro, Beverly Holt, Marcy Hudson, Luce, Jane Poole, Victoria Smith, Peter and Bobbi Stein, and Craig Turner. I also wish to express my gratitude to Maureen Holland and Dawn Franceschini for their support and for the inspiring location that allowed me to write this book.

I owe a special debt to my immensely talented design team—Stephanie Grey and Daryl Smith—for their sustaining vision and confidence in this project. This book could not have been completed in its present form without their close listening, Olympian endurance, and single-mindedness of heart. My abiding gratitude goes to graphic designer Deborah Wieder, who developed the first prototype for this book. Thank you to Claudia Middendorf, Adam Lucas, Leslie Leung, Laura Robinson, and Sara Fix for joining our team and for being fully engaged in our dialogues around design. And to Eric Packer, for his humor and caring, and for graciously offering his conference room for our design meetings.

Finally, I am grateful to the many students who have participated in my seminars and who contributed immeasurably to this work.

Anne West

SPRING 2011
PROVIDENCE, RI

Published by
Moth Press
MFA Archive Project, Maine College of Art
522 Congress Street
Portland, ME 04101-3494, USA
Tel. 207 775 3052
www.meca.edu/mfa/mfa-archive-moth-press

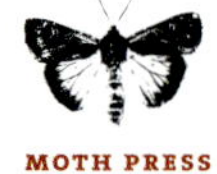

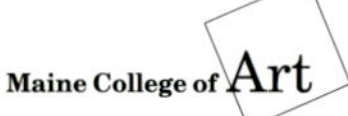

MAPPING THE INTELLIGENCE OF ARTISTIC WORK
AN EXPLORATIVE GUIDE TO MAKING, THINKING, AND WRITING

ISBN 978-0-9834725-0-6

Fourth Edition, 2018

Book Design
Stephanie Grey and Daryl Smith

Typeface: Thesis

Editor
Katarina Weslien

Printed in China

The Moth Press gratefully acknowledges the generous support from the Roderick Dew Fund and the Jenny Fitch Fund.

Grateful acknowledgment is made for permission to quote from the following: From *The Timeless Way of Building* by Christopher Alexander, reprinted by permission of Oxford University Press, Inc. From *I Send You This Cadmium Red* by John Berger and John Christie, reprinted by permission of Actar D. From *Six Memos for the Next Millennium* by Italo Calvino, reprinted by permission of Harvard University Press. From *The Craftsman's Handbook* by Cennino d'Andrea Cennini, reprinted by permission of Dover Publications. From *A Glimpse of the Writing Life* by Annie Dillard, reprinted by permission of HarperCollins Publishers. From "Of Other Spaces" by Michel Foucault in *The Visual Culture Reader*, reprinted by permission of Taylor & Francis Books. From *One Hundred Years of Solitude* by Gabriel Garcia-Marquez, reprinted by permission of Cambridge University Press. From *The Haiku Handbook* by William J. Higginson, with Penny Harter, reprinted by permission of Penny Harter. From *The Big Sea* by Langston Hughes, reprinted by permission of Farrar, Straus and Giroux. From *Conditional Design* by Luna Maurer, Edo Paulus, Jonathan Puckey, and Roel Wouters, reprinted by permission of Luna Maurer. From *Form and Chaos* by Paul Rand, reprinted by permission of Yale University Press. From *What is Found There: Notebooks on Poetry and Politics* by Adrienne Rich, reprinted by permission of W.W. Norton & Company. From "A Shining Example" by Jessica Roundy, reprinted by permission of *Metropolis*. From *The Writings of Robert Smithson,* reprinted by permission of Nancy Holt. From *Reasons for Knocking at an Empty Door* by Bill Viola, reprinted by permission of MIT Press.

idea of artist
tural blind spots
dden clear images
images (or objects) + their stories
ly delving
ough the lens of memory
al pursuits
ratives of place
gin piece
estral lines
notive to begin the work
sing the matter of the world
notations of beauty
t quality of light
rking the dialogue with space
or
out time
ers for the road
lections + organizations of things
finished potential + failures are good
ositioning the familiar
cess
redilection to play
mundane against the fantastic
am quotient
rking with physical materials
play of lightness + weight
ying in the questions
rshalling reference points + models
r reading list
ers of intimacy
ual hopes
fore the "beginning was the word"
gap that drives the work
coming threshold without a map
the collective sphere
ing the doubleness of the work
bidextrous word play
words

EXPLORING

r thinking + working process
trix map
ist statement as origin point
habetical list as inventory
mology
ring words + images
ject-writing
iku sketches
earch sprees
earch as material for the studio
derstanding your processes of understanding
ository of insight
ostwriting interview
ober band project
taphor as an artistic tool

ective grouping
the editor (or author)
og post as extended artist statement
played + preserved work

COMMUNICATING

ur philosophy + teaching strategy
ing on a diet of the work
anifesto, or words to live for
immediate release
stract as convergent process
aphic inspiration
it! launch it!
ving some things unsaid
ence
iew into the studio
akes of breath
voice of now
idea of artist
tural blind spots
dden clear images
images (or objects) + their stories
ly delving
ough the lens of memory
al pursuits
ratives of place
gin piece
cestral lines
notive to begin the work
nsing the matter of the world
nnotations of beauty
at quality of light
rking the dialogue with space
or
out time
ers for the road
lections + organizations of things
finished potential + failures are good
ositioning the familiar
ocess
redilection to play
mundane against the fantastic
am quotient
rking with physical materials
play of lightness + weight
ying in the questions
rshalling reference points + models
ur reading list
ers of intimacy
ual hopes
ore the "beginning was the word"
gap that drives the work
coming threshold without a map
the collective sphere
ing the doubleness of the work
bidextrous word play

ltural blind spots
dden clear images
e images (or objects) + their stories
rly delving
rough the lens of memory
al pursuits
rratives of place
igin piece
cestral lines
motive to begin the work
nsing the matter of the world
nnotations of beauty
at quality of light
orking the dialogue with space
lor
out time
ders for the road
llections + organizations of things
finished potential + failures are good
positioning the familiar
ocess
predilection to play
e mundane against the fantastic
eam quotient
orking with physical materials
e play of lightness + weight
aying in the questions
arshalling reference points + models
ur reading list
yers of intimacy
ual hopes
fore the "beginning was the word"
e gap that drives the work
coming threshold without a map
the collective sphere
eing the doubleness of the work
nbidextrous word play
y words
ur thinking + working process
atrix map
tist statement as origin point
phabetical list as inventory

CHARTING

ymology
iring words + images
ject-writing
iku sketches
search sprees
search as material for the studio
derstanding your processes of understanding
pository of insight
ostwriting interview
bber band project
etaphor as an artistic tool
mbolic language

ur philosophy + teaching strategy
ing on a diet of the work
anifesto, or words to live for
immediate release
stract as convergent process
aphic inspiration
y it! launch it!
aving some things unsaid
ence
iew into the studio
akes of breath
e voice of now
e idea of artist
tural blind spots
dden clear images
e images (or objects) + their stories
rly delving
es
ventive grouping
the editor (or author)
og post as extended artist statement
splayed + preserved work
ur philosophy + teaching strategy
ing on a diet of the work
anifesto, or words to live for

COMMUNICATING

immediate release
stract as convergent process
aphic inspiration
y it! launch it!
aving some things unsaid
rough the lens of memory
al pursuits
rratives of place
igin piece
cestral lines
motive to begin the work
nsing the matter of the world
nnotations of beauty
at quality of light
orking the dialogue with space
lor
out time
ders for the road
llections + organizations of things
finished potential + failures are good
positioning the familiar
ocess
predilection to play
e mundane against the fantastic
eam quotient
orking with physical materials
e play of lightness + weight
aying in the questions

ough the lens of memory
al pursuits
ratives of place
gin piece
cestral lines
notive to begin the work
ısing the matter of the world
nnotations of beauty
at quality of light
rking the dialogue with space
or
out time
ers for the road
lections + organizations of things
finished potential + failures are good
positioning the familiar
ocess
redilection to play
e mundane against the fantastic
eam quotient

EXPLORING

rking with physical materials
e play of lightness + weight
ying in the questions
rshalling reference points + models
ur reading list
ers of intimacy
ual hopes
fore the "beginning was the word"
gap that drives the work
coming threshold without a map
the collective sphere
eing the doubleness of the work
bidextrous word play
y words
ur thinking + working process
trix map
ist statement as origin point
habetical list as inventory
mology
ring words + images
ect-writing
ku sketches
earch sprees
earch as material for the studio
derstanding your processes of understanding
ository of insight
ostwriting interview
ber band project
taphor as an artistic tool
nbolic language
e questions
mbnail catalogue raisonné
ch project descriptions

ır philosophy + teaching strategy
ng on a diet of the work
nifesto, or words to live for
immediate release
stract as convergent process
phic inspiration
it! launch it!
ving some things unsaid
nce
ew into the studio
akes of breath
voice of now
idea of artist
tural blind spots
dden clear images
images (or objects) + their stories
ly delving
es
entive grouping
the editor (or author)
g post as extended artist statement
played + preserved work
ır philosophy + teaching strategy
ng on a diet of the work
nifesto, or words to live for
immediate release
stract as convergent process
phic inspiration **COMMUNICATING**
it! launch it!
ving some things unsaid
ough the lens of memory
al pursuits
ratives of place
gin piece
cestral lines
notive to begin the work
sing the matter of the world
nnotations of beauty
t quality of light
rking the dialogue with space
or
out time
ers for the road
lections + organizations of things
finished potential + failures are good
ositioning the familiar
cess
redilection to play
mundane against the fantastic
am quotient
rking with physical materials
play of lightness + weight
ying in the questions

rough the lens of memory
al pursuits
rratives of place
gin piece
cestral lines
notive to begin the work
nsing the matter of the world
nnotations of beauty
at quality of light
rking the dialogue with space
or
out time
ders for the road
llections + organizations of things
finished potential + failures are good
positioning the familiar
ocess
predilection to play
e mundane against the fantastic
eam quotient
orking with physical materials
e play of lightness + weight
aying in the questions
arshalling reference points + models
ur reading list
ers of intimacy
ual hopes
fore the "beginning was the word"
e gap that drives the work
coming threshold without a map
the collective sphere
eing the doubleness of the work
nbidextrous word play
y words
ur thinking + working process
atrix map
tist statement as origin point
phabetical list as inventory
ymology
iring words + images
ject-writing
iku sketches

CHARTING

search sprees
search as material for the studio
derstanding your processes of understanding
pository of insight
ostwriting interview
bber band project
etaphor as an artistic tool
mbolic language
e questions
umbnail catalogue raisonné
th project descriptions

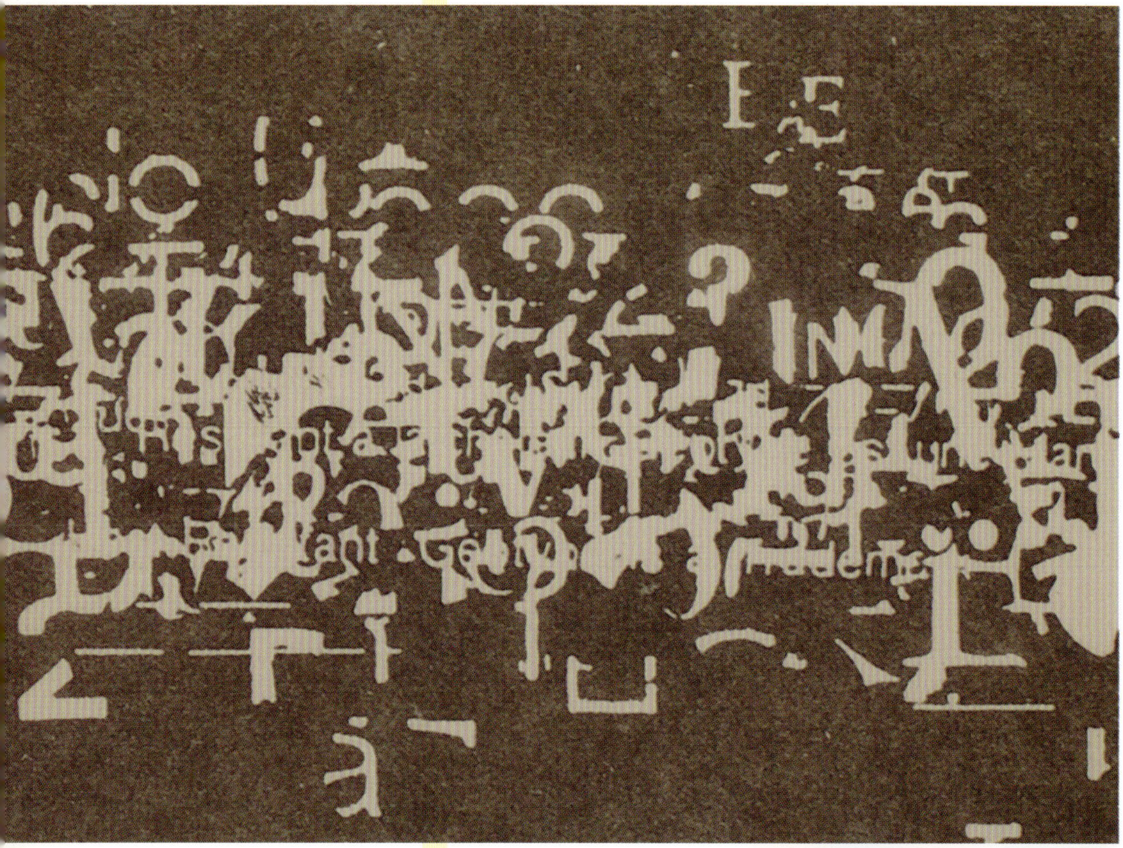

PHOTO BROCKETT HORNE

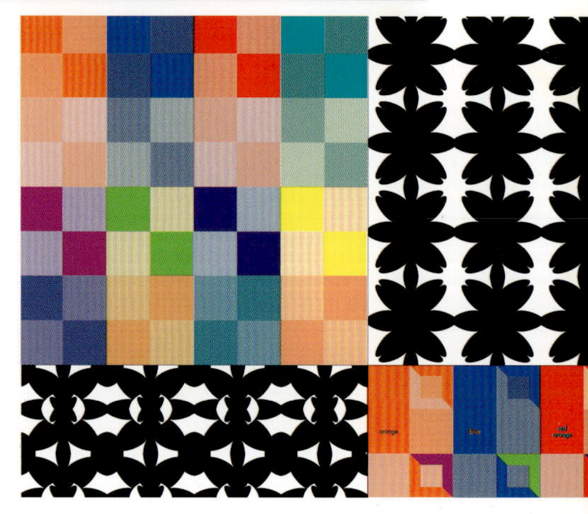

DANNIEL GAIDULA, *DESPERATELY SEE[K]ING SYSTEMS*, 2004